FACTS AT YOUR FINGERTIPS

ANCIENT EGYPT

BROWN BEAR BOOKS

Published by Brown Bear Books Limited

An imprint of:
The Brown Reference Group Ltd
68 Topstone Road
Redding
Connecticut 06896
USA

www.brownreference.com

Library of Congress Cataloging-in-Publication Data available upon request

ISBN-13 978-1-933834-54-2

Editorial Director: Lindsey Lowe
Managing Editor: Tim Cooke
Design Manager: David Poole
Designer: Sarah Williams
Picture Manager: Sophie Mortimer
Picture Researcher: Sean Hannaway
Text Editor: Anita Dalal
Indexer: Indexing Specialists (UK) Ltd

Printed in the United States of America

Picture Credits

Abbreviations: AKG Archiv für Kunst und Geschichte, London; BAL Bridgeman Art Library; C Corbis; MEPL Mary Evans Picture Library; SPL Science Photo Library; b=bottom; c=center; t=top; l=left; r=right.

Front Cover: Shutterstock: Sculpies
Back Cover: iStockphoto: Jan Rihak

iStockphoto: Franck Camhi 5, Dmytro Korolov 36, Matej Michelizza 40, Jan Rihak 42, 61, Karen Moller 50, David Kerkhoff 51, David Parsons 56; **Jupiter Images:** 1, 46–47; **Shutterstock:** Styve Reineck 38, W. H. Chow 38–39.

Artwork © The Brown Reference Group Ltd

The Brown Reference Group Ltd has made every effort to trace copyright holders of the pictures used in this book. Anyone having claims to ownership not identified above is invited to contact The Brown Reference Group Ltd.

CONTENTS

INTRODUCTION

A lasting civilization

This book is about ancient Egypt, one of the great civilizations of the past. The ancient Greeks saw Egypt as the source of all wisdom. Roman emperors traveled to Egypt to marvel at monuments such as the pyramids. Egyptian statues and obelisks were sent to decorate Rome. The worship of Egyptian gods and goddesses such as Isis and Osiris spread through the Roman Empire as far as Britain.

Extensive ruins

The modern fascination with Egypt began in the late 18th century. Since then, a huge number of ancient towns, temples, and tombs have been excavated. No country in the world has so many impressive ancient remains as Egypt does. In the Nile Valley the past seems very close. The people who lived there thousands of years ago have left us a wonderful legacy of art, architecture, and literature.

Structure of the book

Ancient Egypt is divided into two main sections. The first tells the story of Egypt from the union of the country in about 3100 BCE to the coming of the Romans almost 3,000 years later. Archaeologists break up the great span of Egyptian history into a series of periods and "kingdoms."

The Predynastic Period was the era before Egypt was united under a single ruler. From the Early Dynastic Period, Egypt was ruled by dynasties of kings. A dynasty was a sequence of rulers, usually related by blood or marriage. The eras known as kingdoms were times when Egypt was strong and united. The "intermediate periods" between the kingdoms were times when the country was weak and divided. The last dynasties of native Egyptian kings ruled during the Late Period, at the end of Egypt's history as an independent nation. In the Greco-Roman Period, Egypt was first under Greek and then under Roman rule.

History spreads

On each history spread you will find a list of the dynasties that reigned during that period or kingdom. The names and dates of the most important rulers in each dynasty are also given. The exact spelling and pronunciation of most ancient Egyptian names is uncertain because vowels were not written in full. Ideas about how the names should be written out in English have changed as our knowledge of ancient languages has grown. The name that used to be spelled Tutankhamen is now usually written as Tutankhamun or Tutankhamon. It means "Living Image of the god Amon."

The maps in the first part of the book are linked to topics in the text. They show you which places were important in each period or kingdom or sites where objects of a particular date have been found.

Journey down the Nile

The second part of this book, beginning on pages 32–33, takes you on a journey down the Nile. The journey starts in Lower Nubia, a country to the south of Egypt, and ends at the Mediterranean coast. There is a map for each region. These are maps of modern Egypt but they mark all the important ancient sites and structures that survive. For most sites a modern Arabic name and at least one ancient name are given. Some of these ancient names are Egyptian. Others date to the time when the Greeks ruled Egypt. Beside the site names are symbols to show you what kind of ancient remains have been found there.

Abbreviations used in this book

BCE = Before Common Era (also known as BC).

CE = Common Era (also known as AD).

c. = circa (about).

in = inch; ft = foot; yd = yard; mi = mile.

cm = centimeter; m = meter; km = kilometer.

This frieze on the wall of a temple at Karnak, Luxor, shows the 18th-Dynasty pharaoh Amenhotep IV. When he came to the throne in 1353 BCE, the pharoah took the name Akenhaten and tried to get the Egyptians to follow a new religion dedicated to the sun god, Aten. After he died, however, the country returned to its older forms of worship.

TIMELINES

EGYPTIAN HISTORY

Predynastic
Badarian/Tasian culture,
Nile valley c.4500–4000.
Merimda cultures, Delta
c.4800–4100.
Faiyum culture c.5400–4400.

Predynastic
Naqada I, Nile valley
c.4000–3500.
Naqada II–III, Nile valley
c.3500–3100.
Invention of writing.

**Foundation of Egyptian state
c.3100.**
Trade with Mesopotamia.

**Early Dynastic Period
c.2920–2575.**
1st–3rd Dynasties.
First mining expeditions to
Sinai.

Old Kingdom c.2575–2134.
4th–6th Dynasties.
Raids on Libya, Palestine,
and Lower Nubia. Trade
with Upper Nubia.

**First Intermediate Period
c.2134–2040**
7th–11th Dynasties.
Rival dynasties and civil wars.

Hunters from stone palette, c.3000 BCE

*Tomb stela of King Wadj
from Abydos, c.2980 BCE*

*Statue of King Khephren
from Giza, c.2495 BCE*

ARCHITECTURE AND TOMBS

Reed huts.

Graves under hut floors at
Merimda Beni Salama.

Reed shrines.

First buildings in mud-brick.

Walled town and brick-lined
tombs at Hierakonpolis.

Mud-brick "funerary palaces"
at Abydos.

Mud-brick mastaba tombs at
Saqqara.

First stone buildings.

Massive stone pyramids and
stone mastaba tombs at
Giza, Saqqara, and Abusir.

Stone sun temples and obelisks
at Abu Ghurab and Abusir.

*Painted terra-cotta figurine
of a dancer, c.4000 BCE*

Step pyramids at Saqqara.

*Painting of geese from a tomb
at Maidum, c.2560 BCE*

*Step Pyramid of King Djoser
at Saqqara, c.2560 BCE*

ART AND CRAFTS

Fine pottery vessels, clay
figurines, objects carved
from ivory.

Painted pottery, stone palettes
and vessels, terra-cotta and
ivory figurines.

First wall paintings and stone
statuettes.

Large stone statues.

First reliefs in wood and stone.

First stone stelae.

Gold jewelry.

Faience figurines.

Painted tomb reliefs of daily
life.

Royal statues in hard stones
or in copper.

Private statues in stone or
wood.

Furniture in wood and
decorated sheet gold.

Middle Kingdom c.2040–1640.
11th–13th Dynasties.
Reunion of Egypt under Theban dynasty.
Trade with Syria and Palestine.
Occupation of Lower Nubia.

Second Intermediate Period c.1640–1532.
14th–17th Dynasties.
Occupation of Delta by Hyksos from Syria/Palestine.
Kerma culture occupies Lower Nubia. War between the Hyksos and Theban kings.

Statue of King Senwosret III from Deir el-Bahri, c.1850 BCE

Early New Kingdom 1550–1307.
17th–18th Dynasties.
Egypt reunited under Theban dynasty.
Conquest of Lower and Upper Nubia.
Rise of Egyptian empire in Syria and Palestine.

Gold mask from the mummy of King Tutankhamon, c.1325 BCE

Late New Kingdom c.1307–1196.
19th–20th Dynasties. Wars against the Hittites in Syria.
Depopulation of Lower Nubia.
Wars against the Sea Peoples.
Gradual loss of Near Eastern empire.

Colossal statue at the Great Temple of Abu Simbel, c.1270 BCE

Third Intermediate Period c.1070–712.
21st–25th Dynasties.
Egypt divided.
Kings ruling Delta and High Priests ruling Thebes.
Rise of Nubian Kingdom of Napata.
Civil wars among petty rulers.

Late Period 712–332.
25th–30th Dynasties
Egypt reunited by Nubian kings.
Conquest of Egypt by the Assyrians and by the Persians.
Periods of native rule between conquests.

Kneeling Egyptian from statue base of a Persian king, c.500 BCE

Greco-Roman Period 332 BCE–395 CE
Greek rule 332–30 BCE
Egypt ruled by Ptolemies.
Many Greek immigrants. Some Egyptian rebellions.
Roman rule 30 BCE–395 CE
Egypt becomes part of the Roman Empire.
Most of Nubia ruled by Kings of Meroe.

Head of a priest in green schist, c.75 BCE

Stone mortuary temple of Mentuhotep III at Deir el-Bahri.

Mud-brick pyramids in Middle Egypt and at Dahshur.

Rock-cut tombs in Middle Egypt.

Forts in Nubia.

Wooden figurine of a servant from a Theban tomb, c.2020 BCE

Terraced temple of Hatshepsut at Deir el-Bahri.

Rock-cut royal tombs in the Valley of the Kings.

Temples of Amon at Karnak and Luxor.

Palaces and Aten temples at el-Amarna.

Relief from a vizier's tomb at Thebes, c.1360 BCE

Mortuary temples of Ramesses II (The Ramesseum) and Ramesses III (Medinet Habu) at Thebes.

Great Hypostyle Hall at Karnak, Ramesses II.

Great Temple of Abu Simbel and other rock-cut and freestanding temples in Nubia.

Relief of a blind harpist from a Saqqara tomb, c.1300 BCE

Temple of Amon at Tanis with underground royal tombs.

Large tombs with mud-brick pylons at Thebes.

Shaft tombs at Saqqara.

Granite temple of Isis at Behbeit el-Hagar.

Inlaid bronze figure of a high priestess, c.850 BCE

Great Egyptian-style temples at Philae, Kom Ombo, Edfu, Esna, and Dendara.

Greco-Egyptian style "funerary houses" at Tuna el-Gebel.

Underground galleries of tombs at Alexandria.

Facade of the temple of Hathor at Dendara, c.34 CE

Royal portrait sculpture.

Tomb paintings of daily life.

Painted wooden models of daily life.

Fine jewelry in gold and semiprecious stones.

Temple reliefs with royal and religious scenes.

Monumental sculpture.

Tomb paintings and painted reliefs of daily life.

Decorated pottery and faience vessels.

Colossal stone statues.

Temple reliefs with battle and hunting scenes.

Illustrated "Books of the Dead."

Tomb paintings of religious scenes.

Faience bowls and chalices.

Bronze figurines.

Private sculpture in hard stones.

Decorated cartonnage coffins and stone sarcophagi.

Portrait sculpture in hard stones.

Temple reliefs of religious scenes.

Faience and terra-cotta figurines.

Painted "mummy portraits."

EGYPT, GIFT OF THE NILE

Ancient Egyptian civilization was shaped by its geographical location within northeastern Africa. It grew up in the narrow Nile Valley, which was isolated on both sides by desert. Nearby West Asia was where agriculture first began. The ancient Egyptians developed highly efficient ways of farming. They were able to grow enough food to support Egypt's population throughout most of its history. The annual crops depended on the regular flooding of the river. Without the Nile, ancient Egypt would not have come into being more than 5,000 years ago.

A Fertile Corridor

About 12,000 years ago, most of North Africa was covered by grassland (savannah) where animals grazed. Over time, the climate became drier and the savannah turned into desert. The world's longest river—the Nile—flowed through the desert. Even though there was virtually no rainfall in the valley itself, the river's waters supported rich vegetation growing in a narrow strip along its banks.

The Nile valley is a long, narrow corridor that varies in width from 12 miles (19 km) wide to as little as 1 mile (1.6 km) wide. Before it joins the Mediterranean Sea, the Nile splits into lots of small rivers that make up a delta. The delta is 125 miles (200 km) wide.

The Black Land and the Red Land

The ancient Egyptians called their country the Black Land because the rich soil of the Nile Valley was a black color. Over time, the climate changed the valley from a swamp and only the Delta kept large areas of marshland.

Every summer the rains far to the south, where the Nile has its sources, raised the level of the River Nile in what is now Egypt. The Blue Nile rises in the Ethiopian Highlands. The White Nile rises south of Lake Victoria in central Africa and drains water from a large area of southern Sudan. Water levels rose along the whole length of the river.

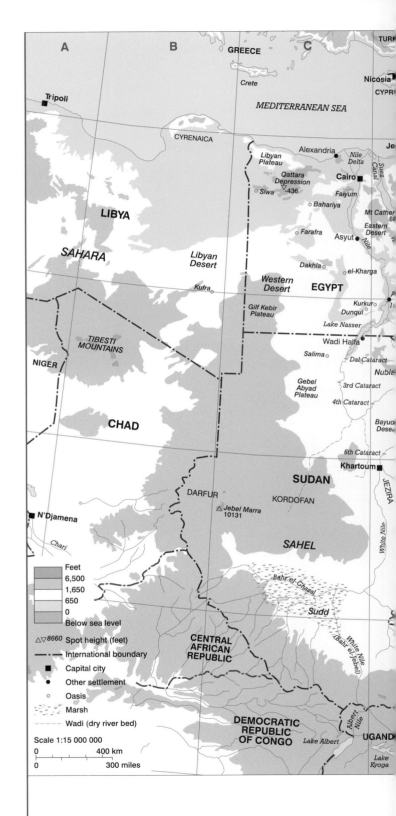

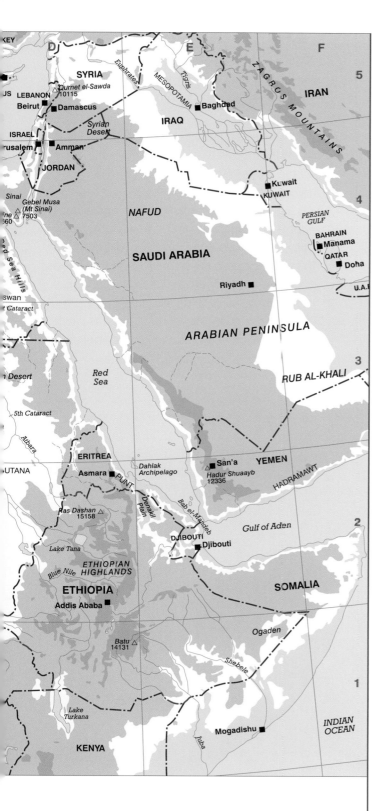

The geography of Egypt today. The Nile is fed by the Blue and the White Nile. Its ultimate source is Lake Victoria, which is located in the south of Uganda.

The Inundation

Within what is now Egypt, the Nile regularly overflowed its banks. It flooded the low-lying fields on either side for about two months each year. The area covered in water was called the floodplain and the event was known as the inundation. When the waters went down, they left a layer of fertile mud. This silt was full of nutrients that made it perfect for growing crops. The level of flooding was crucial, however. Too much and villages might flood; too little and not enough crops would be able to be grown. The ancient Egyptians built nilometers along the river. These structures enabled the Egyptians to measure the height of the river and therefore to be able to predict the seasonal flooding.

The Deserts

Deserts lie to the east and west of the Nile valley. The Egyptians called this the Red Land. To the west, the desert stretched into the huge Sahara. There are few settlements, apart from small areas of fertile land around oases, where water carried in underground layers of rock called aquifers rises to the surface. To the east, the desert rose to a range of mountains, which were cut through by wadis (dry riverbeds). These riverbeds were dry for most of the year, although they filled up with water after heavy rains. Both empty and full, the wadis were important trade routes across the desert and mountains to the coast of the Red Sea.

Natural Protection

The Nile is difficult to sail in the south of Egypt because of a series of rapids, which are known as cataracts. To the north, the marshes of the delta provided natural protection against people arriving from the Mediterranean. These natural barriers, together with the deserts to the east and west, made Egypt a difficult country to invade. They also isolated Egypt from its neighbors, helping to explain how Egypt's unique culture endured for so long.

THE LAND OF GOLD

Ancient Egyptian culture depended on a rich supply of natural resources. Many of them were imported from abroad by traders, but Egypt also possessed many resources of its own. Limestone, sandstone and granite for building temples and tombs came from the desert hills on the edge of the Nile Valley. Rarer stones, such as alabaster, were used for making vases and statues.

The Egyptian deserts also contained mines that extracted semiprecious stones and precious metals, especially gold. One foreign king wrote that in Egypt gold was as common as dust!

The Nile—A Precious Resource

The most precious resource in ancient Egypt was water. Almost no rain falls across Egypt, so the annual flooding of the Nile was vital for growing crops like corn and barley. Another crop was flax, which was used to make linen for clothes. The finest ancient Egyptian linen was spun so finely you could see through it.

People dug irrigation channels to carry water far from the Nile to gardens and orchards. Vegetables like lettuce, onions, peas, and lentils were grown, along with fruits such as figs and pomegranates.

The Nile also gave Egyptians their homes. Bricks were made from wet clay from the riverbank and left in the sun to dry. All Egyptian houses were made from these mud bricks.

The Delta was the only part of Egypt where enough grass grew to feed large herds of cattle. The marshes were rich in bird, fish, and plant life. The Egyptians fished with nets or spears and used boomerangs to hunt birds. Lotus flowers were made into perfume and reeds were made into boats and matting. The stems of papyrus plants were made into a sort of paper, which became one of Egypt's chief exports.

A seated nomarch (governor) oversees the cattle census. Cattle are driven past a kiosk to be counted and recorded by the scribes. The owners are then told how much tax they have to pay.

Main exports of ancient Egypt

Gold – Bags of gold dust, or solid gold made into large rings.

Grain – Corn and any extra grain after a good harvest.

Papyrus – Made into scrolls and ready to write on.

Linens – Made from flax, the best quality was Royal Linen.

Main imports of ancient Egypt

Timber – Including cedar from Lebanon, used for shipbuilding, furniture, and funeral coffins.

Bronze (copper/tin alloy) – Imported as ingots (metal bars) and used to make weapons, vessels, and mirrors.

Iron – Imported after the 1st millennium BCE.

Ivory – From Africa for use in carvings and inlays.

Lapis Lazuli – Semi-precious stone from Afghanistan, used to make jewelry.

Incense – Imported from Punt (possibly present-day Eritrea) and the Yemen. Used for burning during religious rituals.

Oil – Used both for cooking and body oil.

Myrrh – Imported from Punt and Yemen, and used to perfume the inside of mummies.

Exotic Animals – African animals such as monkeys, cheetahs, baboons, and serval cats..

This map shows the very limited area of ancient Egypt that could be used for agriculture. The area of fertile land, particularly within the Delta, varied from season to season, year to year. Also marked are ancient mineral workings on the edges of the Nile valley and in the deserts. The turquoise mines of Sinai were highly prized by the Egyptians. The wadis (dry riverbeds) were used as trade routes.

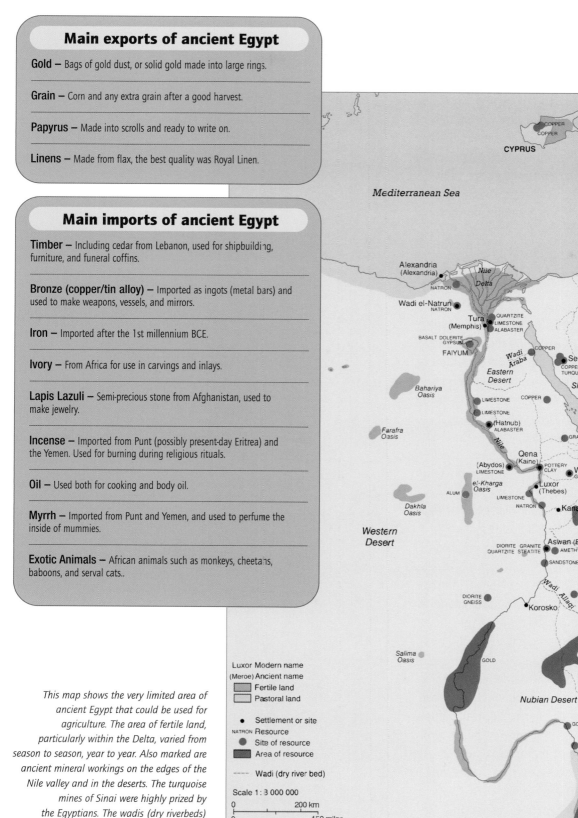

THE TWO KINGDOMS

Ancient Egypt was divided into two regions, known respectively as Upper and Lower Egypt. Upper Egypt was the narrow Nile valley. Lower Egypt was the north of the country, including the Delta region. The two lands were originally separate kingdoms, but were united under one ruler in about 3100 BCE. The rulers of the new kingdom were known as the Lords of the Two Lands. The location of the capital moved as families from different parts of Egypt came to the throne. Several of the capital cities were located near the border of Upper and Lower Egypt. This area was sometimes known as Middle Egypt.

Administrative Centers

For most of the long history of ancient Egypt, its population was probably no more than four million people. For the purposes of government, Upper and Lower Egypt were divided into districts called nomes. Each nome had its own administrative center. These centers were probably quite small. Most Egyptians lived on farms or in small villages. Each village had a headman and each nome had its own governor, known as a nomarch.

The nomarchs ruled their districts on behalf of the kings. The nomarch's duties included maintaining the region's dykes and irrigation channels. This was a very important job because water was so precious. The nomarch also made sure that the grain was stored so that the local people could be fed during times of famine.

The First Civil Servants

Whichever city was the capital, it was home to a large number of officials who worked for the central government. The most important official was the vizier. He was in charge of public works, such as the building of monuments, and justice. At different times, there were two viziers, one for Upper and one for Lower Egypt.

The vizier's office was also responsible for collecting taxes. Until Egypt came under Greek

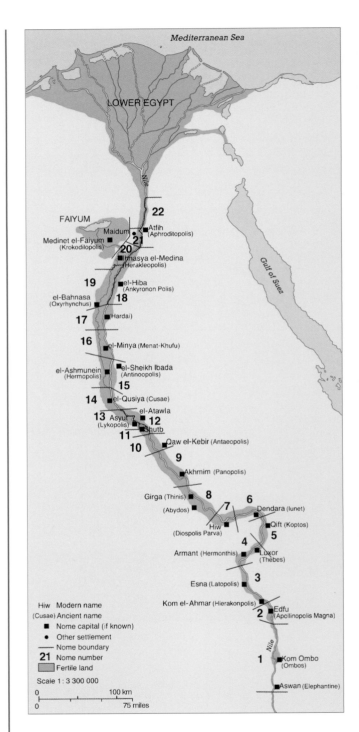

ABOVE: The nomes (districts) of Upper Egypt. The boundaries of the 22 nomes are based on a Middle Kingdom list. Some nomes had more than one capital during their history; in others the site of the capital is uncertain.

RIGHT: Lower Egypt was divided into 20 nomes. This map is based on nome lists in temples of the Greek and Roman (Greco-Roman) periods. Nome boundaries in the Delta were formed by the branches of the Nile.

Upper Egypt

1 9 17

2 10 18

3 11 19

4 12 20

5 13 21

6 14 22

7 15

8 16

Lower Egypt

1 8 15

2 9 16

3 10 17

4 11 18

5 12 19

6 13 20

7 14

Each district, or nome, had a symbol. These symbols, or ensigns, were often derived from the form of a local god or goddess. In temple reliefs (carved scenes) the symbols are worn on the heads of figures that represent the nomes.

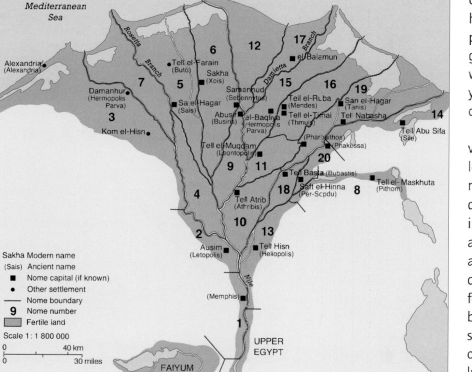

control in 332 BCE, it did not have coins. Instead, taxes were paid with valuable goods, like grain or cattle. All land ownership was registered and every two years all the cattle in Egypt were counted for the register.

Officials who worked in the vizier's office had to be good at lots of different jobs. One official noted in an inscription that during his career he was an inspector of pyramids, a judge, and a tax collector. He also led an army, and oversaw the digging of canals and the quarrying of stone for pyramid building. He later became the governor of all of southern Egypt. Successful officials were well rewarded with luxury goods and country estates.

EGYPT BEFORE THE PHARAOHS

The very earliest Egyptians were nomads who hunted the wild animals that lived on the savannah while also herding their own domesticated animals. Over time, possibly because of the changing climate that made the savannah drier, people moved down into the Nile Valley. They began to settle in small communities along the river and raised crops for food. We know very little about these early people and how they lived, but we do know that there were different groups who followed different ways of life.

Predynastic Middle and Lower Egypt

In around 5400 BCE, one group of nomads settled in the region of the Faiyum, a large lake in the middle of Egypt. This community grew some crops but its main source of food came from fishing in the lake. From other ancient sites excavated in Lower Egypt, archaeologists have learned that other groups of settlers grew corn, hunted desert animals, and fished in the Nile.

At the oldest of the northern sites, Merimda Beni Salama in the western delta, people lived in clusters of huts made from reeds. They used stone tools, made simple clay pots, and spun cloth into textiles for their clothes. At a later site near the southern end of the delta, Ma'adi,

there is evidence that people practiced farming, herding, and metalworking.

Predynastic Upper Egypt

In the south, the Badarian/Tasian culture spread along the Nile valley. These people lived in small villages scattered over the floodplain. They left many traces of their lives in the articles that they buried with their dead in cemeteries on the edge of the valley, where it met the desert. The grave goods were precious items for the dead, suggesting that the people practiced a religion that believed in an afterlife. They included decorated pots, bead necklaces, linen clothing, and clay figures of people and animals, as well as amulets, ivory spoons, and combs.

The Naqada Cultures

The Naqada I (or Amratian) culture was descended from the Badarian/Tasian people. The people were skilled stone workers who used flint to make rippled knives and arrowheads and made clubs from harder stones. The weapons were used for hunting desert animals, which were an important food source. Metal was still a rare material.

The Naqada II (or Gerzean) people were more technologically advanced than their ancestors. They lived in large tribal communities

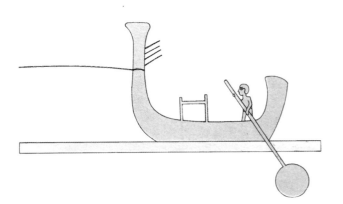

River traffic and trade on the Nile became important before dynastic times in Egypt. This Predynastic boat was made from papyrus reeds woven together. It had a tall prow and stern and was steered with a single large oar.

By the time of the Old Kingdom, boats had evolved into wooden craft with distinctively shaped hulls and double-footed masts that supported sails that were taller than they were wide.

that seem to have fought frequently among each other. Some of their burial goods suggest that the ruling classes of this period had grown very wealthy. The goods included jewelry made from gold and lapis lazuli, elaborate slate palettes used to grind eye paint, as well as beautiful ivory combs and knife handles.

Trade in the Predynastic Period

By the Naqada III period a series of chieftains, who called themselves kings, had emerged to rule all of Upper Egypt. These kings are sometimes known as Dynasty 0, to suggest that they were very similar to the first dynasty to rule all of Egypt. Some objects from the period are decorated with designs from Mesopotamia (modern-day Iraq). Ancient Mesopotamia was then a sophisticated urban society.

Archaeologists used to think that the rapid changes that took place in ancient Egypt at the end of the Predynastic Period were a result of the influence of newcomers. Foreigners may have invaded from the east and taken power, bringing Mesopotamian ideas with them. There is, however, no real evidence of an invasion but the different goods found in tombs proves the Egyptians were trading goods and ideas with people to the east.

About this time, the Upper Egyptians probably started to mine and export gold. The important early town of Ombos, near Naqada, was close to a major gold mining area.

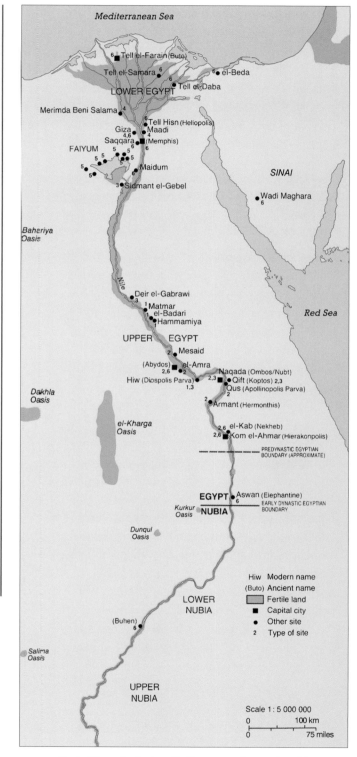

Most of the major Predynastic sites were on the margins of the desert. By Early Dynastic times many of these sites had been abandoned and new settlements were founded on the Nile's floodplain. The key numbers on the map relate to the numbers in the box at left.

MAJOR PREDYNASTIC AND EARLY DYNASTIC SITES

Dates for Predynastic cultures are uncertain. The development of Upper and Lower Egypt cannot easily be related. The numbers in the list refer to the numbers on the map.

1. Badarian/Tasian – c.4500–4000 BCE

2. Naqada I – c.4000–3500 BCE

3. Naqada II – c.3500–3000 BCE

4. Lower Egypt – c.4800–3000 BCE

5. Faiyum – c.5400–4400 BCE

6. Naqada III and early Dynasties – c.3200–2575 BCE

THE FIRST PYRAMIDS

Ancient Egyptian legend recorded that Upper and Lower Egypt were first united by a king named Menes. According to the story, Menes was a king of Upper Egypt who conquered Lower Egypt and founded a new capital at Memphis. The real identity of Menes remains a mystery. Two early kings have both been identified as the legendary founder. Their names, Narmer and Aha, are found on their tombs in the sacred city of Abydos. Events that actually took place during the reigns of both the kings may have added to the legend of Menes and the founding of the First Dynasty.

Early Dynastic Egypt

From the founding of the First Dynasty, historians are able to trace Egyptian history more closely, because the Egyptians themselves increasingly began to record events. They used a kind of picture writing known as hieroglyphics, which was only used in Egypt and was probably the oldest form of writing in the world.

During the First Dynasty, towns appeared alongside the traditional small villages, and homes made from mud bricks replaced reed huts. Tombs for important officials were made from mud bricks at Saqqara, the cemetery for the town of Memphis. The brick tombs (mastaba) were large rectangular flat-topped structures, which contained storerooms full of goods close to the burial chamber. Stone stelae, which were pillars carved with inscriptions, were placed next to the wall of one of the mastaba tombs at the spot where offerings were made to the dead. It was not unusual for some of the servants of a dead king to be killed and buried near his body so that their spirits could continue to serve him in the next life.

Khasekhemwy

Despite the development of the hieroglyphs, little is known about the history of Early Dynastic Egypt. It seems likely that during the Second Dynasty there was a civil war between two kings named Peribsen and Khasekhemwy. The kings were followers of two rival gods, Set and Horus, When

<table>
<tr><td colspan="2">SELECTED KINGS OF THE EARLY DYNASTIC PERIOD 3100–2575 BCE</td></tr>
<tr><td>1st Dynasty 3100–2770</td><td>Ninetjer</td></tr>
<tr><td>Menes (=Aha?)</td><td>Peribsen</td></tr>
<tr><td>Djer</td><td>Khasekhemwy</td></tr>
<tr><td>Djet</td><td></td></tr>
<tr><td>Den</td><td>3rd Dynasty 2649–2575</td></tr>
<tr><td>Semerkhet</td><td>Nebka 2649–2630</td></tr>
<tr><td></td><td>Djoser 2630–2611</td></tr>
<tr><td>2nd Dynasty 2770–2649</td><td>Sekhemkhet 2611–2603</td></tr>
<tr><td>Hetepsekhemwy</td><td>Khaba 2603–2599</td></tr>
<tr><td>Reneb</td><td>Huni 2599–2575</td></tr>
</table>

Khasekhemwy emerged as the victor, he included the names of both the gods in writing with his name. This was possibly a peace gesture toward his defeated rival and his followers.

Khasekhemwy is the earliest Egyptian king for whom a stone statue survives. Unfortunately, grave robbers have robbed all the royal tombs of the First and Second Dynasties. Among the few objects to escape the robbers are treasures that reveal a high degree of skill. In the tomb of King Djer at Abydos, archaeologists found four bracelets made of gold, lapis lazuli, and turquoise. The bracelets were still attached to an arm torn from a mummy in ancient times by tomb robbers.

Imhotep and the Step Pyramid

The reign of King Djoser from 2630 to 2611 BCE, during the Third Dynasty, was remembered by later ancient Egyptians as a golden age. One of Djoser's most important government officials was a man named Imhotep. Modern scholars often identify Imhotep as the first known individual from history who deserves the description of "genius." Imhotep is thought to have written books about medicine and was later worshiped by the Egyptians as a god of healing.

Later Egyptians also credited Imhotep with inventing stone architecture using mud bricks. That is highly unlikely, but Imhotep may deserve credit for designing Egypt's first pyramid—the Step Pyramid at Saqqara—for King Djoser. Imhotep's name has been found inside the Step Pyramid enclosure, suggesting that he may well have been the chief architect of this remarkable group of stone buildings. The pyramid started as a normal mastaba but later more mastabas were added to it. Eventually, it consisted of six terraces, or steps, that rose 200 feet (60 m) into the sky. The whole structure was originally clad with smooth white limestone.

The Step Pyramid, like the later pyramids, was both a royal tomb and a temple where the spirit (or ka) of the dead king could be worshiped.

Djoser's statue was found in a sealed chamber near the pyramid's northeastern corner. Although the Step Pyramid was the first of the Egyptian pyramids, building it was clearly a huge effort that took huge resources and thousands of workers. The cost and effort that went into building the structure shows how important the cult of the divine king was.

The Step Pyramid at Saqqara—the first pyramid to be built—was begun in about 2630 BCE. Under the pyramid is Djoser's tomb. It had been robbed in ancient times, so the granite sarcophagus is now empty.

The architect of the Step Pyramid began with a large mastaba tomb (1), but then had the idea of building a pyramid in steps. The pyramid increased in size several times (2-3), until the finished structure had six steps and was 200 feet (60 m) high (4). Changes were made in the design of the substructure when underground tombs were added for other royal family members

THE OLD KINGDOM

During the Fourth Dynasty, members of the ruling royal family held the key positions in government. The first king of the dynasty was Snofru. He was supposed to have been a kind ruler. He was responsible for building at least two true (straight-sided) pyramids for himself. One of the pyramids is known as the "Bent Pyramid," because halfway up its height it changes angle abruptly.

During Snofru's reign, the Egyptians built a fortified town at Buhen in Nubia to the south. From there, they were able to exploit the Nubian gold fields and to control trade routes into Africa. Unlike Snofru, the next ruler, Khufu (Cheops), who is best-known as the builder of the Great Pyramid at Giza, was remembered as a cruel and mean ruler. Later, the pharaohs Khephren and Menkaura also built huge pyramids at Giza.

Tombs of queens, princesses, and officials were built around the pyramids. Human sacrifice had once been practiced during royal burial rites but was now abandoned. Statues of the Fourth Dynasty kings show them as serene figures, who were not only absolute rulers but also living gods. However, many only ruled for a short period. Some experts think that might mean that they died in wars with rivals. The peaceful appearance of the statues may be misleading.

The Old Kingdom was a high point in Egyptian art. Beautiful statues and reliefs

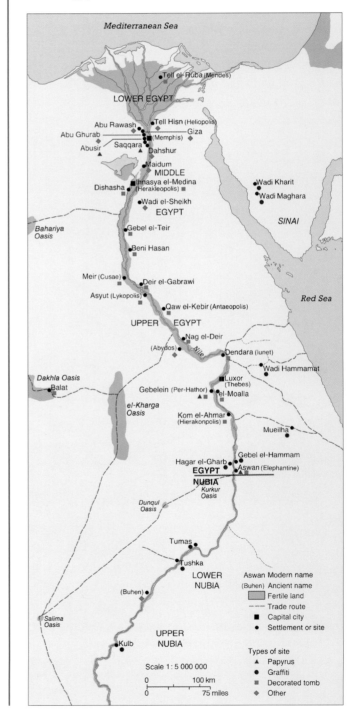

Egypt and Nubia in the Old Kingdom and the First Intermediate Period. The major Fourth- and Fifth-Dynasty sites are clustered near the capital, Memphis. Lower Nubia was almost uninhabited until it was settled by the "C-Group" during the Sixth Dynasty.

Old Kingdom and First Intermediate Period

Papyrus sites Papyrus was probably first used for writing on in the Old Kingdom. Old Kingdom papyri include legal documents and temple records.

Graffiti sites These consist of names and titles scratched on rocks by members of Egyptian mining and trading expeditions. Most date from the Sixth Dynasty.

Decorated tomb sites By the late Old Kingdom important officials were building themselves elaborate tombs in provincial cemeteries. This shows the increasing wealth and independence of the regions. The decoration in First Intermediate Period tombs is crude compared with Old Kingdom art.

SELECTED KINGS OF THE OLD KINGDOM, 2575–2134 BCE

Fourth Dynasty 2575–2465
Snofru 2575–2551
Khufu (Cheops) 2551–2528
Djedefra 2528–2520
Khephren 2520–2494
Menkaura 2490–2472
Shepseskaf 2472–2467

Fifth Dynasty 2465–2323
Userkaf 2465–2458
Sahura 2458–2446
Neferirkara 2446–2426
Shepseskara 2426–2419
Raneferef 2419–2416
Neuserra 2416–2392
Menkauhor 2396–2388
Djedkara 2388–2356
Wenis 2356–2323

Sixth Dynasty 2323–2150
Teti 2323–2291
Pepy I 2289–2255
Merenra 2255–2246
Pepy II 2246–2152

Seventh/Eighth Dynasties
2150–2134
Numerous kings

First Intermediate Period
2134–2040 BCE

9th/10th Dynasties 2134–2040
Kings ruling from Herakleopoli- Ity, Merykara, Khety

11th Dynasty 2134–2040
Kings ruling from Thebes, including
Inyotef I 2134–2118
Inyotef II 2118–2069
Inyotef III 2069–2061
Nebhepetra Mentuhotep 2061–2010

(raised images) were carved in stone. Subjects like math, astronomy, and engineering flourished during the Old Kingdom. Perhaps the complex job of building a pyramid helped to promote both artistic and scientific advances.

Pyramid Building

The pyramids required a huge amount of labor to build. Some of the builders belonged to a permanent workforce of craftsmen. Many others were peasants who worked on royal projects for the two months of the year when the fields were flooded and it was impossible for them to farm. Up to 100,000 men may have worked for as many as twenty flood seasons to build a single pyramid. To build such enormous structures required a stable and rich country as well as a well-organized workforce. The vast civil service that developed to cope with the pyramid building remained an important feature of ancient Egyptian civilization.

Pyramids built during the Fifth Dynasty were smaller in scale than earlier pyramids. Several kings built magnificent stone temples to the sun god Ra. The pyramid of the last king of the Fifth Dynasty, Wenis, was the first to have the famous spells known as the Pyramid Texts carved onto it. The spells were meant to help the king become a god in the afterlife and to help him take his place among the stars.

Rise of the Nomarchs

In the Sixth Dynasty, royal power declined. The government was no longer controlled by princes. Important officials continued to build lavish tombs for themselves, but they described themselves with humble titles such as "Keeper of the King's Nail Clippings."

All the land in Egypt originally belonged to the king but over time the kings gave it away to support temples and reward officials. Estates could belong to the cults of gods or to dead ancestors. This meant little or no tax was paid on any wealth the estates gathered. Over time, royal wealth disappeared. Their political power was also threatened by the gradual rise in the power of the nomarchs. The office of nomarch had started to pass from father to son.

The Slide Into Chaos

Pepy II, who reigned for more than 90 years, was the last ruler of the Sixth Dynasty. After a number of poor flood seasons caused famine and some nomarchs declared themselves kings, Egypt started to split into a number of smaller states. Chaos followed. During the First Intermediate Period poverty and violence became the norm, as a later 13th Dynasty poem summed up, "All happiness has disappeared, the land is bowed down in misery."

THE MIDDLE KINGDOM

The First Intermediate Period ended only after nearly a century of upheaval. A king from Thebes reunited Egypt. Under Nebhepetra Mentuhotep II, the kingdom grew wealthy again. Once more, the government organized large-scale building projects. The reign of the 11th Dynasty was short, however. After just two more kings, power changed hands. Thanks either to violence or a peaceful succession, the throne passed to the vizier, Amenemhet.

Amenemhet founded a new dynasty, the 12th, which ruled from a new capital city called Itjawy (near el-Lisht). He selected the location to give him a more central powerbase. To keep control, he reorganized the administration. He kept the nomarchs, who had supported his seizure of power, but took away power from the regional governors. After he had ruled for 20 years, he made his son, Senwosret, his co-ruler. Egyptian territory expanded under their rule into Nubia and they constructed a long chain of forts along the Nile. Later 12th Dynasty rulers followed Amenemhet's example. Amenemhet was murdered while his son was away fighting the Libyans, but the system of government was strong enough to prevent the country falling into civil disorder.

The Careworn Kings

The greatest of the 12th Dynasty kings was Senwosret III. He conquered more of neighboring Nubia than any of his ancestors and spread Egyptian influence as far north as Palestine. He took away power from the nomarchs and increased the power of the central government.

Although the pyramids from this period were poorly built, the artwork of the 12th Dynasty was of a very high quality. It also showed a different idea of kingship. Statues of Senwosret III and his son, Amenemhet III, show them with very tired looking faces. Their faces are much more human-like than the god-images of the earlier dynasties, which had set out to illustrate the divine nature of the kings. Even the writings from the Middle Kingdom stressed how hard it was for the king to rule.

The Reign of the Hyksos

The last ruler of the 12th Dynasty was a queen, Nefrusobek, which suggests the royal family had probably died out because of the lack of a male heir. During the 13th Dynasty, Egypt continued to prosper, although no king stayed in power for very long. It may be that the real power lay in

---

SELECTED KINGS OF THE MIDDLE KINGDOM, 2040–1640 BCE

11th Dynasty 2040–1991
Nebhepetra Mentuhotep II
  2061–2010
Mentuhotep III 2010–1998
Mentuhotep IV 1998–1991

12th Dynasty 1991–1783
Amenemhet I 1991–1962
Senwosret I 1971–1926
Amenemhet II 1929–1892
Senwosret II 1897–1878
Senwosret III 1878–1841
Amenemhet III 1844–1797

Amenemhet IV 1799–1787
Queen Nefrusobek 1787–1783

13th Dynasty 1783–1640
About 70 kings, most with short reigns. Best known include:
Sobekhotep I c.1750
Hor c.1748?
Sobekhotep III c.1745
Neferhotep I c.1741–1730
Sobekhotep IV c.1730–1720
Sobekhotep V c.1720–1715
Aya c.1704–1690

Second Intermediate Period
1640–1550 BCE

14th Dynasty
Minor kings contemporary with dynasties 13 and 15

15th Dynasty
Hyksos kings ruling from Avaris:
Salitis
Sheshi
Khian
Apophis c.1585–1542
Khamudi c.1542–1532

16th Dynasty
Minor Hyksos kings contemporary with 15th Dynasty

17th Dynasty 1640–1550
Numerous Theban kings. The best known are:
Inyotef V c.1640–1635
Seqenenra c.1560–1555
Kamose 1555–1550

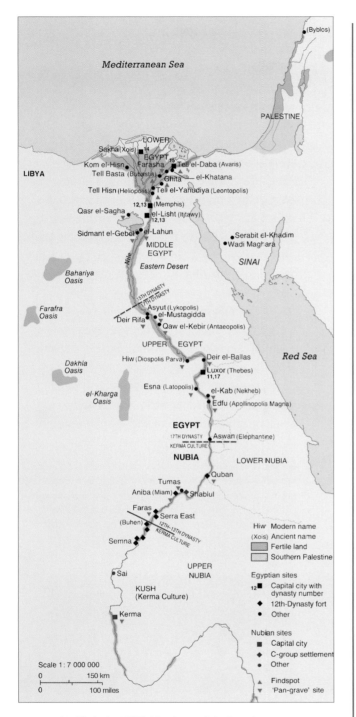

Egypt and Nubia in the Middle Kingdom and the Second Intermediate Period. The map shows capital cities and changing centers of power during the 11th to 17th Dynasties. These include areas of Nubia controlled by Egypt's line of forts along the Nile, and major sites of the Nubian culture groups.

Middle Kingdom and Second Intermediate Period

Find spots The finds include bronze weapons and distinctive pottery of the Middle Bronze Age culture of Palestine and those parts of Egypt settled by the Hyksos.

Dynasty capitals The centers of power often changed with dynasties. The local god of a dynastic capital became an important deity.

"Pan-grave" sites The "Pan-grave" people were nomads from the Eastern Desert who served as mercenary soldiers in Egypt and Nubia.

12th Dynasty forts and "C-group" settlements – The Egyptians built forts to control the "C-group" culture people from the Lower Nubia and to create a buffer zone against the fierce "Kerma culture" people of Kush (Upper Nubia). In the Second Intermediate Period, the Princes of Kush ruled Lower Nubia and attacked Upper Egypt.

the hands of officials like the vizier. Rival dynasties started to challenge for power. One of them was a foreign dynasty known as the Hyksos. They founded the 15th Dynasty.

The Hyksos had originated in Palestine but moved south to Egypt, where they settled in the Delta. They lived according to their own laws in their own communities. The Hyksos kings soon expanded their power until they controlled all of Egypt, They also made an alliance with Kush, an area of Upper Nubia, which was also ruled by local princes.

During the Second Intermediate Period, local rulers still held power in much of the Nile Valley. The Hyksos kings tolerated them, as long as they continued to pay tribute (a tax) to the Hyksos in their capital of Avaris. A new dynasty of Theban kings arose to the south of the delta. They, too, paid tribute to the Hyksos, but they had ambitions to free Egypt from foreign rule.

A Theban king named Seqenenra led an army against the Hyksos, but he died after a battle. His mummy showed terrible ax wounds. His successor, Kamose, continued the fight against the Hyksos and the Nubians of Kush.

THE NEW KINGDOM

It was the first king of the 18th Dynasty, a ruler named Ahmose, who finally got rid of the Hyksos from Egypt and the Prince of Kush from Lower Nubia. As a consequence of Ahmose's victories, by the end of the reign, Egypt controlled an area that stretched from Palestine to Upper Nubia.

Thutmose I led the armies of Egypt farther north than they had ever gone. He founded an empire in Palestine and Syria. His successor, Thutmose II, died young. Thutmose II's widow and sister, Hatshepsut, acted as regent for the boy king, Thutmose III, her husband's son by a lower-ranking wife. After several years, she declared herself king. Hatshepsut claimed the equivalent power to a male pharaoh. Statues show her wearing the traditional clothing of male kings. Hatshepsut's reign appears to have been peaceful and prosperous. Images in her beautiful temple at Deir el-Bahri show an expedition returning to her kingdom from a land the Egyptians named Punt (probably in present-day Eritrea) with valuable goods such as incense trees.

After Hatshepsut's death, Thutmose III fought a series of battles to consolidate Egypt's rule in both Palestine and Syria. Tribute paid from across the empire and gold from Nubia made Egypt the wealthiest place anywhere in the ancient world. The 18th Dynasty kings used this wealth to build magnificent temples to a range of both local and more widespread dieties. The most popular god was Amon. His temple at Karnak in Thebes became the largest in Egypt.

Akhenaten, the Sun King

The dominance of Amon was challenged temporarily during the reign of one of the 18th Dynasty's most remarkable rulers, Akhenaten. Akhenaten's father, Amonhotep III, built more lavishly than his ancestors as the remains of his palace at Thebes shows. His son, Amonhotep IV, changed his name to Akhenaten and made Aten (the sun disk) the main god of Egypt. Moving his capital to el-Amarna, he declared Aten the only god and closed down the temples of other gods.

Akhenaten broke with tradition. He allowed himself to be pictured by artists and sculptors in informal family scenes, kissing his beautiful wife, Nefertiti, or playing with his daughters.

Akhenaten's rule was unpopular, and during the reign of Tutankhamon, the new capital was abandoned and the old religious order restored.

Ramesses II's army in camp. Chariot horses are tethered in rows waiting to be fed and watered, while close by a chariot is being repaired. A company of foot soldiers is drilled by its standard-bearer, and the king's pet lion is being taken for a walk. None of the soldiers has a helmet; thick wigs or bushy hairstyles cushioned the head from the enemy's blows. The weapons shown include shields made of cowhide stretched on wooden frames and a bow made from two antelope horns lashed together.

Capital Cities of the New Kingdom and Later

Thebes The New Kingdom religious capital and the royal burial place.

Memphis Administrative capital for most of the 18th Dynasty and early 19th Dynasty.

El-Amarna New capital begun in year five of Akhenaten's rule. Abandoned 15 years later under Tutankhamon.

Pi-Ramesses Built under Ramesses II. The probable site is the Qantir district near Tell el-Daba in the northeast of the Delta.

Tanis Capital and burial place of kings of the 21st and 22nd Dynasties.

Bubastis City of origin and religious capital of the 22nd Dynasty.

Leontopolis Capital and probable burial place of some 23rd Dynasty rulers.

Akhenaten's name was carefully scratched off any monuments where it had been engraved. The capital at el-Armana was abandoned.

The Ramessid Pharaohs

After Tutankhamon, who died when he was still a young teenager, the throne passed to a series of officials. The third was a general, Ramesses, who founded the 19th Dynasty. His son, Seti I, was a strong ruler but it was his grandson, Ramesses II (1290–1224 BCE), who became one of the greatest of all the Egyptian pharaohs. He ruled for 66 years and erected more buildings and huge statues than any other Egyptian king.

Under the Ramessids, Egypt was prosperous, but its borders were increasingly under threat. The Libyans and other invaders threatened Ramesses II's successor, Merneptah. Ramesses III, the second king of the 20th Dynasty (1196–1070), fought land and sea battles against invaders who were known to the Egyptians as the Sea Peoples. During the 20th Dynasty, Egypt's power started to decline as the power of the priesthood at Thebes started to rival that of the king.

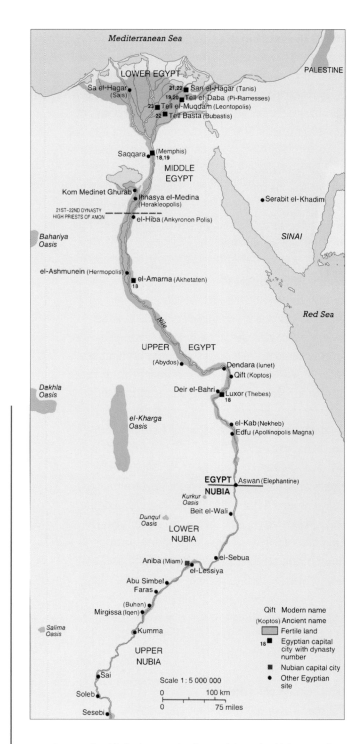

Egypt and Nubia in the New Kingdom and the early Third Intermediate Period. During the latter period the High Priests of Amon at Thebes controlled the area between Aswan and el-Hiba while the kings of the 21st and 22nd Dynasties ruled the north. The sites marked in Nubia are towns or temples built by the Egyptians during the New Kingdom.

The Egyptians believed that they were more important than all the other races with whom they came into contact. When foreigners appeared in Egyptian art, it was usually to show them in humble situations such as paying tribute or as bound prisoners. The Nubians to the south, the Libyans to the west, and the "vile Asiatics" to the east were pictured on the pharaoh's footstool or on the sole of his sandals, so that he symbolically trod on Egypt's enemies. In reality, however, some of Egypt's North African and West Asian neighbors were indeed potential threats.

Legacy of the Hyksos

Toward the end of the Middle Kingdom, large numbers of Asiatic peoples were allowed to settle in Egypt. Their presence had made it easier for the Hyksos kings to take power. The new immigrants brought with them new bronzeworking techniques, as well as improved types of looms and potter's wheels. They also introduced new types of weapons, as well as the tactic of fighting from horse-drawn chariots.

The Theban kings of the 17th and 18th Dynasties drove the Hyksos from Egypt into Palestine and Syria, which were then divided into small states, each with its own ruling prince. The Egyptians easily terrorized these princes into acknowledging the reign of the pharaoh and paying tribute to the Egyptian treasury. Northern Syria, however, was beyond the reach of the Egyptian kings. It belonged to the powerful kingdom of Mitanni (Naharin), an Indo–Iranian empire based in northern Mesopotamia.

Mitanni and the Hittites

Thutmose I attacked Mitanni and led his Egyptian army as far north as the Euphrates River. He celebrated his victory with a great elephant hunt at Niya. Keeping control of this new addition to the empire was troublesome, however. Egypt often had to send an army to recapture rebel states or to threaten Mitanni. Thutmose III fought 14 major campaigns in Palestine and Syria to restore order

among Egypt's tributary states. Inscriptions in the temple of Karnak show some of the loot carried off during these campaigns, and a relief shows exotic plants, birds, and animals collected for the pharaoh in Syria.

Eventually, Egypt and Mitanni came to a relatively peaceful coexistence. The pharaoh Thutmose IV and his son, Amonhotep III, both married princesses from Mitanni and sent wedding gifts of gold north to the rulers of Mitanni. Under the reign of Akhenaten, however, the pharaoh was so busy with his new religion that he largely ignored foreign affairs. Once again the empire of Mitanni broke away from Egyptian control.

The Hittites

By the 19th Dynasty, Mitanni had declined and Egypt's main rival in the Near East was now the Hittite Empire. The Hittites were a warlike people whose homeland was the mountains of Anatolia, now in modern-day Turkey, more than 600 miles (965 km) north from Thebes. The Hittites fought with Seti I and Ramesses II for control of Syria.

The battle of Qadesh in about 1285 BCE pitched the forces of Egypt under Ramesses II

Northern Frontiers of the Egyptian Empire

1. Farthest point reached by Thutmose I.

2. Frontier at the end of Thutmose III's reign.

3. Frontier in year 7 of Amonhotep II.

4. Frontier under Thutmose IV.

5. Frontier under Tutankhamon.

6. Frontier in year 21 of Ramesses II.

Egypt and the Near East (c.1530–1190 BCE). Egypt traded with Cyprus, Crete, and Mycenaean Greece. The great Near Eastern powers were the Mitannis, Hittites, Babylonians, and Assyrians. The numbers on the map refer to the box above.

against the Hittites led by Muwatalli II for control of Syria. Ramesses II won the battle—the first in history for which there is a contemporary account—but only a few years later he signed a peace treaty with the Hittites and married a

Hittite princess. The Hittite empire was destroyed in the 12th century BCE by a mass arrival of migrants identified as the Sea Peoples. Egypt itself narrowly avoided being overthrown by the Sea Peoples, but lost all of its Near Eastern empire.

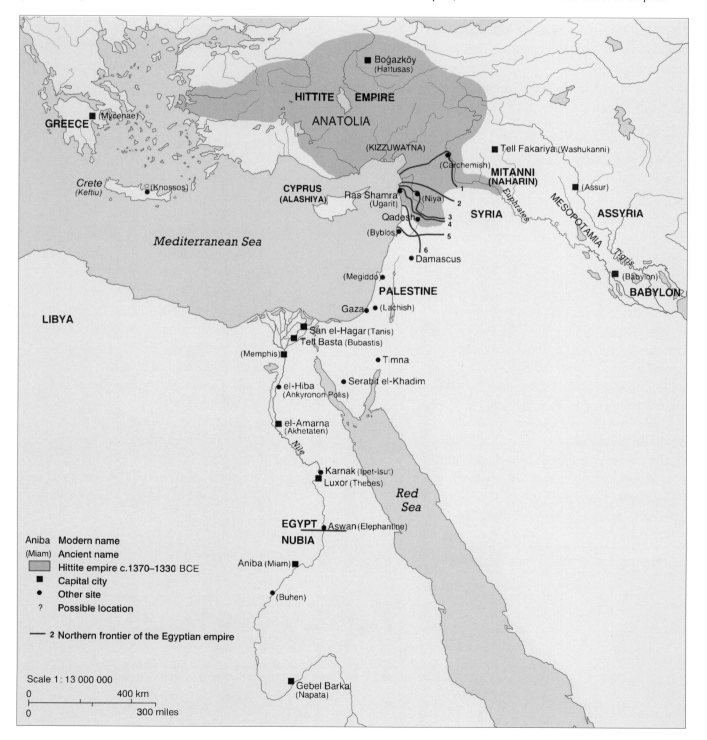

GREECE ■ (Mycenae)

■ Boğazköy (Hattusas)

HITTITE   EMPIRE
ANATOLIA

(KIZZUWATNA)

■ Tell Fakariya (Washukanni)

(Carchemish)

MITANNI
(NAHARIN)

(Assur)

Crete (Keftiu)   ● (Knossos)

CYPRUS (ALASHIYA)

Ras Shamra (Ugarit)   ● (Niya)   1   2

SYRIA

ASSYRIA

MESOPOTAMIA

Euphrates

Mediterranean Sea

Qadesh   3   4   5
(Byblos)

6

● Damascus

Tigris

● (Babylon)

BABYLON

(Megiddo) ●

PALESTINE

Gaza ● (Lachish)

LIBYA

San el-Hagar (Tanis)
Tell Basta (Bubastis)
(Memphis) ■

● Timna

● Serabit el-Khadim

● el-Hiba
(Ankyronon Polis)

■ el-Amarna
(Akhetaten)

Nile

Karnak (Ipet-Isut)
Luxor (Thebes)

Red Sea

EGYPT   ● Aswan (Elephantine)
NUBIA

Aniba (Miam) ■

(Buhen)

Aniba   Modern name
(Miam)   Ancient name
▨   Hittite empire c.1370–1330 BCE
■   Capital city
●   Other site
?   Possible location

—2   Northern frontier of the Egyptian empire

Scale 1 : 13 000 000
0   400 km
0   300 miles

■ Gebel Barkal
(Napata)

EGYPT DIVIDED

By the end of the 20th Dynasty, Egypt had lost much of its outlying territory. It had lost Nubia to the south as well as the Near Eastern empire in what are now Syria and Lebanon. The kings of the late 20th Dynasty, based in their Delta capital, had little influence even over Upper Egypt. The High Priest of Amon, who controlled the huge wealth of the temple of Karnak in Thebes, was the effective ruler of the south. The office of high priest had by now become hereditary: It was always held by a member of the same family.

The Third Intermediate Period

With the death of the last 20th Dynasty ruler, the so-called Third Intermediate Period began when a king called Smendes claimed power in the north of the country. He established his capital at Tanis in the northeastern Delta. The 21st Dynasty kings brought statues, obelisks, and decorated blocks created during earlier reigns to decorate the new capital.

The dynasty of high priests, based in Thebes, recognized the claims of the 21st Dynasty kings to power, but continued to effectively rule the south. Soon, however, the pharaohs' power in the Delta region was also disputed.

Dynastic Rivalries

During the late New Kingdom, a large number of settlers from neighboring Libya arrived in Lower Egypt, where they became a powerful political force. The first king of the 22nd

A Legacy of Warring kKings

The Victory Stela of Piye From c.730 BCE the Theban area was under the power of Nubian kings from Napata. One of these kings, Piye, recorded his victorious campaign in Egypt on a stela set up in the temple of Amon at Napata, southern Nubia. The stela is our main source for the history of this period.

Cities taken by Tefnakhte The cause of Piye's campaign was the expanding power of Tefnakhte of Sais, in the western Delta, who called himself "Chief of the West." The cities taken over by Tefnakhte are listed on Piye's victory stela.

Dynasty came from a family of Libyan descent. Shoshenq I was a strong ruler who won back a number of Egypt's former territories in Palestine.

By this time, the Jews had established the kingdom of Judah in the region. Shoshenq attacked Judah and removed a lot of treasure from the temple at Jerusalem. Details about the conquests were recorded in the buildings that Shoshenq added to the temple at Karnak. To protect his power base, Shoshenq installed his son as the high priest at Thebes, bringing the whole of Egypt once again under the control of a single dynasty. The unification lasted for about a century. Then, rebellions in the south started and a rival dynasty, the 23rd, was established in the Delta.

Egypt started to split into small areas, each with its own local ruler who called himself king. Two of the most important of these kings were the rulers of Hermopolis and Herakleopolis. King Orsokon IV of the 23rd Dynasty tried to take control of the south by getting rid of the by-then

SELECTED KINGS OF THE THIRD INTERMEDIATE PERIOD 1070–712 BCE

21st Dynasty 1070–945	22nd Dynasty 945–712	23rd Dynasty ca 828–712	24th Dynasty 724–712
Smendes 1070–1044	Shoshenq I 945–924	Rulers of Thebes, Hermopolis, Herakleopolis, Leontopolis, and Tanis. The order of these kings is unknown and some ruled at the same time. They include	Rulers of Sais:
Amenemnisu 1044–1040	Osorkon II 924–909		Tefnakhte 724–717
Psusennes I 1040–992	Takelot I 909–?		Bocchoris 717–712
Amenemope 993–984	Shoshenq II ?–883		
Osorkon I 984–978	Osorkon III 883–855	Pedubaste I 828–803	**25th Dynasty 770–712**
Siamun 978–959	Takelot II 860–835	Orsokon IV 777–749	Ruling Nubia and the Theban area:
Psusennes II 959–945	Shoshenq III 835–783	Peftjauawybast 740–725	Kashta 770–750
			Piye 750–712

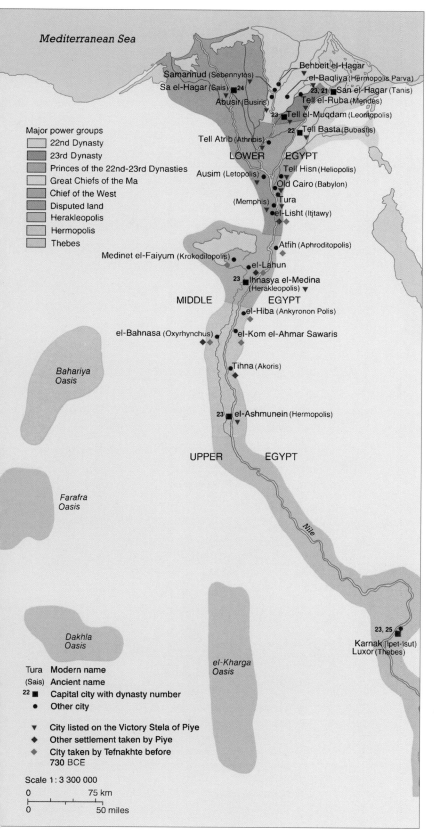

Major power groups
- 22nd Dynasty
- 23rd Dynasty
- Princes of the 22nd-23rd Dynasties
- Great Chiefs of the Ma
- Chief of the West
- Disputed land
- Herakleopolis
- Hermopolis
- Thebes

Mediterranean Sea

Samannud (Sebennytos)
Sa el-Hagar (Sais) 24
Behbeit el-Hagar
el-Baqliya (Hermopolis Parva)
23, 21 San el-Hagar (Tanis)
Abusir (Busiris)
Tell el-Ruba (Mendes)
23 Tell el-Muqdam (Leontopolis)
Tell Atrib (Athribis)
22 Tell Basta (Bubastis)
LOWER EGYPT
Ausim (Letopolis)
Tell Hisn (Heliopolis)
Old Cairo (Babylon)
(Memphis) Tura
el-Lisht (Itjtawy)
Atfih (Aphroditopolis)
Medinet el-Faiyum (Krokodilopolis)
el-Lahun
23 Ihnasya el-Medina
(Herakleopolis)
MIDDLE EGYPT
el-Hiba (Ankyronon Polis)
el-Bahnasa (Oxyrhynchus)
el-Kom el-Ahmar Sawaris
Tihna (Akoris)
23 el-Ashmunein (Hermopolis)
UPPER EGYPT

Bahariya Oasis

Farafra Oasis

Nile

Dakhla Oasis

el-Kharga Oasis

23, 25 Karnak (Ipet-Isut)
Luxor (Thebes)

Tura Modern name
(Sais) Ancient name
22 ■ Capital city with dynasty number
● Other city
▼ City listed on the Victory Stela of Piye
◆ Other settlement taken by Piye
◆ City taken by Tefnakhte before 730 BCE

Scale 1 : 3 300 000
0   75 km
0   50 miles

Egypt in the late Third Intermediate Period. All the major power groups and their capitals are shown. The Great Chiefs of the Ma were Libyans. The exact boundary between the territories ruled by the local kings of Hermopolis and Herakleopolis is uncertain.

hereditary office of the high priest of Amon. He did this by making his daughter high priestess. The high priestess was supposed to be the bride of the god Amon. This meant that she could not marry a man—and therefore she could not found a dynasty that would rival that of the royal family.

Kings Out of Nubia

To the south, the kings of Napata now ruled all of Nubia. Although they were Nubian by birth, the Napatans had adopted Egyptian culture and religion. They built pyramids and worshiped Amon. One of the 25th Dynasty Nubian rulers, Kashta, took control of the region between Aswan and Thebes.

Kashta's successor, Piye, invaded Upper Egypt on the pretext that he was restoring order and the proper worship of the gods. Egyptian practices and dieties were highly popular among the Nubians. Nubian rulers adopted many aspects of Egyptian culture, including building royal tombs in the shape of pyramids.

Piye forced the high priestess at Thebes to adopt his sister as her successor. He defeated the local ruler of Hermopolis and led his armies as far north as Memphis. After a fierce battle, King Piye entered the city, where he gave thanks for his victory in the temple of Ptah.

Tefnakhte, a chieftain who ruled the western Delta, was among the Egyptian rulers who had to acknowledge the rule of Piye and send him tribute in the form of payments of gold and other treasure. But after the Nubian king returned south, Tefnakhte continued to dominate the Delta. He was the first 24th Dynasty ruler of Sais.

THE LAST EGYPTIAN RULERS

The next 25th Dynasty king after Piye was Shabaka. He defeated the pharaoh in Sais who claimed rule over the Delta, and destroyed all other opposition. Shabaka then ruled a united kingdom of Egypt and Napata from Memphis. Reunification brought a period of renewed prosperity to Egypt. It ended as the whole region entered a period of great turmoil, which saw great empires rise and fall throughout the whole of West Asia.

The Assyrian Conquest of Egypt

In the seventh century BCE, the Assyrians of Mesopotamia were trying to expand their empire westward into Palestine. Egypt formed a defensive alliance with the kingdom of Judah there, which earned it the hostility of the Assyrians. They invaded Egypt. Initially the invasion failed but, sometime around 671 BCE, the Assyrian king Esarhaddon captured the important city of Memphis.

With the Assyrians in control, the 25th Dynasty king Taharqa fled south to Napata, and Egypt found itself forced to pay tribute to the Assyrians. In return for acknowledging the superiority of the Assyrians, the local ruler of Sais, Necho, was allowed to retain the title of king. He was killed fighting Tantamani, Taharqa's successor.

Conquest in the Late Period

The annals of Assurbanipal This Assyrian king left detailed records of his wars. He lists the Egyptian cities whose rulers paid homage to him. These local rulers are described as kings, showing how divided Egypt had become.

The route of Psammetichus's Army The route most likely taken by Psammetichus II when he invaded Napata in 591 BCE. Evidence for the route comes from the graffiti left by his army. Many of the soldiers were Greek mercenaries.

Stelae of Darius The Persian king Darius I completed a canal begun by Necho II. The canal linked a branch of the Nile River to the Red Sea. Darius set up four stelae recording this achievement along the banks of the canal.

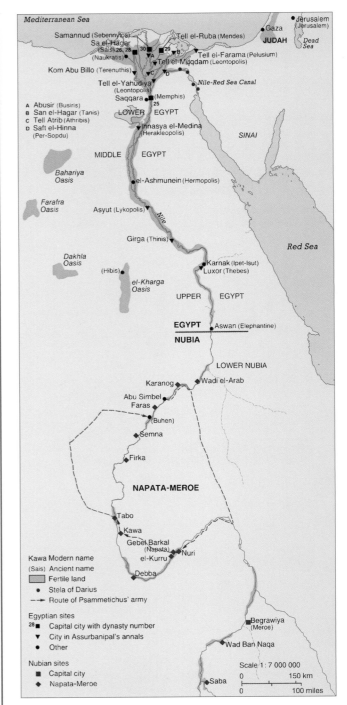

Egypt and the kingdom of Napata–Meroe, united under Shabaka before the Assyrian conquest. Meroe became the Nubian capital in around 591 BCE. At its peak, Meroe controlled territory that reached as far as Lake Chad, on the border of modern-day Nigeria, Niger, and Chad. The kingdom of Meroe endured until the fourth century CE.

SELECTED KINGS OF THE LATE PERIOD, 712–332 BCE

25th Dynasty 712–657
Ruling Egypt and Nubia:
Shabaka 712–698
Shebitku 698–690
Taharqa 690–664
Tantamani 664–657

26th Dynasty 664–525
Kings from Sais:
Necho I 672–664
Psammetichus I 664–610
Necho II 610–595

Psammetichus II 595–589
Apries 589–570
Amasis 570–526
Psammetichus III 526–525

27th Dynasty 525–404
(First Persian Period)
Cambyses 525–522
Darius I 521–486
Xerxes I 486–466
Artaxerxes I 465–424
Darius II 424–404

28th Dynasty 404–399
Amyrtaios 404–399

29th Dynasty 399–380
Nepherites I 399–393
Hakoris 393–380

30th Dynasty 380–343
Nectanebo I 380–362
Teos 365–360
Nectanebo II 360–343

Second Persian Period
Artaxerxes III 343–338
Arses 338–336
Darius III 335–332

The next Assyrian king, Assurbanipal, pushed Tantamani back to Napata and sacked Thebes. Necho's son, Psammetichus, was left as a puppet ruler in the Delta and waited for an opportunity to take control if the Assyrians found themselves distracted by trouble in other parts of their empire. When Psammetichus finally got his chance, he seized it. He drove the Assyrians from Egypt, reclaimed the throne for the Saite 26th Dynasty, and made himself king of all of Egypt.

Egypt Allies with Greece

Under the Saite kings of the 26th Dynasty, art and literature flourished in Egypt. The country was rarely at peace, however, as the balance of power shifted throughout West Asia. Babylon in Mesopotamia had risen to become a greater power than its neighbor Assyria. In 601 BCE, the Egyptian pharaoh Necho II had to defeat an attempted invasion led by the Babylonian ruler Nebuchadnezzar.

The next king, Psammetichus II, led an army deep into Nubia to intimidate the ruler of Napata. His successor, Apries, was deposed by an Egyptian general, Amasis. By this time, there were many Greeks serving in the Egyptian army and Amasis encouraged Greeks to establish a trading post at Naukratis, on a branch of the Nile in the west of the Delta.

The Persian Invasion

By the late sixth century BCE, Persia (modern-day Iran) had become the main power in West Asia. In 525 BCE, the Persian ruler Cambyses II invaded Egypt. He was helped in his conquest when the commander of the Egyptians' Greek allies switched sides to support the invaders. Cambyses successfully overthrew the Egyptian pharaoh, Psammetichus III, to become the first ruler of the 27th Dynasty, known as the First Persian Period.

Cambyses shocked the ancient world with the brutality and cruelty he showed toward his conquered subjects. He also showed contempt for the Egyptians' local deities, although he adopted the title and traditions of the pharaohs. His successor, Darius I, was a more moderate pharaoh, but the Egyptians nevertheless resented Persian rule. As a result, there were a number of rebellions against Persian rule, led by a series of Egyptian dynasties. None was successful for very long.

Persian rule in Egypt lasted until the late fourth century BCE. Then the young king of Macedon in Greece, Alexander the Great, conquered the whole of the Persian Empire. As part of his campaign he captured Persian naval bases farther north before marching in triumph into Egypt, where he was heralded as a savior by the Egyptians.

GREEK AND ROMAN RULE

When Alexander the Great died in 323 BCE, his mighty empire stretched across Asia to modern India. It soon started to break up. Ptolemy, a Macedonian general, brought Alexander's body to Egypt and built a tomb for him in the new city of Alexandria, founded by the emperor himself in the Delta. In 304 BCE, Ptolemy declared himself king of Egypt, beginning a dynasty that ruled for more than 250 years. The male rulers were all known as Ptolemy.

Artists and scholars were encouraged to come to Alexandria, where Ptolemy established a large library. Many Greeks and Macedonians were also given parcels of land in Egypt. The Ptolemies almost always appointed Greek rather than Egyptian officials.

A Murderous Family

It was usual for Ptolemaic kings to marry their sisters. The royal ladies often acted as co-rulers with their husband-brothers. There were frequent power struggles within the family. Many of the rulers seized or kept hold of power by murdering their relatives to prevent opposition.

Although there were some rebellions against Greek rule in Upper Egypt, the Ptolemies tried to keep their Egyptian subjects happy by building splendid temples to their Egyptian gods.

By the first century BCE, Rome had become the greatest power in the ancient world. The Romans set their sights on Egypt, which they wanted for its gold and grain.

Queen Cleopatra VII

In 48 BCE, the great Roman general Julius Caesar intervened in an Egyptian civil war to support Cleopatra as ruler. Cleopatra was the first Ptolemy to learn Egyptian (the others had spoken Greek). Caesar was attracted by Cleopatra's wit and beauty. They had a son.

Following Julius Caesar's murder in Rome, another Roman general, Mark Antony, also fell in love with Cleopatra. Antony and Cleopatra ruled until they were attacked by Julius Caesar's heir, Octavian (Augustus). Defeated, they were forced to take their own lives.

Roman Rule

As a province of the Roman Empire, Egypt was now ruled by prefects, who were appointed by the emperor. Temples continued to be built to the Egyptian gods, however. The worship of the

---

Desert Finds and Roman Roads

Papyrus Sites Sites at which papyri or ostraca written on in ancient Greek were found. They include plays and poems, books on medicine and mathematics, as well as many personal letters. Many great works of Greek and Roman literature survive only in copies that were preserved by the hot, dry climate of Egypt. Papyrus production was a major industry in Alexandria.

Roman Way-Stations The Romans built a road network in the Eastern Desert. Way-stations were provided with water supplies to make it easier for expeditions to cross the desert. The Romans quarried granite and porphyry, a stone used to make statues and vessels, and mined for emeralds. The roads led to ports on the Red Sea. The Persian-built canal linking the Nile River to the Red Sea was improved under the emperor Trajan.

SELECTED RULERS: THE GRECO-ROMAN PERIOD, 332 BCE–395 CE

Macedonian Dynasty 332–304	Ptolemaic Dynasty 304–30		
Alexander the Great 332–323	The reigns of most later Ptolemies were interrupted by civil wars.	Ptolemy VII 145	Ptolemy XII 80–58 & 55–51
Philip Arrhidaeus 323–316	Ptolemy I 304–284	Ptolemy VIII 170–163 & 145–116	Ptolemy XIII 51–47
Alexander IV 316–304	Ptolemy II 285–246	Queen Cleopatra III & Ptolemy IX 116–107	Ptolemy XIV 47–44
	Ptolemy III 246–221	Queen Cleopatra III & Ptolemy X 107–88	Queen Cleopatra VII 51–30
	Ptolemy IV 221–205	Ptolemy IX 88–81	
	Ptolemy V 205–180	Queen Cleopatra IV 81–80	**Roman Rule**
	Ptolemy VI 180–164 & 163–145	Ptolemy XI 80	30 BCE–395 CE
			Rule by prefects appointed by the emperor.

goddess Isis actually spread throughout the empire. Greek and Roman settlers in Egypt also adopted some Egyptian burial customs.

However, native Egyptians had very little power in their country. They lived under Roman law and were taxed heavily so that most Egyptian people were forced to live in extreme poverty. The ancient Egyptian culture—some parts of which had existed for thousands of years—was finally destroyed when Christianity became the official religion of the Roman Empire in the fourth century CE.

Egypt in the Greco-Roman Period. During the Ptolemaic era most of the country's wealth was centered on Alexandria, the capital. Land reclamation schemes and improved irrigation transformed the Faiyum into a prosperous agricultural area. Many Greeks settled there. Group tombs full of gilded mummies have been found at Bahariya Oasis.

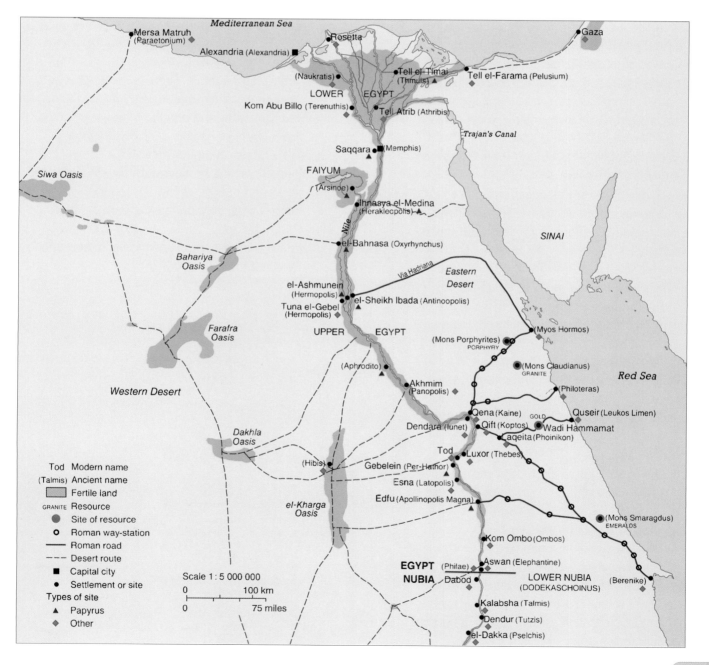

NUBIA

In most of ancient Nubia, the Nile Valley consisted of a narrow strip on either side of the riverbanks. Some Nubian groups settled in the few areas of land that were fertile enough to support crops and raise livestock. Other people lived as nomads in the deserts. During the Old Kingdom, the Egyptians often raided Lower Nubia to capture people and cattle. They also wanted to gain control of the profitable trade routes into Africa and the gold mines of the Nubian desert.

In the Middle Kingdom, Egypt conquered all of Lower Nubia as well as part of Upper Nubia (in present-day Sudan). The Egyptians tried to control their conquests by building a series of forts along the Nile River, mainly in the area of the Second and Third Cataracts. Egypt later lost control of Nubia, although some Egyptians continued to live there.

During the New Kingdom, Egypt once again conquered its southern neighbor. This time, instead of building forts, they built towns and temples. The population of Lower Nubia was very small by the end of the New Kingdom, perhaps as a result of years of drought.

From the Late Period, a native dynasty ruled the whole of Nubia. Influenced by the Egyptians, they continued to build temples and pyramids at their capitals in Napata and later Meroe. They built in the Egyptian style for hundreds of years. In the later Greco-Roman Period, a few temples to Egyptian and Nubian gods were built in Lower Nubia. One Nubian tribe, the Blemmyes, still worshiped the goddess Isis long after Egypt had become a Christian state.

Flooding of Nubia in Modern Times

The decision by the Egyptian government to build the new Aswan High Dam across the Nile River in the 1960s meant that much of what was Lower Nubia had to be flooded to create a giant reservoir, known as Lake Nasser. Before the flooding took place, however, the United

Nations organized a huge salvage campaign, funded by international donations, to save all the area's main archaeological ruins. This involved digging up and recording every item at the ancient sites. The urgent project brought together an international team of archaeologists to save as much as they could of the Nubian heritage. In fact, the concentrated burst of activity also allowed them to make many exciting finds and to learn a lot of new information about life in ancient Nubia.

Many of the most important monuments were physically removed to positions safely above the waterline. Some temples, such as Abu Simbel and Amada, were simply dismantled stone-by-stone and rebuilt on higher ground in the same area. Others, such as Kalabsha, were rebuilt at entirely new sites. Some of the temples were even removed from their sites and re-erected outside Egypt. The temple of Dabod, for example, now stands in a park in Madrid. At the Metropolitan Museum of Art in New York, a new wing was built specifically to house the temple of Dendur.

Much of what was Lower Nubia is now flooded by Lake Nasser, the reservoir created by the building of the Aswan High Dam in the 1960s. Some old sites such as Abu Simbel were reconstructed in safe locations. Moving the temple at Old Kalabsha to a new site—New Kalabsha—involved dismantling, transporting, and rebuilding some 13,000 blocks of stone. The original temple was the largest free-standing structure in all of Lower Nubia.

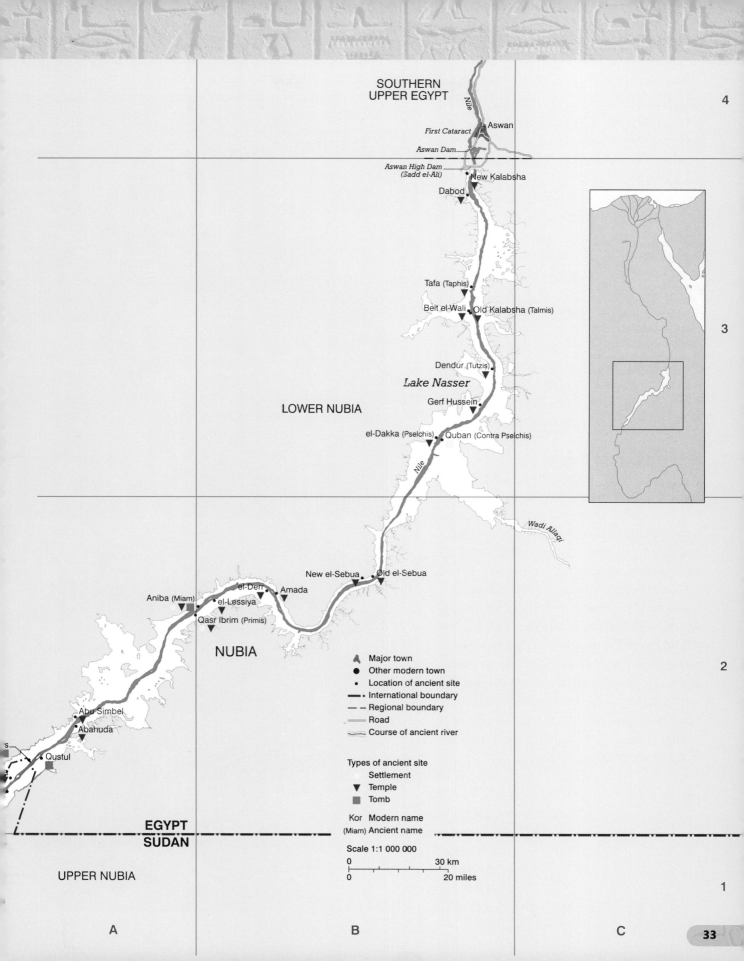

SOUTHERN
UPPER EGYPT

Nile

First Cataract • Aswan

Aswan Dam

Aswan High Dam
(Sadd el-Ali) ▼ New Kalabsha

Dabod ▼

Tafa (Taphis) ▼

Beit el-Wali ▼ ▼ Old Kalabsha (Talmis)

Dendur (Tutzis) ▼

Lake Nasser

LOWER NUBIA

Gerf Hussein ▼

el-Dakka (Pselchis) ▼ ▼ Quban (Contra Pselchis)

Nile

Wadi Allaqi

New el-Sebua • • Old el-Sebua

el-Derr ▼
Aniba (Miam) ▼ ■ • Amada
• el-Lessiya ▼

Qasr Ibrim (Primis) ▼

NUBIA

Abu Simbel •
Abahuda •
s

Qustul ■

EGYPT
SUDAN

UPPER NUBIA

🏛 Major town
● Other modern town
• Location of ancient site
▬ ▪ International boundary
▬ ▬ Regional boundary
═══ Road
〰〰 Course of ancient river

Types of ancient site
○ Settlement
▼ Temple
■ Tomb

Kor Modern name
(Miam) Ancient name

Scale 1:1 000 000

0 ———————— 30 km
0 ———————— 20 miles

4

3

2

1

A   B   C

Abu Simbel

Ramesses II built seven major temples in Nubia in the 19th Dynasty. The two most famous of these are the temples at Abu Simbel, known as the Great Temple and the Small Temple. They are built into a sandstone cliff.

Carved out inside the cliff are two pillared halls decorated with rock-cut reliefs. Some of the reliefs show the pharaoh in his chariot fighting the Hittites at Qadesh. Ramesses was very proud of his role in the victory and wanted to show off his military prowess.

The Great Temple was designed so that twice a year, during the summer and winter solstices, the rising sun would shine through its entrance and reach the inner part of the temple, lighting up the statues of the gods. In the beautiful Small Temple, the Great Royal Wife, Nefertari, is shown being crowned as a goddess.

The Rescue of the Temples

In the 1960s, the temples of Abu Simbel were threatened with destruction. They would have been submerged under the rising waters of Lake Nasser when the Aswan High Dam was built. In order to save them, people and governments across the world raised the sum of $40 million. The Great Temple was cut into 807 large blocks and the Small Temple into 235 blocks. Meanwhile, an artificial cliff was built 215 feet (66 m) above the original site. The blocks were moved to the new site and put back together again exactly as before; they were covered by a huge concrete dome. The operation took four and a half years. Now Abu Simbel is not only a wonder of the ancient world but also a wonder of modern technology.

1 Terrace
2 Grand entrance with colossi
3 Great pillared hall
4 Side rooms
5 Small pillared hall
6 Anteroom
7 Sanctuary with niche for cult statues

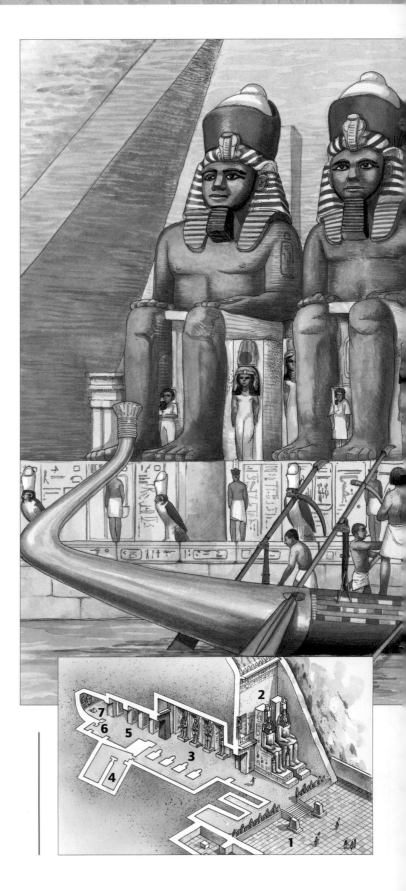

LEFT: A cutaway view showing the plan of the Great Temple. Most Egyptian temples had a walled forecourt, a grand entrance, one or more pillared (hypostyle) halls, and a sanctuary that housed the cult statues.

ABOVE: Priests and a high official arrive at the Great Temple of Abu Simbel for the festival of the sun god. The most important festivals were on the two days of the year when the sun's rays shone through the entrance and along the main axis to the sanctuary. In ancient times the temples would have looked much more colorful than they do today. The rock-cut facade of the Great Temple has four 70-foot- (21-m-) high statues (colossi) of Ramesses II. His mother, his chief wife, and eight of his 140 children are shown on a much smaller scale at the feet of the statues.

SOUTHERN UPPER EGYPT

In ancient times the border between Egypt and Nubia lay at Biga. The island was submerged after the building of the Aswan High Dam. In the first four nomes, or districts, of Upper Egypt, the Nile Valley is narrow and the desert is very close to the riverbanks.

There was not much land to grow crops and vegetables, but the deserts were very rich in valuable minerals. Sandstone, granite, diorite, quartzite, and steatite (used for buildings and statues) were quarried from sites close to Aswan. An amethyst mine was also located in the same area. Gold was found in both the Eastern and Nubian Deserts.

A Temple From Earliest Times

The dry climate of Southern Upper Egypt is perfect for preserving ancient remains and preventing decay. Experts therefore know more about ancient southern Egypt than about the north, where the land is more marshy, making both excavation and preservation difficult.

The first four nomes of Upper Egypt were important in Predynastic times. Hierakonpolis (now known as Kom el-Ahmar) was one of the earliest towns to be built along the Nile. The Predynastic settlement was a lively city that extended more than 3 miles (5 km) along the edge of the Western Desert.

In the First Dynasty, a new town and temple were built on the floodplain. The temple is the oldest in Egypt that historians know about in detail. Treasures found in the temple include mace heads and palettes. They are the only record of some of the early Egyptian rulers. There were also ivory figurines, a golden hawk, and life-size copper statues of two Sixth Dynasty kings.

This ancient relief of deities and a ruler is on the wall of the Greco-Roman temple overlooking the River Nile at Kom Ombo. Half of the temple was dedicated to Sobek, the crocodile god, and the other half to Haroeris, who was a form of the falcon god Horus. Sacred crocodiles were reared in a pool inside the temple grounds. There was also a cemetery for mummified crocodiles.

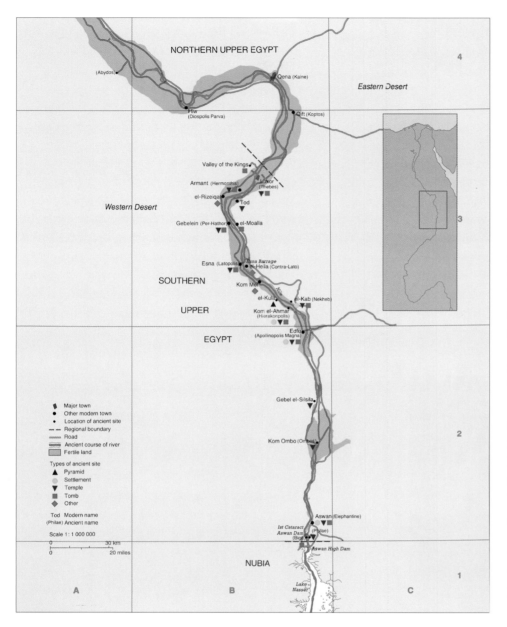

This map shows the most important historic centers of Southern Upper Egypt. The leading archaeological sites—Aswan, Philae, Biga, Edfu, and Thebes, are described in more detail on the following pages.

people were cut into the desert cliffs.

Every large town in ancient Egypt contained a necropolis, or "city of the dead." Its streets were lined with tombs instead of houses. The desert necropolises often survived long after their towns on the floodplain disappeared.

Greco–Roman Temples

The most spectacular remains in Southern Upper Egypt consist of a series of impressive temples dating back to the Greco-Roman period late in Egyptian history. There are examples at Philae, Aswan, Kom Ombo, Edfu, el-Kab, Esna, and Tod. Although the temples were built when the country was under foreign rule, they are traditionally Egyptian in style.

Edfu is the most famous and probably the best preserved of all the temples, but the temples at Esna and Kom Ombo are also outstanding examples of temple architecture. Esna was dedicated to the ram god Khnum. A calendar inscribed on the walls tells us about the many festivals that were celebrated there. The temple at Kom Ombo is unusual because the left side of the structure is dedicated to one deity (the falcon god Haroeris, also known as Horus the Elder), and the right side to another, the crocodile god Sobek.

An Ancient Town

Nekheb (modern-day el-Kab) is another important site dating from Predynastic times. This settlement developed into a typical Egyptian town. The houses were built close together inside a huge mud-brick enclosure wall. The main temple, dedicated to the local vulture goddess, was situated inside the town. It was rebuilt many times over a period of about 3,000 years. Smaller temples were built on the edge of the desert, while the tombs of important

City of Aswan

Aswan took its ancient name of Elephantine from the elephant-ivory trade. The main part of the city was situated on Elephantine Island in the middle of the Nile River. Aswan was close to the border between Egypt and Nubia. Troops were stationed there to protect the border and to take part in mining and trading expeditions. All the gold from the Nubian mines passed through Aswan. Donkey trains took desert routes to trade with African peoples.

In a Sixth-Dynasty tomb at Aswan there is an account of some trading trips. The tomb owner was a courtier named Harkhuf. He tells how his explorations took him south. Each trip took seven or eight months. On the third trip he returned

Reliefs at the temple of Edfu tell the story of how Horus, the hawk-headed god, defeated the god Seth.

home with 300 donkeys carrying precious goods such as ivory, ebony, incense, and leopard skins.

Best of all, he had brought back a pygmy to dance for the king. Harkhuf quotes a letter from King Pepy II. The king, who was a young boy, was thrilled. He ordered Harkhuf to hurry to the palace by boat. The pygmy was to be guarded day and night. "Check on him 10 times a night!" wrote Pepy. "My Majesty wants to see this pygmy more than all the treasures of Sinai and Punt!"

Holy Islands

Philae and Biga are a pair of islands in the Nile River just below Aswan. On Biga Island was the Abaton, a mound that was linked with the god Osiris.

When Set murdered Osiris he tore the body into many pieces. Biga was said to be the place where the left leg of Osiris was buried. In one version of the myth Isis, the wife of Osiris, collected the pieces and joined them by magic. Several places claimed to be the site where the whole body of Osiris was buried. Biga was one. The soul of Osiris was thought to haunt the island in the form of a bird. Biga was so holy that only priests could land there.

Philae was sacred to Isis. The temple of Isis was the largest of several temples and shrines on the island. Most of the buildings date to Greco-

Roman times. Pilgrims came from all over the Roman Empire to worship Isis here.

The last known inscriptions in ancient Egyptian are at Philae. The religion of Egypt survived here for longer than in any other place.

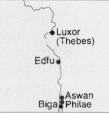

Many of the buildings were in excellent condition until building of the first Aswan Dam began in 1898. Once the dam was finished, Philae and Biga were flooded for most of each year. When the second Aswan Dam was constructed they were permanently submerged. The temples of Philae were reassembled on Agilika Island about 600 yards (550 m) from their original site and are now well above the water level again.

There was a walled town at Edfu from the Old Kingdom onwards. The site was ideal for settlement because it was near the the river but on high ground that was safe from flooding. Walls surround the site of the city, most of which has not been excavated.

The site is now famous for its Temple of Horus. Few buildings from the ancient world are as well preserved as this temple. It was almost completely intact when it was first excavated in the 1860s. Inscriptions give many construction details. It was begun under Ptolemy III in 237 BCE and took about 180 years to complete. The massive pillars of the hypostyle (Greek for "bearing pillars") hall were designed to imitate a thicket of marsh plants. On some pillars the figures of the Egyptian gods were damaged by early Christian visitors and have been almost erased. Within the temple, the pillars add to a subtle pattern of light and darkness. Some rooms are entirely dark; others are lit by shafts of light that shine between the pillars.

On the great pylon (gateway) Ptolemy XII strikes a group of prisoners with a mace. Egyptian kings had been shown in this pose for nearly 3,000 years. Inside the temple are reliefs depicting Horus fighting the enemies of his father, Osiris. The evil god Set turns himself into a hippopotamus, but Horus fearlessly hunts him down with a magical harpoon. This story was acted out each year during the festival of The Victory of Horus. Inside the pylon is a large temple courtyard, which is the only one preserved in Egypt. The decorated walls of the courtyard continue to form an enclosure behind the temple.

A colonnade leads to the pylon, or gateway, of the reconstructed temple of Isis at Philae. The colonnades that welcomed pilgrims and led them toward the sanctuary were probably later additions to the temple. The first structures on the island were built during the 2th Dynasty, in the seventh century BCE.

Thebes

During the period of the Old Kingdom, Thebes was little more than a small provincial town. When a local dynasty reunited Egypt following the First Intermediate Period, however, Thebes soon grew to become an important administrative and religious center. From the New Kingdom onwards, it was one of the largest urban areas in all of Egypt. Its magnificent buildings were famous throughout the ancient world. Thebes is actually a Greek name; the Egyptians called the city Waset.

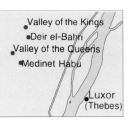

Thebes covered an area of about 3 square miles (8 sq km) and was located on both sides of the River Nile. The east bank was reserved for the living, while the west bank was mainly for a necropolis for the dead. Today, the site of

Floodlights illuminate the forecourt of Amenophis III in the temple at Luxor. Amenophis was largely responsible for building the inner part of the temple. The forecourt leads to a series of antechambers, including a shrine celebrating the king's birth.

Eastern Thebes is largely covered by the modern city of Luxor. Little remains of the ancient houses and splendid palaces that once stood on the site, although some of the great stone temples have survived.

The City of the Dead

A mountain, known as "The Peak," loomed over Western Thebes. The Egyptians believed the mountain was an entrance to the Underworld where people went after death. They therefore positioned as many of the royal tombs as close to the foot of the mountain as possible. The tombs were cut into the cliffs and ravines close to the Peak. The necropolis was known as "The Place of Truth."

The builders, artists, and sculptors who constructed, decorated, and maintained the royal tombs lived in a settlement at Deir el-Medina in housing provided by the government. Their homes, shrines, and family tombs have been well preserved and extensively excavated. Today we know more about these people than about any other ancient Egyptian community.

The Valley of the Kings

The pyramid burials of Old and Middle Kingdom rulers were soon robbed of their treasures. From the 18th Dynasty onwards, the rulers tried instead to hide their burial places. Enene, the chief architect of Amonhotep I and Thutmose I, tells us: "I oversaw the cutting out of the rock tomb of his Majesty in a lonely place where nobody could look on." This lonely place was the Valley of the Kings, located in Western Thebes.

Throughout the New Kingdom, rulers were buried in tombs hidden in the valley. Mortuary temples were built on the west bank to serve the cult of the dead kings. Some rulers also built palaces in Western Thebes. The largest was the palace of Amonhotep III at Malqata.

Thebes: the city and temples on the east bank of the Nile River and the tombs, temples, and palaces on the west bank.

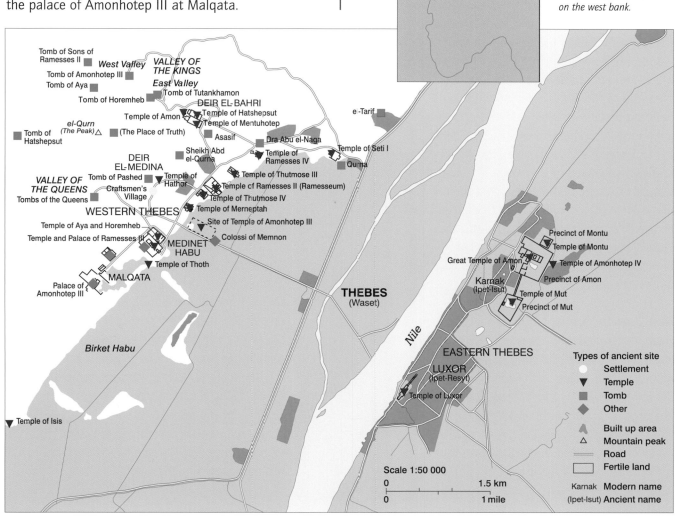

Tomb of Sons of Ramesses II
West Valley
VALLEY OF THE KINGS
Tomb of Amonhotep III
Tomb of Aya
East Valley
Tomb of Horemheb
Tomb of Tutankhamon
DEIR EL-BAHRI
Temple of Amon
Temple of Hatshepsut
Temple of Mentuhotep
e -Tarif
el-Qurn (The Peak) △
(The Place of Truth)
Tomb of Hatshepsut
Asasif
Dra Abu el-Naga
Temple of Seti I
Sheikh Abd el-Qurna
Temple of Ramesses IV
DEIR EL-MEDINA
Qurna
Temple of Thutmose III
Tomb of Pashed
Temple of Hathor
Temple of Ramesses II (Ramesseum)
VALLEY OF THE QUEENS
Craftsmen's Village
Temple of Thutmose IV
Tombs of the Queens
WESTERN THEBES
Temple of Merneptah
Site of Temple of Amonhotep III
Temple of Aya and Horemheb
Colossi of Memnon
Temple and Palace of Ramesses III
MEDINET HABU
Temple of Thoth
MALQATA
Palace of Amonhotep III
Precinct of Montu
Temple of Montu
Great Temple of Amon
Temple of Amonhotep IV
Precinct of Amon
Karnak (Ipet-Isut)
Temple of Mut
Precinct of Mut
Birket Habu
THEBES (Waset)
Nile
EASTERN THEBES
LUXOR (Ipet-Resyt)
Temple of Isis
Temple of Luxor

Types of ancient site
- ○ Settlement
- ▼ Temple
- ■ Tomb
- ◆ Other
- ⧉ Built up area
- △ Mountain peak
- ═ Road
- ▭ Fertile land

Karnak Modern name
(Ipet-Isut) Ancient name

Scale 1:50 000
0 — 1.5 km
0 — 1 mile

Luxor

The god Amon was the local diety of Thebes. After the ruler of Thebes had expelled the Hyskos from Egypt and founded the 18th Dynasty, Amon became an important fertility god throughout Egypt.

The god had two main temples in Thebes: Karnak in the north, and Luxor in the south. Most of the Luxor temple was built in the 18th Dynasty during the reign of Amonhotep III. Ramesses II later added a courtyard and pylon, or a gateway supported on pillars. The avenue of sphinxes that joined Luxor to Karnak was added during the Late Period.

The Luxor temple has one of the most impressive entrances of any Egyptian temple. The pylon has carvings that illustrate Ramsesses II's bravery at the battle of Qadesh against the Hittites. Outside the pylon stand some huge statues of Ramesses II. The temple is built around two courtyards. A narrow colonnade, which formed a route for processions, links them. The walls were decorated with scenes from the Festival of Opet, one of the most important of all the festivals held in Thebes.

During the annual festival, the Amon of Karnak visited Luxor for 11 days. The cult statues of Amon, his wife Mut, and their sons Khons were placed in beautiful decorated boats on the Nile. Watched by huge crowds, the vessels were towed from Karnak to Luxor. Musicians, dancers, and acrobats formed a procession on the riverbank.

New Uses for Ancient Temples

Deep inside the temple is a room decorated with reliefs that tell the story of the birth of Amonhotep III. Close to this room is an area of the temple that was turned into a shrine to the Roman emperors in around 300 CE. Nearly 1,000 years later a mosque (Muslim place of worship) was built in the courtyard of Ramesses II. The mosque is still in use today.

Temple at Karnak

Karnak is the site of a group of temples that cover an area of about one square mile (1.6sq km). The most important temple was the Great Temple of Amon. The name Amon means 'the hidden one'. He was the god of invisible forces like the wind. He became an important god during the Middle Kingdom. Few

Most pillars in the Great Hypostyle Hall at Karnak, built in the 13th century BCE, fell down during earthquakes but were reconstructed in the 19th century.

Middle Kingdom temples survive because each pharaoh wanted to please Amon by building a new temple to him. They knocked down existing temples and reused the stones. The Great Temple was continually enlarged and rebuilt over a period of 2,000 years.

The Triumph of Amon

In the early 18th Dynasty, Thebes became the capital of Egypt. Amon was linked with the sun god, Ra, and the new deity Amon-Ra was credited with creating the world.

During the New Kingdom, Karnak became the largest and richest temple complex in Egypt. The complex included a sacred lake, smaller temples and shrines surrounded by a mud-brick enclosure. The eastern part is the oldest. Successive kings built new entrances so the temple now has ten huge pylons (gateways).

The most famous part of the temple is the Great Hypostyle Hall. Begun by Seti I and finished by Ramesses II, the huge hall has 134 columns. In one of its many courtyards 751 stone statues and stelae and 17,000 bronze figurines were found buried.

The other main buildings at Karnak include temples to the god Montu and the creator god Ptah. The temple of Mut once held more than 700 granite statues.

Thebes West Bank Sites

After King Mentuhotep reunited Egypt in 2040 BCE, he built himself a tomb and temple on the west bank at Deir el-Bahri. Nearly 600 years later, Queen Hatshepsut built her temple against the cliff face of Deir el-Bahri. Other pharaohs also built here, including Ramesses II. His temple is called the Ramesseum and was the site of the first strike over wages, in 1165 BCE, by necropolis workers.

A town grew up around the great temple of Ramesses III at Medinet Habu, the best-preserved mortuary temple of Thebes. Its strong fortifications meant that Medinet Habu was used as a safe place in times of unrest.

The funeral procession of Tutankhamon. The royal coffins, weighing more than 2,900 lb (1,315 kg), lie on a frame inside a bark (boat) shrine. The shrine, mounted on a sled, is dragged along by courtiers and a team of oxen. The courtiers wear white headbands, a sign of mourning. Next comes an alabaster shrine shouldered by priests. This holds the four canopic jars containing the liver, lungs, stomach, and intestines of the king.

All kinds of people were buried in the Theban necropolis. One 11th Dynasty tomb held the bodies of 60 soldiers killed in battle. Paintings in royal tombs usually showed traditional rituals while the art in private tombs showed everyday life. The Tombs of the Nobles were for those of high office. Many contain magnificent paintings and some remained unfinished because their owners suddenly fell from royal favor.

Members of the royal families were buried in the Valley of the Queens. The finest tomb there belonged to Queen Nefertari.

The Royal Mummies

Sixty-three tombs have been found in the Valley of the Kings. In most, rock-cut passages and stairways lead to the burial chamber. The walls are decorated with religious scenes. Seti I and Ramesses VI had the most elaborate tombs.

Each king was buried with valuable funerary objects. By the end of the New Kingdom, most of the tombs had been robbed. Under the 21st Dynasty, many of the royal mummies were moved to a secret hiding place where they remained hidden until 1881. Now the rulers rest in the Egyptian Museum in Cairo.

Northern Upper Egypt was the heartland of ancient Egypt. It was where the ancient Egyptian civilization first emerged. The Badarian/Tasian and Naqada cultures, the early predecessors from whom the Egyptians developed, are named after sites in this region that have yielded evidence of early settlement. The discovery of easily mined gold in the Eastern Desert was a key factor in the rise of an early kingdom centered on Northern Upper Egypt. Just as important as the presence of gold were the trade routes that led east from this part of the Nile across the desert to the Red Sea and the shipping routes that began there. The major route was the Wadi Hammamat, which ran along a dry riverbed.

Gold mines and stone quarries lay along the wadi. Ship parts and cargo boxes dating back over 4,000 years have recently been found in caves on the Red Sea coast. The physical evidence confirmed what archaeologists studying ancient trade have long suspected. Ships that carried goods on the Nile were dismantled and carried through the wadi on the 100-mile (160 km) journey to the Red Sea. At the coast, the ships were put back together for the journey north to carry turquoise miners to Sinai or south to Yemen or Punt (possibly modern-day Eritrea) to trade for spices and incense. On the return journey, the ships were taken apart again to be carried back to the Nile.

A Holy Place

Another site in northern Upper Egypt that started to be important in early times was Abydos. It was a religious rather than a political center. Some of the predynastic and first and second Dynasty kings were buried in tombs close to Abydos. The city's main god was Khentanetiu (Chief of the Westerners). The Westerners were the spirits of the dead who had reached the Egyptian paradise—"the beautiful West." From the late Old Kingdom, Khentamentiu was linked to the god Osiris.

During the Middle and New Kingdoms, Abydos was the most important of a number of places that claimed to be the burial site of Osiris. Every year, a festival was held there that told the story of Osiris's murder and rebirth. Pilgrims came from all over Egypt to attend, and every Egyptian wanted to visit Abydos at least once in their life. The festival was a favorite subject in tomb paintings, so that a person who had not managed to make the journey in life would be able to make it after death.

Another belief was that by building a tomb or monument at Abydos a person could share in the resurrection of Osiris. Not only kings but also ordinary Egyptians put up stelae (carved pillars) so their spirits could join Osiris.

The Shadow of Thebes

From the Middle Kingdom onward, the town of Thebes grew rapidly, overshadowing all the other towns of Northern Upper Egypt. New Kingdom rulers did build temples at Abydos, Koptos, and Dendara but they were far outshone by the size and wealth of the temples at Thebes. Thebes remained the most important political and religious center in the region until the end of the Late Period.

Under Greek and Roman rule other towns flourished. During the Greco-Roman period, many fine temples were built at sites like Dendara, Nag el-Madamud, Akhmim, and Hiw. These temples usually replaced earlier, simpler buildings. The god Min was worshipped at Koptos for 3,500 years, and his temple was rebuilt many times during that period. Among the objects found in this temple were three huge statues of Min. They are the oldest colossal stone statues in the world.

Northern Upper Egypt was the heartland of Egypt's earliest dynasties, which had political and religious centers at Naqada, Qift, and Abydos. During the Old Kingdom, Dendara was important. The Middle Kingdom was dominated by Abydos, while the New Kingdom saw the rise of Thebes. Dendara and Abydos are described in more detail on the following pages.

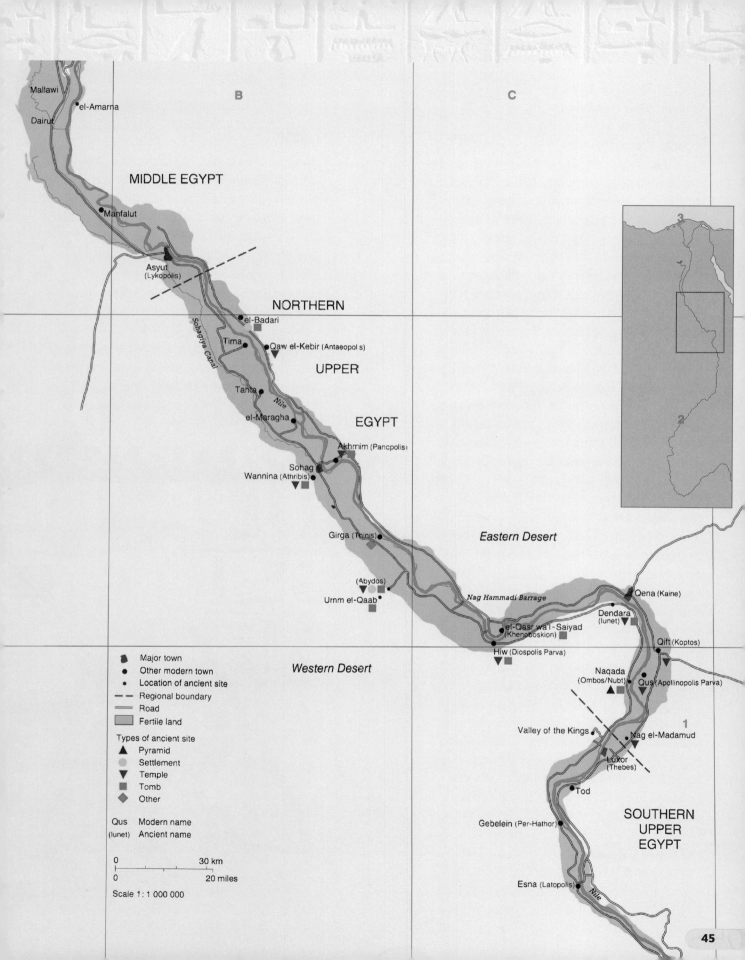

Mallawi
el-Amarna
Dairut

MIDDLE EGYPT

Manfalut

Asyut
(Lykopolis)

NORTHERN

Sohagiya Canal

el-Badari
Tima
Qaw el-Kebir (Antaeopolis)

UPPER

Nile

Tanta
el-Maragha

EGYPT

Akhmim (Panopolis)

Sohag
Wannina (Athribis)

B

C

3

Eastern Desert

Girga (Thinis)

(Abydos)
Umm el-Qaab

Nag Hammadi Barrage

Qena (Kaine)

Dendara
(Iunet)

el-Qasr wa'l-Saiyad
(Khenoboskion)

Qift (Koptos)

Hiw (Diospolis Parva)

Western Desert

Naqada
(Ombos/Nubt)

Qus (Apollinopolis Parva)

1

Valley of the Kings

Nag el-Madamud

Luxor
(Thebes)

Tod

SOUTHERN
UPPER
EGYPT

Gebelein (Per-Hathor)

2

Esna (Latopolis)

Nile

	Major town
●	Other modern town
•	Location of ancient site
– – –	Regional boundary
	Road
	Fertile land

Types of ancient site
▲ Pyramid
⬤ Settlement
▼ Temple
◼ Tomb
◆ Other

Qus   Modern name
(Iunet) Ancient name

0   30 km
0   20 miles
Scale 1 : 1 000 000

45

Dendara

During the Old Kingdom and the First Intermediate Period, Dendara was a very important town in Northern Upper Egypt. It was the capital of the 6th nome of Upper Egypt, but its main importance was due to its religious connections. It was the main cult center of Hathor, who was a popular goddess of birth and death. Hathor was originally worshiped as a personification of the Milky Way and later as a cow-deity whose milk helped nourish humankind. Various cow burials have been found in the necropolis. The goddess was also connected with love, music, foreign lands, and precious metals.

Every year, the cult statue of Hathor made a ritual journey from Dendara to Edfu for the festival of her "marriage" to the god Horus, who later became associated with the sun-god Ra. Horus and the couple's son, Ihy, each had their own temple at Dendara. Today, only the temple complex of Hathor still stands.

The Sacred Area

A sacred lake lay inside the enclosure wall of the Hathor temple. Priests washed in the lake to purify themselves before entering a sanctuary. Among the buildings near the temple are a sanatorium (hospital) and two "birth houses." Sick people slept in the sanitorium in the hopes that Hathor would tell them in a dream how to cure their sickness. Patients also drank or bathed in sacred water to heal themselves.

A birth house was a special shrine that celebrated the birth of a deity or god. At Dendara, reliefs in the two birth houses show Hathor giving birth to her son Ihy. Pregnant Egyptian women prayed to Hathor, Lady of Dendara, to bring them safely through the process of giving birth.

The Temple of Hathor

The temple of Hathor at Dendara was built and decorated between the second century BCE and the first century CE. It was the largest and most elaborately decorated temple built anywhere in Egypt during the period. There are two wonderful columned halls. At the top of the columns were capitals in the form of a sistrum, a musical instrument sacred to the goddess. Several shrines were also built on top of the flat roof. Two were dedicated to the god Osiris. They were reached by staircases built inside the temple walls. The roof is quite rare among Egyptian ruins. Very few ceiling structures survive in ancient Egyptian temples.

Sacred treasures were once hidden in small underground rooms near the sanctuary. On the back wall of the temple, Cleopatra VII appears with her son by Julius Caesar. In the middle of this wall is a huge symbol of Hathor. Most visitors prayed to the goddess at this spot.

Abydos

Excavations in the southern part of Abydos have revealed the presence of a Middle Kingdom and Second Intermediate Period town. Little of

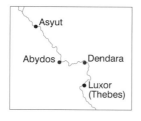

the main temple of Osiris, located in central Abydos, remains. The necropolis (city of the dead) of Abydos spreads along the desert edge for about one mile (1.6km). The first burials were made there in the fourth millennium BCE.

The Mother of Pots

The earliest royal tombs at Abydos were underground palaces with brick-lined rooms. They are near the area known as Umm el-Qaab (which means "Mother of Pots") and date to the little-known Dynasty O. Some First-Dynasty kings built tombs at Umm el-Qaab and huge brick enclosures nearer to the town. The tomb of King Djer was later mistaken for the tomb of Osiris.

Umm el-Qaab gets its name from the thousands of pieces of pottery left by pilgrims in what they thought was Osiris' tomb.

The Temple of Seti I

Several kings built mortuary temples in the southern part of Abydos. The best preserved of these is the temple of King Seti I. Known as the Memnonium, it was built of fine white limestone. Originally, there were two pylons, two courtyards and two columned halls. The plan of the inner area is unique. It has seven sanctuaries side by side.

One sanctuary was for the worship of the cult of Seti, another was dedicated to Osiris. Its walls are decorated with scenes from the myth of Osiris. The reliefs are some of the most beautiful in all of Egyptian art. They show ceremonies associated with the gods. In another part of the temple, Seti is shown with his heir, Ramesses II, making offerings to royal ancestors. Ramesses completed his father's tomb and built his own nearby.

Behind Seti I's temple is a mysterious building known as the Osireion. It was probably started by Seti I and finished by his grandson, Merneptah. The main feature was an underground hall built in red granite. In the middle of the hall there was an artificial island and a canal was dug to surround the island with water. A sarcophagus was placed on the island. The building could have been a dummy royal tomb, a model of the tomb of Osiris or a re-creation of the first mound of land rising above the waters of chaos.

This painting from Abydos was created in about 1413 BCE, during the 18th Dynasty, to decorate the tomb of Sennefer, the mayor of Thebes. It shows oarsmen rowing a Nile boat under the watchful eye of an overseer. At the back of the vessel is the helmsman.

The term Middle Egypt describes an area of some 180 miles (290 km) of the Nile Valley from Asyut in the south to Memphis in the north. Asyut was the most southern part of the Herakleopolitan kingdom during the First Intermediate Period. It lay near the traditional boundary between the southern and northern administrative areas of Upper Egypt. Middle Egypt also includes the Faiyum, a large area of fertile land jutting out into the Western Desert. A branch of the Nile River flowed through the Faiyum into Lake Moeris. This lake was much bigger in ancient times than it is today. The Faiyum became an important area during the Middle Kingdom and retained its importance for the rest of the ancient period.

During the Third Intermediate and Late Periods Middle Egypt benefited from its position at the meeting point between the delta and the south. In late antiquity it prospered as a commercial center, trading with the oases in the desert.

Royal Tombs and Cities

Although there are relatively few large temples in Middle Egypt, there are a lot of interesting tombs. Some kings were buried in this area during the late Old Kingdom and the first Intermediate Period in tombs dug into cliffs at the edge of the desert plateau. There is a Third/Fourth Dynasty royal pyramid at Maidum, and Middle Kingdom rulers built pyramids at el-Lisht, el-Lahun, and Hawara.

These 12th-Dynasty pyramids were generally poorly constructed and are now in ruins. The huge mortuary temple of Amenemhet III at Hawara was famous throughout the ancient world as "The Labyrinth." Almost nothing of it survives today. No trace has been found of the 12th-Dynasty capital, Itjtawy, which lay somewhere near el-Lisht. In the 18th Dynasty, another capital city and royal necropolis was built in Middle Egypt at el-Amarna. It was only the royal residence for a few years, however, as part of an Egyptian king's attempt to reform Egyptian religion. The religious reforms did not outlast their creator. The pharaoh's name was scratched off the stone monuments and his capital city was abandoned only 15 years after it was built. The brief period of occupation means that the city is of great interest to archaeologists. Although few ruins stand today, experts have been able to excavate traces of the town plan, which was not obscured by later building and rebuilding.

The Nomarchs of Middle Egypt

Form the Sixth Dynasty to the late 12th Dynasty, the nomarchs of Middle Egypt enjoyed much power and independence. They built themselves magnificent rock-cut tombs along the edges of the desert and were buried in coffins painted with maps that would help their souls find the way through the Underworld after death. The nomarchs of Herakleopolis called themselves kings in the First Intermediate Period.

Herakleopolis and Hermopolis were both the capital towns of some minor kings during the Third Intermediate Period. Hermopolis, which the Egyptians called the City of the Eight (meaning eight gods), was located on the west bank of the Nile River, between Thebes and Memphis. It was the main center of the god, Thoth, the god of the moon, wisdom and writing. A huge temple complex once stood here. The monuments that survive include two huge statues of Thoth as a baboon. Sacred baboons and ibises, the bird of Thoth, were buried in underground galleries in the necropolis at Tuna el-Gebel. There were painted tombs from the Greco-Roman period in the necropolis.

Middle Egypt was the northern part of what was traditionally called Upper Egypt, and comprised the length of the Nile from Asyut in the south to Memphis in the North. Some of the major sites—Meir, Maidum, Beni Hasan, and Akhenaten's short-lived capital at el-Amarna—are described in more detail on the following pages.

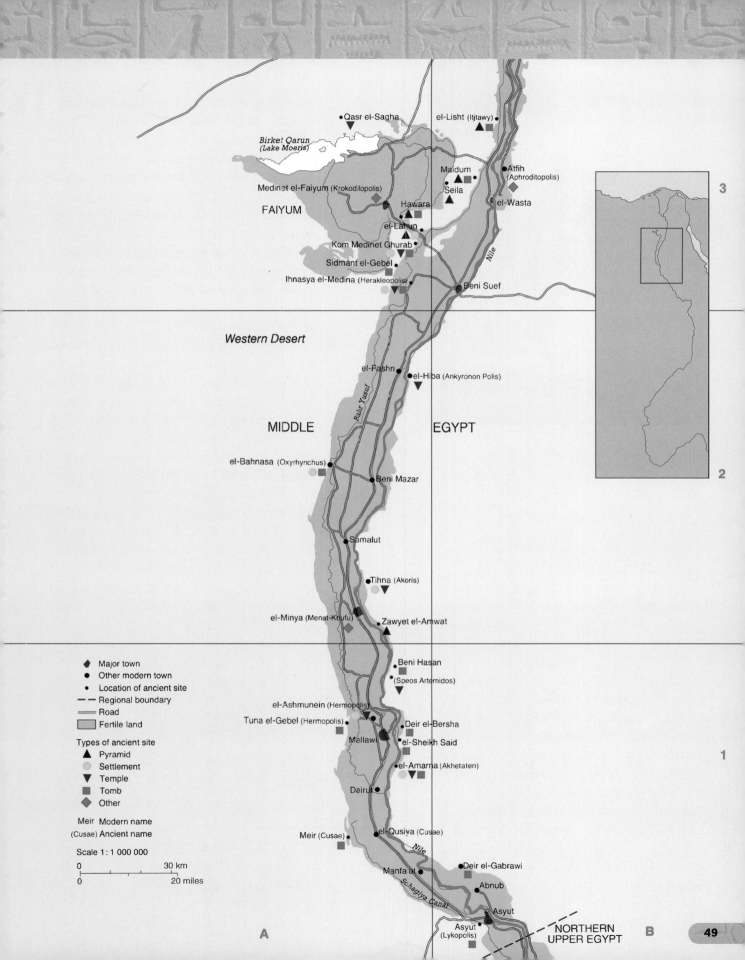

Meir

Traditional feluccas sail near the town of Asyut. With their distinctive triangular sails, which make them easier to sail into the wind, feluccas have been used to carry passengers and cargo on the Nile for many hundreds of centuries.

Meir is the site of the necropolis for the ancient town of Cusae, of which there are no remains. The town, which is located about 30 miles (50 km) northwest of Asyut, was the administrative center of a nome. The rock-cut tombs at Meir belong to the nomarchs of the Sixth and 12th Dynasties.

Each tomb comprised a large room cut directly into the cliff face. There are niches for statues and offerings and deep shafts for the coffins. The walls are decorated with painted reliefs. Common pictures include hunting in the desert and fishing in the marshes. Other images include vase-making and harvesting.

A festival, associated with Hathor, is depicted in several of the tombs. The late 12th Dynasty tomb of Wekh-hotep has some of the most delicate paintings that survive from the Middle Kingdom. They show the nomarch spearing fish and throwing a boomerang at marsh birds.

Maidum

Maidum is the site of a mysterious building disaster. All that remains of an early attempt to build a true pyramid—rather than a step-pyramid—is a strange-looking tower that rises out of a mound of rubble. The pyramid was the earliest to be built with a related pyramid complex. The original size of the pyramid itself was 472 feet (144 m) square and 138 feet (42 m) high. It was probably begun for Huni, who was the last king of the Third Dynasty, but according to graffiti created in the New Kingdom, it may have been completed by his successor Snofru.

The Maidum pyramid was first created as a seven-stepped structure. Then an eighth step was built. The steps were filled in and a limestone casing was added to create a smooth-sided pyramid. Unfortunately, the outer cladding was not applied properly: it did not bond to the sides of the existing structure and it had no proper foundations. As a result, the outer parts of the pyramid collapsed. We do not know whether this happened just after the pyramid was finished or hundreds of years later; it may have been the latter, as a necropolis of early Fourth Dynasty mastaba (flat-roofed tombs) grew up nearby, which would be unlikely if the pyramid had already collapsed.

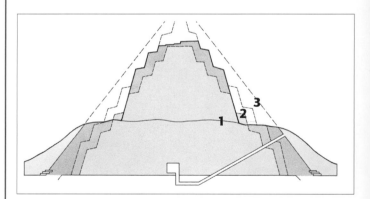

A section showing the three stages of the Maidum pyramid:
1 Seven-stepped pyramid.
2 Eight-stepped pyramid.
3 True geometric pyramid.

Beni Hasan

Decorated rock-cut tombs belonging to Middle Egyptian nomarchs survive at sites at Asyut, Deir el-Gabrawi, Meir, el-Sheikh Said, and Deir

el-Bersha. The most interesting are the group found at Beni Hasan. There are 39 tombs here, dating from the 11th to the late 12th Dynasties. Wooden coffins, statuettes, and models have been found in them. At least eight of the tombs belonged to the nomarchs of the Oryx nome. They were powerful in the region until the 12th Dynasty kings centralized power. The more elaborate tombs are made up of an outer court and portico and a rock-cut main room with elegant pillars. The walls were painted rather than carved. The ceilings, too, are painted. They feature geometric patterns that imitate woven matting or textiles.

Scenes showing daily life cover most of the walls. Unusual paintings of battles and sieges illustrate wars between nomes. Other scenes show girls playing ball, men and baboons picking figs, and the arrival of a group of traders from Palestine. The paintings became badly deteriorated but have since been restored.

In a nearby valley, almost 1 mile (1.5 km) to the south of Beni Hasan, Queen Hatshepsut built a small temple. This unfinished rock-cut temple is known as Seos Artemidos and was dedicated to a lioness goddess called Pakhet. Her name means "she who scratches."

In inscriptions, the names of rulers were inscribed in lozenge-shaped features that Egyptologists call "cartouches." The cartouche contains a series of hieroglyphs that give the king's name and describe the qualities associated with him.

El Amarna

One of the great cities of ancient Egypt was el-Amarna in Middle Egypt. Its power only lasted for about 15 years. Its Egyptian name was Akhetaten, which means "The Horizon of the Sun Disk." When the pharaoh Akhenaten decided to build a new capital to complement the new religion he had founded, dedicated to the Sun god Aten, he chose a site on a flat stretch of land beside the Nile valley that had never been inhabited. About 1349 BCE, work began, and the city soon spread rapidly to cover an area of about two square miles (5 sq km). The city's population was probably around 30,000 or more. Akhenaten lived there with his queen Nefertiti.

A reconstruction of the villa of a high official at el-Amarna. Such villas were like miniature farms. Fruit and vegetables were grown in the gardens. There were beehive-shaped grain bins (center right), a cattle yard, and stalls and stables for chariot horses. Each villa had a shrine for worship of the Aten and the royal family (bottom left).

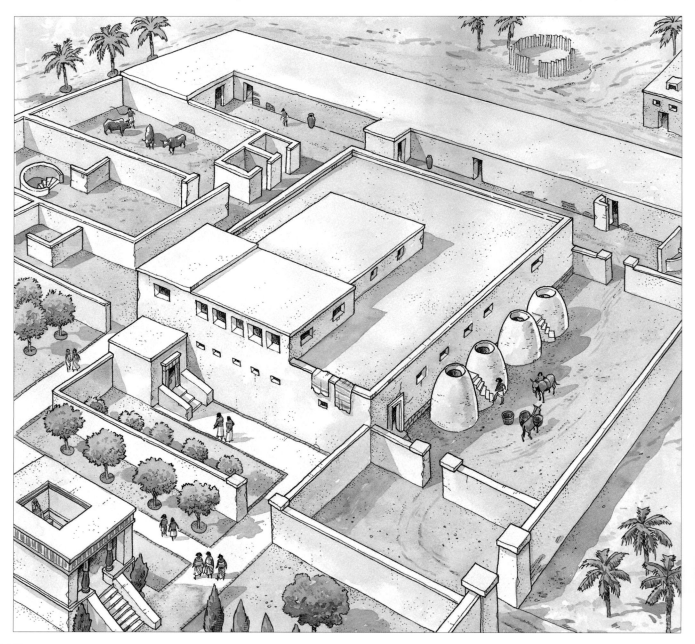

Palaces, Temples, and Tombs

El-Amarna became the chief royal residence and the center of government. There were at least five palaces, many official buildings, and several necropolises, as well as a number of zoos and gardens. In the palaces, floors and ceilings were painted or tiled in brilliant colors. One room in the North Palace had a beautiful painting of birds in a papyrus thicket that covered three walls. Akhenaten's private apartments were decorated with charming pictures of Queen Nefertiti and the little princesses. Important officials, like the

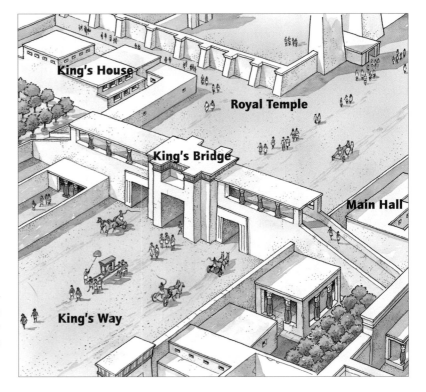

RIGHT: This picture shows part of the central city c.1340 BCE. The King's Way was 130 feet (40 m) wide. It passed under the King's Bridge, linking the Great Palace to Akhenaten's private apartments (the King's House). The Great Palace had a series of stone courts and halls. The Royal Temple, built for the Aten, was the second largest in the city.

BELOW: Plan of the areas of el-Amarna excavated so far. The temples and altars marked were all dedicated to the Sun Disk (Aten). The purpose of some buildings, such as the Maru Aten, is uncertain. The workmen's village continued to be lived in for some time after the main city was abandoned.

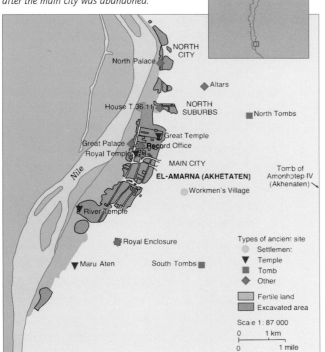

vizier, also had magnificently decorated homes at el-Amarna. The only gods worshiped at el-Armarna were the Aten (the Sun Disk) and Akhenaten himself. A new type of temple was built for Aten. Unlike other temples, these temples had huge courtyards with hundreds of altars open to the sun.

Tombs were cut in the desert hills for the royal family and favored courtiers, but most were never used. Their paintings show the official view of life in el-Amarna. In many scenes the rays of the Sun Disk end in hands holding out the symbol of life to Akhenaten.

The Deserted City

Akhenaten's new ideas were not popular. After his death, people called him "The Great Criminal." During Tutankhamon's reign the city was abandoned and never lived in again. Everything of value was taken away. Portraits of the disgraced royal family, including the famous head of Nefertiti, were left behind in a sculptor's workshop.

MEMPHIS

Memphis was the first capital of a united Egypt. Today little survives, but for three thousand years it was one of the country's greatest cities. Ancient Memphis is now buried under silt from the Nile and modern towns. Around the palm groves of the village of Mit Rahina are the remains of a few major buildings. A colossal statue of Ramesses II lies where it was found but it is now surrounded by a museum.

Ptah, the creator god, was the main deity of Memphis. A small part of the temple complex dedicated to Ptah has so far been excavated. It was once one of the largest temples in Egypt. Among the kings to be crowned there was Alexander the Great. The remains of palaces built by 19th and 26th Dynasty kings have been found at Mit Rahina.

A Sacred Bull

A sacred bull, known as the Apis Bull, represented Ptah. To be considered sacred, the bull had to have a white triangle on a black forehead, a scarab shape under its tongue, and a further 27 special marks. If it fulfilled these requirements, the bull lived in great luxury. Each year, it led a procession at the festival of "The Running of the Apis Bull." When the bull died, it was mummified and put in a stone sarcophagus.

From the rule of Ramesses II, bulls were buried in underground galleries at Saqqara, which was part of the necropolis of Memphis. Above these galleries was a temple, known as the Serapeum. From the third century BCE, the main god of the temple was Serapis, created from Greek and Egyptian gods.

Other animals were also buried at Saqqara, including cows, which had given birth to the Apis Bulls, as well as sacred dogs, cats, and ibises. People believed that by paying for the mummification and burial of an animal they would please the gods. Archaeologists have found the mummified bodies of many sacred ibises. In ancient Egypt, the ibis was thought to be an incarnation of the god Thoth.

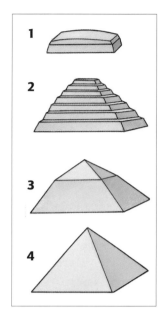

Tomb types in the Memphis necropolis:

1 Mastaba tomb, First-Sixth Dynasties.
2 Step pyramid, Third Dynasty.
3 Bent pyramid, Fourth Dynasty.
4 True pyramid, Old and Middle Kingdoms.

The Great Necropolis

The necropolis for the town of Memphis stretches for 18 miles (30 km) along the edge of the Western Desert between Dahshur and Abu Rawash. It is probably the largest cemetery in the world, as befits the status of Memphis. As well as the temples at Giza, there are around 50 smaller tombs. The royal tombs consist of step pyramids and true pyramids. From the Fourth Dynasty, each pyramid had two temples adjoining it, the valley temple and the mortuary temple.

The valley temple was located on the edge of the floodplain so it could be reached by boat. From the valley temple, the royal coffin was transported via an enclosed causeway to the mortuary temple. It was usually situated on the east side of the pyramid because the king hoped to be reborn like the rising sun. Priests made offerings to the king's spirit in the mortuary temple. This cult continued long after a king died. Towns were built to accommodate the priests who continued to serve the dead king.

Smaller pyramids were also part of the pyramid complex. By the Middle Kingdom, royal ladies were buried in these pyramids. In the Old Kingdom, the smaller pyramids had been used to bury the king's vital organs. The mastaba tombs of high officials and lesser members of the royal family are organized around the Old Kingdom pyramids.

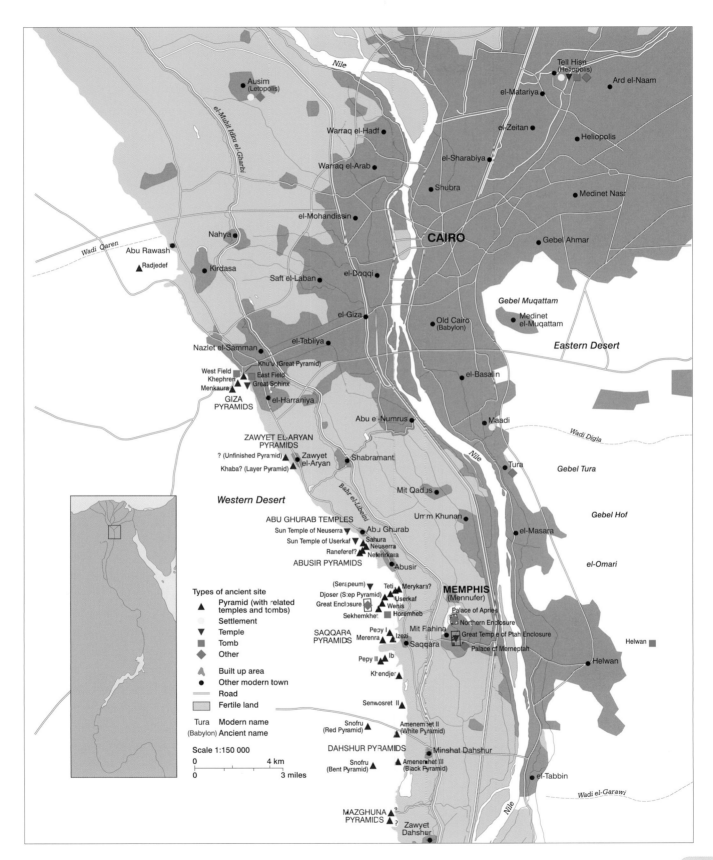

Nile

Tell Hish
(Heliopolis)

Ard el-Naam

Ausim
(Letopolis)

el-Matariya

el-Zeitan

Heliopolis

Warraq el-Hadf

el-Sharabiya

Medinet Nasr

Warraq el-Arab

Shubra

CAIRO

el-Mohandissin

Gebel Ahmar

Nahya

Abu Rawash

▲ Radjedef

el-Doqqi

Kirdasa

Saft el-Laban

Old Cairo
(Babylon)

Medinet
el-Muqattam

Gebel Muqattam

el-Giza

Eastern Desert

el-Tabliya

Nazlet el-Samman

Khufu (Great Pyramid)

West Field
Khephren ▲
Menkaura ▲

East Field ▲
Great Sphinx ▼

el-Basatin

**GIZA
PYRAMIDS**

el-Harraniya

Abu el-Numrus

Maadi

Wadi Digla

**ZAWYET EL-ARYAN
PYRAMIDS**

? (Unfinished Pyramid) ▲ Zawyet
Khaba? (Layer Pyramid) ▲ el-Aryan

Shabramant

Tura ◆

Gebel Tura

Western Desert

Mit Qadus

Gebel Hof

ABU GHURAB TEMPLES

Umm Khunan

Sun Temple of Neuserra ▼ Abu Ghurab
Sun Temple of Userkaf ▼ Sahura
Raneferef? ▲ Neuserra
Neferirkara

el-Masara

ABUSIR PYRAMIDS

Abusir

el-Omari

(Serapeum) ▼ Teti ▲ Merykara
Djoser (Step Pyramid) ▲ Userkaf
Great Enclosure ▲ Wenis
Sekhemkhet ▲ Horemheb

MEMPHIS
(Mennufer)

Palace of Apries
Northern Enclosure

**SAQQARA
PYRAMIDS**

Pepy I ▲ Izezi
Merenra ▲ Mit Rahina

Great Temple of Ptah Enclosure

Helwan

Saqqara

Palace of Merneptah

Pepy II ▲ Ib

Khendjer ▲

Helwan

Senwosret II ▲

Snofru
(Red Pyramid) ▲

Amenemhet II
(White Pyramid) ▲

DAHSHUR PYRAMIDS

Snofru
(Bent Pyramid) ▲

Amenemhet III
(Black Pyramid) ▲

Minshat Dahshur

el-Tabbin

Wadi el-Garawi

**MAZGHUNA
PYRAMIDS** ▲ ?
▲ ?

Zawyet
Dahshur

Types of ancient site

▲ Pyramid (with related
temples and tombs)

○ Settlement

▼ Temple

■ Tomb

◆ Other

▲ Built up area

● Other modern town

━━ Road

Fertile land

Tura — Modern name
(Babylon) — Ancient name

Scale 1:150 000

0   4 km

0   3 miles

Dahshur

Snofru, the first king of the Fourth Dynasty, built two stone pyramids at Dahshur, which is located in the southernmost part of the necropolis of Memphis.

The Bent Pyramid

This pyramid was most likely the first royal tomb to be designed as a true pyramid. When it was half finished, the angle of the outer surface was made smaller to give the sides a gentler slope. Also, a new way of laying the casing stones was used. The changes were probably made to stop the pyramid from collapsing like the one at Maidum. The Red Pyramid (named for the red limestone used to build it) is a huge true pyramid. It was built at the same angle as the upper part of the Bent Pyramid.

Royal Treasures

Three 12th Dynasty rulers—Amenemhet II, Senwosret III, and Amenemhet III—each built mud-brick pyramids, finished in stone, at Dahshur. Two lesser 13th Dynasty kings were buried nearby. In a pit close to the pyramid of Senwosret III, archaeologists have discovered six wooden boats.

The tombs of the royal women were located around the 12th Dynasty pyramids. Wonderful jewelry made from gold and precious stones have been found at seven of the burial sites.

Saqqara

For more than three thousand years, Saqqara was an important cemetery. From as early as the Second Dynasty, kings were buried here. The most famous monument is the Step Pyramid. There are 13 other pyramids built between the Third and 13th Dynasties.

The Writing on the Walls

The pyramid of the last king of the Fifth Dynasty, Wenis, was the earliest to be inscribed with the Pyramid Texts, a series of magic spells, written in vertical columns in hieroglyphic script. The spells were to help the king become a god in the afterlife.

Reliefs decorate the causeway that connected the pyramid to the valley temple. They show workers bringing stone columns to Saqqara from Aswan, and workers collecting honey. There is also an inscription noting that a later pharaoh repaired the pyramid about 1,200 years after it was originally built.

Decorated Tombs

From the Early Dynastic times, high officials were buried in mastaba tombs at Saqqara. The best were built in the Fifth and Sixth Dynasties. The small rooms of the tombs were highly decorated to show the owner enjoying life. The mastaba of the vizier Mereruka was the biggest with 32 rooms. Its reliefs in the family tomb show scenes from daily life including a hippopotamus hunt.

The next great period of tomb building at Saqqara was in the late 18th and early 19th Dynasties. High officials had rock-cut tombs or large stone tombs with pillared courts and chapels with miniature pyramids on top.

In the Late Period, tombs were made to be "robber-proof." Coffins were put in deep shafts and then covered with sand.

The huge step pyramid at Saqqara towers over a passing horse and rider. The pyramid was built for Djoser, a king of the Third Dynasty in the Old Kingdom, in about 2650 BCE. Its six steps were the forerunner of the later "true" pyramids.

Abusir and Abu Ghurab

The four pyramids built in the Fifth Dynasty at Abusir were poorly made. The outer cladding was taken off and reused, or made into lime.

The Pyramid of Sahura

Most of the reliefs that once decorated the temples of King Sahura have been lost. The few that survive show scenes from royal life. Sahura's successor, Neferirkara, planned a huge complex but it was never finished. The next king, Neuserra, used the causeway for his pyramid complex. King Raneferef built the fourth Abusir pyramid. The largest mastaba tomb belonged to the vizier Ptahshepses.

Sun Temples

Userkaf, founder of the Fifth Dynasty, built a huge temple to the sun god Ra. It looks like a pyramid complex because it has a causeway and a valley temple.

A well-preserved sun temple, dating from the reign of Neuserra, contains an open court with an altar and giant obelisk. The obelisk was a copy of a sacred stone in the temple of Ra at Heliopolis. The stone was a symbol of the first mound of land and the rays of the sun.

Pyramids at Giza

On the edge of modern Cairo is the plateau of Giza. The largest of the Egyptian royal tombs were built here in the Fourth Dynasty.

The Great Pyramid

The Great Pyramid is the popular name for the pyramid of Khufu (Cheops). Built almost 4,500 years ago, it was 482 feet (147 m) tall and covered an area of 2,800 square yards (2,341 sq m). There were five boat pits nearby, three subsidiary pyramids and many mastaba tombs.

The Second and Third Pyramids

The slightly smaller pyramid next to the Great Pyramid belonged to Khufu's son, King Khephren. The much smaller third pyramid was that of King Menkaura.

Near the valley temple of Khephren, a huge outcrop of limestone was carved into a sphinx 240 feet (73 m) long. Built with the body of a lion and the head of a king, the Great Sphinx was worshiped as the sun god. Pilgrims left offerings of miniature sphinxes and lions.

A reconstruction of Sahura's pyramid complex at Abusir. A causeway joins the riverside valley temple to the courtyard of the mortuary temple. There is one subsidiary pyramid.

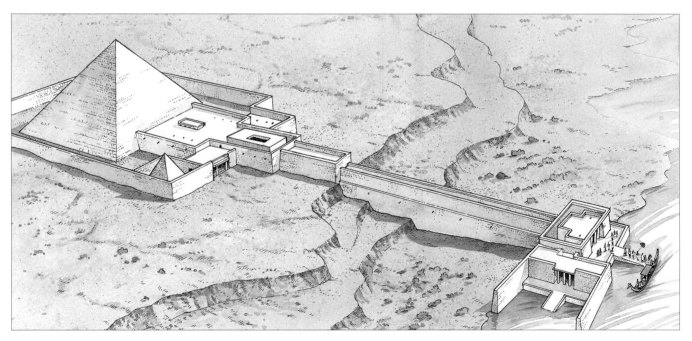

THE DELTA

The damp climate and marshy delta of Lower Egypt are not good for preserving ancient remains. The channels of the Nile have changed, course, destroying towns. Stones from ancient temples and tombs were re-used, and mud-bricks were turned into fertilizer. As a result, little is known about Lower Egypt than Upper Egypt.

Remains of Religious Sites

At Buto, the Delta goddess Wadjit was worshiped for three thousand years. The buried remains of a Predynastic settlement have produced pottery and building materials that show that the culture of Upper Egypt gradually overwhelmed the local culture.

Houses and tombs from the Old Kingdom have been found at the important religious sites of Bubastis and Tell el-Ruba (ancient Mendes). Archaeologists at Mendes have found a burned building full of bodies. This may be evidence of a civil war at the end of the Old Kingdom.

The Hyksos, foreign invaders, seized power in the delta in the Second Intermediate Period. They built the walled city of Avaris (modern Tell el-Daba). The early 18th Dynasty rulers who defeated the Hyksos erected a new palace at Avaris. It was decorated with wall paintings in the Cretan style.

Unrobbed Tombs

During the late New Kingdom and for much of the Third Intermediate Period, the delta ruled Egypt. Many kings, princes, and queens were buried inside temple enclosures in delta cities. Lots of treasures have been discovered in undisturbed royal tombs at Tanis and Tell el-Muqdam, and in the temple area at Bubastis.

Once the Delta had temples that were as impressive as the temples that still stand today in southern Egypt. The temple of the goddess Neith at Sais was famous in the ancient world but today little remains. Most of the great temple of Ra at Heliopolis was lost beneath the sprawling suburbs of modern Cairo.

Mediterranean Sea

Alexandria (Raqote)

Abusir (Taposiris Magna)

Rosetta Mouth

Lake Idku

Kafr el-Dauwar

Lake Mariut

Dam (Hermopolis)

A Major city or town
● Other modern town
• Location of ancient site
– – Regional boundary
═══ Road
▢ Fertile land

Types of ancient site
▲ Pyramid (with related temples and tombs)
▢ Settlement
▼ Temple
■ Tomb
◆ Other

Zifta Modern name
(Buto) Ancient name

Scale 1:1 000 000
0 ──────── 30 km
0 ──────── 20 mi

B C D

...etta

Lake Burullus

Damietta Mouth

Damietta

Lake Manzala

Port Said

el-Balamun
(Diospolis Inferior)

Tell el-Farain (Buto)

Shirbin

el-Matariya

Kafr el-Sheikh

Tell el-Farama
(Pelusium)

...nhur
(...arva)

Behbeit el-Hagar (Iseum)

el-Mansura

Sa el-Hagar (Sais)

Tell el-Ruba (Mendes)

San el-Hagar (Tanis)

el-Mahalla el-Kubra

(Naukratis)

Samannud
(Sebennytos)

el-Baqliya
(Hermopolis Parva)

Tell el-Timai (Thmuis)

Tell Nabasha (Imet)

Tell Abu Sifa (Sile)

Kom el-Hisn
(Imu)

el-Simbellawein

Sweet Water Canal

LOWER EGYPT

el-Khatana

Qantir (Pi-Ramesses)

Tanta

Zifta Mit Ghamr

Abu Kebir

Tell el-Dab'a
(Avaris)

Tell el-Muqdam
(Leontopolis)

Saft el-Hinna
(Per-Sopdu)

Tell el-Maskhuta
(Pithom)

Ismailia

Lake Timsah

Shibin el-Kom

Tell Basta
(Bubastis)

Zagazig

Wadi Tumilat

Ismailia Canal

Kom Abu Billo
(Terenuthis)

Minuf

Tell Atrib
(Athribis)

Benha

Great Bitter Lake

Little Bitter Lake

Bilbeis

Merimda Beni Salama

Rosetta Branch

Damietta Branch

Sweet Water Canal

Tell el-Yahudiya (Leontopolis)

Tell Hisn
(Heliopolis)

Ausim
(Letopolis)

Cairo

el-Giza

Suez

Nile

Tura

MEMPHIS

Helwan

Zawyet Dahshur

MIDDLE EGYPT

Suez Canal

*Birket Qarun
(Lake Moeris)*

Sinnuris

FAIYUM

Medinet el-Faiyum

el-Wasta

Gulf of Suez

el-Lahun

Ihnasya el-Medina

Beni Suef

59

Town at Bubastis

From the Old Kingdom onward, Bubastis was an important town. It stood in an important strategic location where it controlled the trade routes from Memphis to the Sinai peninsula and further east to Asia. The town was also the main cult center for Bastet, the lioness goddess. It reached its greatest influence during the 22nd Dynasty. The kings of the dynasty came from Bubastis, where they erected beautiful buildings in honor of the goddess. The main temple to Bastet was rebuilt many times. During the Late Period the town was the capital of one of the nomes of Lower Egypt. It entered a decline in the first centuries CE.

Worshiping Bastet

The annual festival of Bastet was one of the most popular in all of Egypt. People traveled from all over Egypt to sing, dance, and feast in honor of the cat goddess. One Greek writer said, "More wine is drunk at this festival than in the whole of the rest of the year" (Herodotus, *History* II). Herodotus also described the main temple dedicated to the goddess. In the middle of the fifth century BCE, when he wrote, the temple stood on a far lower level than the surrounding city. It stood on an island created from two arms of a sacred lake. Although archaeologists working at the temple confirm that Herodotus's description was accurate, they have been unable to determine even the size of the building; it was anything from 650 to 980 feet (200–300 m) long.

Cat Cemetery

Starting in the Third Intermediate Period, sacred cats were bred in the temple. They were buried in a special cat cemetery to the north of the town. Although the exact number of cats buried in the cemetery is unknown it is thought to run into millions. During the 19th century, thousands of cat mummies from Bubastis were shipped to Europe. Their remains were ground up and used as fertilizer.

Harbor at Alexandria

Alexandria was the capital of the Ptolemies, the Greek dynasty that ruled Egypt from 332 to 30 BCE. It was founded by Alexander the Great and became a lively international center. Its culture owed more to Greece and the Mediterranean than to Egypt. Although many Egyptians lived in the city, it was governed by Greeks; there was also a large and influential Jewish community. The city was the most important port in the Hellenistic world, and it played a key role in the spread of information about ancient Egypt during the Classical age.

Ancient Wonder

A tall lighthouse that stood on the island of Pharos in the busy harbor was considered one of the Seven Wonders of the Ancient World. It was topped by a huge flame that never went out. Alexandria had other important buildings, including the tomb of the city's founder, Alexander the Great, and a library that contained the largest collection of books in the ancient world. Under the Romans, villas, a sports stadium, and public bathhouses were also built.

Archaeologists have found underground tombs close to the temple of the Greco-Egyptian god Serapis. The tombs show Greek style paintings of scenes from Egyptian religion. The Greeks borrowed some ideas from the Egyptians. Statues and other objects from older Egyptian buildings were brought to Alexandria to decorate the city, including a pair of obelisks from Heliopolis. One of the most famous remains is a stone column that is known as "Pompey's pillar." Like other ruins at Alexandria, it dates from the Roman period. However, the city was also home to many pieces of ancient Egypt statuary, such as sphinxes.

Parts of the ancient city have disappeared under the modern city. Earthquakes and gradual coastal erosion have destroyed other parts. Marine archaeologists are still excavating the harbor seabed, where they have already found many Egyptian and Hellenistic statues.

Treasures of Tanis

The most impressive ruins of the whole Delta region are found at Tanis. It was the capital of Egypt for much of the Third Intermediate Period. A great temple of Amon, founded by King Psusennes I, lies inside a double mud-brick enclosure wall. The temple was added to by successive Third Intermediate Period kings.

Remains, such as stone blocks, columns, obelisks and statues, from much earlier periods have been found at Tanis. They were taken from older buildings at other sites and were brought to Tanis to give it instant authority and splendor as the new capital.

A Golden Discovery

In 1939, a French archaeologist called Pierre Montet discovered underground tombs near the southwest corner of the temple. The tombs of four Intermediate Period kings lay there, and some of the burials were intact. Funeral objects included spectacular gold and silver jewelry as well as gold and silver vessels, including drinking cups. King Psusennes I was buried in a solid silver coffin and had a gold mummy mask.

City at Qantir

At two points the Qantir area was very important in Egyptian history. In the Second Intermediate Period, it was the site of Avaris, the capital of the Hyksos kings. Avaris was probably located in the south part of the Qantir district, close to present-day Tell el-Daba. The Theban king Ahmose took the city and partially destroyed it around 1540 BCE.

The Ramessid family came from this part of the Delta. Ramesses II built a new city called Pi-Ramesses close to modern Qantir. In its day, it was one of the largest and most splendid cities of ancient Egypt. The palace area covered almost 22 acres (9 ha) or the equivalent of nine soccer fields.

Today, almost nothing remains. Many of the major buildings were later taken apart to provide stone and statues for Tanis. It may have been the use of forced labor on the building of Pi-Ramesses that led to the Exodus of the Jews from Egypt.

The many channels and islands have long made the Delta Egypt's most fertile area. Agricultural production supported the rise of numerous local dynasties, some of which ruled all of Egypt.

GLOSSARY

Book of the Dead Spells written on papyrus and placed in tombs from the New Kingdom to the Greco-Roman Period. No single copy contains all 192 spells.

canopic jars Set of four jars to hold the vital organs removed from a mummy. The organs were the liver, lungs, stomach, and intestines.

cartouche A sign representing an oval knot of rope. From the Fourth Dynasty, the king's two most important names were written inside cartouches. Cartouches were used on the king's documents and made into reliefs on the king's buildings and statues as a kind of seal.

Cataracts Stretches of dangerous rapids in the Nile River. There were six Cataracts between Aswan and Khartoum in Sudan.

colonnade A double row of columns roofed to form a passage, or a single row of columns joined by a roof to a wall.

cuneiform The Mesopotamian script, written on clay tablets with wedge-shaped strokes. Cuneiform tablets were found at el-Amarna.

deity A god or goddess. Egyptian deities can have human, semihuman, and animal shapes.

demotic An Egyptian script for everyday use, developed in the seventh century BCE. It is one of the three scripts on the Rosetta Stone.

dynasty A series of rulers, usually related to each other by blood or marriage. The order of the dynasties is known from the third-century BCE historian Manetho and from ancient Egyptian lists of kings.

figurine A small statue of a god or goddess, a person, or an animal. Figurines could be made of stone, wood, metal, faience, or pottery.

hieroglyph A sign in the oldest Egyptian script. Most hieroglyphic signs are pictures of people, animals, plants, or things. The word is Greek and means "sacred carving."

inundation The annual flooding of the Nile River between July and October. A "good Nile" was a flood that covered all the agricultural land, leaving behind a fertile layer of mud. If the flood was too high, it swept away houses.

If the flood was too low, it would not cover all the fields. These were "bad Niles."

ka The spirit or "double" of a living person. After death the *ka* needed offerings to survive. A dead person also had a *ba* (soul), shown as a human-headed bird.

mastaba A type of Early Dynastic and Old Kingdom tomb with a flat-roofed rectangular superstructure. The name comes from the Arabic word for a bench.

mummification The artificial preservation of bodies. Drying out the body was usually the most important part of the process.

natron A natural mixture of carbonate, bicarbonate, chloride, and sodium sulfate. It was used in mummification and was an ingredient of faience.

necropolis A Greek term meaning "city of the dead." It is used for large and important burial areas, mainly on the edge of the desert.

nome Greek word for an administrative province of Egypt. The governor of a nome was a nomarch.

obelisk A tapering stone shaft with a tip shaped like a pyramid; a symbol of the sun's rays. Pairs of obelisks were often set up outside temples.

oracle A shrine where a god or goddess answered questions from worshipers, or a sign that was given by a deity in answer to a question.

papyrus A marsh plant (*Cyperus papyrus*) and a type of paper made from it. Also a scroll made from sheets of papyrus gummed together.

pharaoh A title for the king of Egypt from the late 18th Dynasty onward. It means "The Great House"—the Palace.

pylon The grand entrance to a temple, consisting of towers flanking a doorway.

pyramid A tomb in the shape of a geometric pyramid. This shape may have symbolized a stairway to heaven, the sun's rays, or the first mound of land.

relief A scene carved in stone or wood.

sacred bark A special boat used by a statue of a deity on river journeys. Statues were often carried in model boats known as bark shrines.

sarcophagus Used in this book to mean the stone chest that a coffin was placed inside. A sarcophagus was rectangular or anthropoid (human body-shaped).

scarab A carving in the form of a scarab beetle (dung beetle). It represented Khepri, god of the rising sun. This "sun beetle" was a very popular amulet shape. Scarabs were often inscribed with royal names.

scribe A person trained to read and write. Most scribes worked for the government.

shabti (or ushabti) Small figurines, usually in the shape of a mummy, placed in burials. Their magical purpose was to carry out any work the dead person might be told to do in the afterlife.

sphinx An Egyptian sphinx usually had the body of a lion and the head of a king or queen. It was a symbol of royal power and a form of the sun god.

stela A slab of stone or wood, usually with carved and painted texts and scenes. Stelae were set up in the outer areas of tombs and in temples somewhat like gravestones or commemorative plaques.

uraeus A symbol of kingship in the shape of a rearing cobra.

vizier The highest official in the Egyptian government. There were sometimes two viziers, one based at Memphis, the other at Thebes.

FURTHER RESOURCES

PUBLICATIONS

Ardagh, P. *The Hieroglyphs Handbook* (Scholastic, 2001).

Clare, J. D. *Pyramids of Ancient Egypt* (Harcourt Brace Jovanich, 1992).

Cohen, D. *Ancient Egypt* (Doubleday, 1990).

Galford, E. *Hatshepsut: The Princess Who Became King* (National Geographic, 2005).

Harris, G. *Gods and Pharaohs from Egyptian Mythology* (Shocken, 1983).

Harris, G., and D. Pemberton. *The British Museum Illustrated Encyclopaedia of Ancient Egypt* (NTC, 2000).

Hart, George. *Ancient Egypt: Eyewitness Books.* (Dorling Kindersley, 2008).

Hawass, Z. *Tutankhamun: The Mystery of the Boy King* (National Geographic, 2005).

Ikram, S. *Egyptology* (Amideast, 1997).

Millard, A. *Going to War in Ancient Egypt* (Franklin Watts, 2001).

Pemberton, D. *Egyptian Mummies: People from the Past* (Harcourt, 2000).

Rubalcaba, Jill. *Ancient Egypt: National Geographic Investigates.* (National Geographic Society, 2007)

Tiano, O. *Rameses II and Egypt* (Henry Holt & Co., 1996).

Reference books for adults

Baines, J., and J. Malek. *Cultural Atlas of Ancient Egypt* (Checkmark Books, 2000).

Ikram, S., and A. Dodson. *The Mummy in Ancient Egypt* (W. W. Norton & Co., 1998).

Lehner, M. *The Complete Pyramids* (W. W. Norton & Co., 1997).

Pinch, G. *Handbook of Egyptian Mythology* (ABC–Clio, 2002).

Redford, D. (ed.). *The Oxford Encyclopaedia of Ancient Egypt* (Oxford University Press, 2001).

Shaw, Ian. *The Oxford History of Ancient Egypt* (Oxford University Press, 2004).

Taylor, J. H. *Death and the Afterlife in Ancient Egypt* (University of Chicago Press, 2001).

WEB SITES

http://www.ancientegypt.co.uk
Pages about Egypt on the Web site of the British Museum, London.

http://griffith.ashmus.ox.ac.uk
The Griffith Institute of Oxford, England, includes links for young people.

http://www.carlos.emory.edu/ODYSSEY/index.html
An interactive journey through ancient Egypt.

http://www.oi.uchicago.edu/OI/MUS/ED/kids.html
The Oriental Institute of the University of Chicago education program.

http://www.guardians.net/egypt/kids
Fun and interesting Egypt links especially for children.

http://www.historyforkids.org
Community service learning project from Portland State University. Click on link to Pyramids.

http://www.horus.ics.org.eg
Egyptian Web site designed and developed specially for kids around the world.

http://www.metmuseum.org/explore
The Metropolitan Museum of Art "Explore and Learn" pages with links to ancient Egyptian art under the "Themes and Cultures" link.

INDEX

Earth's Changing Environment

Compton's by Britannica®

ENCYCLOPÆDIA
Britannica®

CHICAGO   LONDON   NEW DELHI   PARIS   SEOUL   SYDNEY   TAIPEI   TOKYO

Learn & Explore series
Earth's Changing Environment
Compton's by Britannica

Library of Congress Control Number: 2007908762
International Standard Book Number: 978-1-59339-429-5

Printed in Malaysia

Britannica may be accessed at http://www.britannica.com on the Internet.

Front cover (top to bottom) and table of contents (left to right): Courtesy, Image Science & Analysis Laboratory,
NASA Johnson Space Center, photo no. ISS001-421-24; Carlos Navajas—Stone/Getty Images;
Photos.com/Jupiterimages; Ablestock/Jupiterimages; back cover (top to bottom): NASA; AP;
The Image Bank/Getty Images; AP; Jeremy Woodhouse/Getty Images

www.britannica.com

EDITOR'S PREFACE

The first edition of *Compton's Encyclopedia* was published in 1922. At that time its stated purpose was "to inspire ambition, to stimulate the imagination, to provide the inquiring mind with accurate information told in an interesting style, and thus lead into broader fields of knowledge." This is still true today. In this volume we address the broad topic of climate change and global warming in a way that we trust will honor that ongoing Compton's tradition.

Earth's Changing Environment pulls together several article titles from *Compton's Encyclopedia* that have some relationship to the topic of climate change. These articles have been expanded and given new treatment expressly for the purposes of this book. Several of the titles are new and do not yet appear within *Compton's Encyclopedia*. The material is presented in four parts with each part having a specific focus or common theme. Part one presents a focus on climate featuring articles on climate, greenhouse effect, global warming and the Kyoto Protocol. Part two explores the delicate web of life with articles on ecology, biogeography, biodiversity, endangered species, deforestation, and desertification. The effects of environmental pollution and efforts to protect the environment and to conserve its resources are addressed in part three with articles on environmental pollution, conservation, environmentalism, and environmental law. The final part examines the planet Earth and its interconnected systems. Two of the articles in part one have been reviewed by Susan Hassol, a climate change communicator, analyst, and author who frequently discusses the subject on radio and television as well as writing about it for film, journals, books, and a variety of other reports. Her introduction to this volume can be found on page *vi*.

Compton's challenges and inspires readers of all ages and this subject matter is one that should concern everyone on the planet. The articles within these pages have been supplemented with sidebars, tables, maps, charts and graphs, artwork, and photographs that are certain to engage the reader. By helping to make reading pleasurable and exciting, we hope to spark independent study and the habit of lifelong learning.

PART I   II   III   IV

TABLE OF CONTENTS

EARTH'S CHANGING ENVIRONMENT

This introduction was contributed by Susan Joy Hassol, Director of Climate Communication, who has been engaged in research and writing on the environment for two decades, focusing primarily on the impacts of and solutions to global warming. She recently authored Impacts of a Warming Arctic, *the synthesis report of the Arctic Climate Impact Assessment, and wrote HBO's global warming documentary* Too Hot Not to Handle. *In September 2006, she was honored by the Climate Institute with its first ever award for excellence in climate science communication.*

INTRODUCTION

Do you think of the environment as something "out there," separate from yourself, as opposed to something vital to your existence? Do you think of environmentalists as "tree-huggers" who care mainly about whales and polar bears? While some people do feel a deep connection to the natural world and seek to protect it for its own sake, for those who do not, it is important to recognize that nature must also be protected for our sake.

Nature is ultimately the source of everything we need: the food we eat, the water we drink, the air we breathe. We can no longer afford to push aside concern over the environment while we deal with more immediate concerns. As the world's population has quadrupled in the past 100 years, to over six billion people, it is time to re-think how we interact with and use the environment and to develop a new relationship with nature because, ultimately, nothing less than our survival is at stake.

Our world is a living system, and this system is now under such stress from human activities that it threatens to fail in serious and irreversible ways. For example, our intensive use of coal and oil is overloading Earth's atmosphere with greenhouse gases, changing climate so rapidly that neither human societies nor natural systems will be able to evolve quickly enough to keep up. As a result, some species are being driven to extinction, while the quality of life of others, including human beings, is at increasing risk. Broadly understood, global warming is not an environmental issue but an issue that is central to human health, the economy, and national security.

Some people have assumed that we must choose between protecting the environment and enhancing the economy, but this is a false dichotomy. What is good for the environment is also good for the economy in the long term. For example, increased energy efficiency and greater reliance on renewable energy sources like solar and wind power would build a new economic engine for the economy. Studies show that many more jobs would be created in these budding industries than would be lost in the older, more polluting ones. Furthermore, these new jobs would be healthier and more sustainable jobs because the resources on which they are based are clean and inexhaustible.

Another way taking care of the environment benefits the economy is that a healthy natural world provides us with many free goods, like food and materials, as well as services, like purifying air and water, that we either cannot get any other way or that would be astronomically expensive if we had to create them artificially and pay for them monetarily. A degraded environment provides less of these goods and services that benefit humanity.

As we look back on the past century of human interaction with nature, it is worth noting that we did not damage the environment intentionally. We used coal and oil as energy sources and used a wide variety of chemicals for many purposes because they made our lives easier. The negative environmental consequences of these actions were not deliberate. But now that we understand the consequences, we can act to reduce these impacts, to take responsibility as good stewards of the environment. As we look forward to the rest of this century, will we create a society that is more in harmony with nature, for its benefit, as well as our own?

Courtesy Image Science & Analysis Laboratory, NASA Johnson Space Center, No. ISS001-421-24

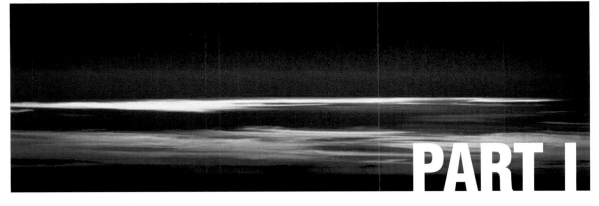

PART I

CLIMATE

The aggregate, long-term weather—or state of the atmosphere—of any place is known as its climate. For example, a description of weather might be "It rained yesterday in Phoenix," while "Phoenix gets only 10 inches of rain per year" would be a statement about climate. Descriptions of climate include such weather elements as temperature, precipitation, humidity, wind, cloudiness, and snow cover. The study of climate is known as climatology.

Climate Statistics

A location's climate can be described by various statistical measures of the elements of weather and climate. Mean, or average, values are usually computed for a fairly long time period, such as 30 years. These means are often calculated for each month and for the year as a whole.

Extreme maximum and minimum figures help convey the degree of climate variability. Information on the frequency of various events, such as the number of days per year with thunderstorms or the number of frosts in a typical winter, is also important.

Temperature is one of the most important climate elements. Daily mean temperatures may be computed as the average of the daily maximum and minimum temperatures or as the average of temperatures from all 24 hours. These daily means can then be used to compute the mean value for a given month or for the entire year. Normal daily maximum and minimum temperatures for a given date or month are also frequently cited. The average difference between nighttime low temperatures and afternoon highs may be less than 10° F (6° C) in cloudy climates or at sea but over 30° F (17° C) in deserts. The highest and lowest

temperatures ever recorded at a site give an idea of the range of temperatures one might experience living a lifetime in that location.

Precipitation data are also very important in describing a location's climate. Mean and extreme monthly amounts are often cited, with snow often included as "liquid equivalent" precipitation. Snow cover and evaporation data are also important. Mean wind speed and prevailing direction, humidity, and daily hours of sunshine help complete the climate picture.

Climate Controls

The various controls of climate include latitude, land and water distribution, prevailing winds and belts of high and low pressure, ocean currents, altitude, topography, clouds, and cyclonic activity.

Energy received from the Sun is greater near the equator than near the poles because the Sun's rays are more concentrated at the equator and pass through less of the atmosphere.

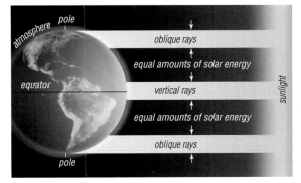

This article was contributed in part by Melvin E. Kazeck, Professor and Chairman, Faculty of Earth Sciences, Southern Illinois University; and by Thomas J. Ehrensperger, physics, astronomy, and meteorology upper school instructor and developer of the Weather Simulator (WXSIM) software.

Hours of Daylight

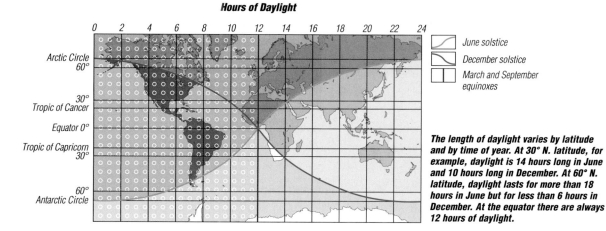

June solstice

December solstice

March and September
equinoxes

*The length of daylight varies by latitude
and by time of year. At 30° N. latitude, for
example, daylight is 14 hours long in June
and 10 hours long in December. At 60° N.
latitude, daylight lasts for more than 18
hours in June but for less than 6 hours in
December. At the equator there are always
12 hours of daylight.*

Latitude. Great amounts of energy are required for the massive movements of the air in the atmosphere and for the exchange of heat and moisture between the atmosphere and Earth's land and water surfaces that are the essence of weather and climate. This energy comes from the Sun. Incoming solar radiation, or insolation, is not evenly distributed. Much more is received in the low latitudes, near the equator, than in the high latitudes, near the poles. This is mainly because latitude, the primary control of climate, determines the angle at which the Sun's rays strike Earth's surface. Latitude also determines the length of daylight, or the time during which solar energy reaches Earth at any angle.

Only in the tropics—those areas around the equator between 23½° N. latitude (the Tropic of Cancer) and 23½° S. latitude (the Tropic of Capricorn)—does the Sun ever appear directly overhead. For that reason, only those areas ever receive the rays of the Sun vertically (at an angle of 90°). The average angle of the Sun's rays decreases toward the poles. As a result, the solar energy is spread over a greater area at high latitudes than at low latitudes, and less solar energy reaches Earth's surface at high latitudes because more is absorbed and reflected by the atmosphere.

The length of daylight is about 12 hours everywhere on Earth at the time of the equinoxes (about March 21 and September 23). This is not the case year-round, however, because Earth's spin axis is tilted (*see* Earth). The length of daylight is always about 12 hours at the equator but increases toward each pole in summer, reaching a maximum at the time of the summer solstice (about June 21 in the Northern Hemisphere and about December 21 in the Southern Hemisphere). Likewise, the length of daylight decreases toward each pole in winter, reaching a minimum at the winter solstice (about December 21 in the Northern Hemisphere and about June 21 in the Southern Hemisphere).

The area on Earth where the Sun appears directly overhead at noon shifts north and south as the planet orbits the Sun, reaching the Tropic of Cancer at the June solstice and the Tropic of Capricorn at the December solstice. The zone of maximum insolation swings back and forth over the equator along with the area where the

Sun is directly overhead. Because of the additional heating from the longer periods of daylight toward the poles in summer, however, the zone of maximum insolation moves beyond the tropics to between 30° and 40° N. latitude in July and 30° and 40° S. latitude in January.

In the lower latitudes, Earth gains more heat by radiation from the Sun than it loses to space by radiation from Earth. In the higher latitudes, Earth gives off more heat than it receives from the Sun. This unequal heating and cooling would result in ever-increasing temperatures in the tropics and ever-decreasing temperatures in the polar regions if it were not for the continuous transfer of heat from low latitudes to high latitudes by winds and ocean currents.

Land and water distribution. The irregular distribution of land and water surfaces is a major control of climate. Air temperatures are warmer in summer and colder in winter over the continents than they are over

Earth absorbs about 47 percent of total insolation, the atmosphere about 19 percent. About 34 percent is reflected back into space— 23 percent by clouds, 9 percent by the atmosphere, and 2 percent by Earth's surface.

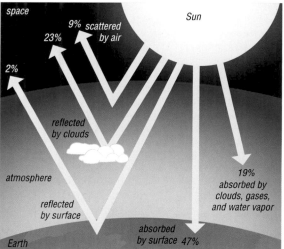

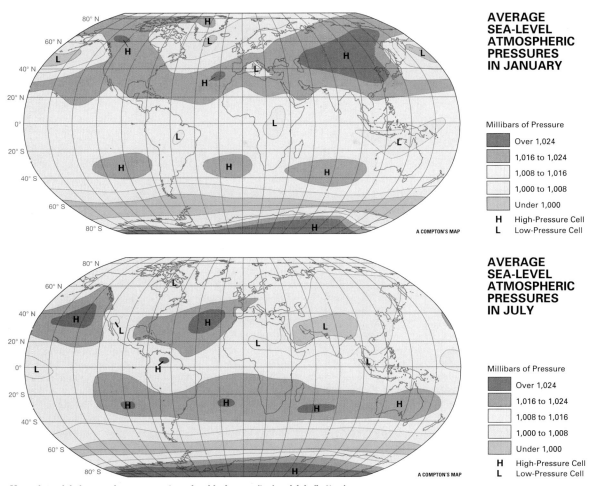

Maps show global mean air pressures at sea level in January (top) and July (bottom).

the oceans at the same latitude. This is because landmasses heat and cool more rapidly than bodies of water do. Bodies of water thus tend to moderate the air temperatures over nearby land areas, warming them in winter and cooling them in summer. The interiors of large landmasses such as Eurasia (Europe and Asia) are affected least by the oceans and so have greater annual temperature ranges than do coastal areas and the interiors of small landmasses. Large permanent ice surfaces reflect away most of the Sun's energy and then affect climate by chilling the air over them and the land and water surrounding them.

Prevailing winds and pressure belts. Prevailing winds and pressure belts are major climate controls. A belt of low pressure known as the intertropical convergence zone (ITCZ) lies along the equator. On either side of the equatorial low, between 25° and 30° latitude in each hemisphere, is a belt of high-pressure centers over the oceans. From the equatorial side of these subtropical highs—such as the Hawaiian high over the North Pacific—blow the warm, moist tropical easterlies (winds blowing from east to west), or trade winds.

From the polar side of the subtropical highs, to about 60° latitude in each hemisphere, blow the moist but cooler prevailing westerlies. At about 60° latitude are belts of low pressure, with centers over the oceans. Into these subpolar lows—such as the Aleutian low over the North Pacific—blow not only the westerlies but also cold easterly winds from polar high-pressure centers located over the Arctic Ocean and Antarctica.

The pressure and wind belts shift along with the area where the Sun appears directly overhead at noon—to the north when the Northern Hemisphere has its summer and to the south when the Southern Hemisphere has its summer. As is true with temperature patterns, the east-west alignment of pressure patterns is greatly modified by the arrangement of the world's landmasses and oceans. Most notable are the intense winter high over northern Asia and the summer low over southwestern Asia. These pressure centers are major influences on the monsoon winds that blow out of Asia in the winter and into it in the summer.

Ocean currents. The major ocean currents also are a climate control. They follow the prevailing winds that circle the oceanic subtropical highs—clockwise in the

Northern Hemisphere and counterclockwise in the Southern Hemisphere. Wherever these currents flow toward the polar regions—on the western sides of the lows—they carry warm water away from the equatorial regions. Where they flow toward the equator—on the eastern sides of the lows—they carry cold water from the polar regions. Ocean currents such as the Gulf Stream and the North Atlantic Current carry warm water northward and eastward around the Azores high, which moderates the climate of western Europe. There are similar warm currents around the Hawaiian high in the North Pacific and around the highs in the South Atlantic, South Pacific, and Indian oceans.

Altitude. Another climate control is altitude, or elevation. Just as there is a gradual decrease in average temperature with increasing latitude, there is a decrease in temperature with increasing elevation. High mountains near the equator, for example, may have tropical vegetation at their bases but permanent ice and snow at their summits. The reasons for this are somewhat different for mountains as opposed to wide, elevated areas, such as plateaus. Mountains are exposed to atmosphere that is far above the surrounding lowlands. This air receives little heat from the ground far below, so that it is colder by about 3.6° F for every 1,000 foot increase in elevation (about 6.5° C per 1,000 meters). Plateaus are effectively "on the ground," but there is less air above to trap heat, so that such places are about 2.4° F cooler per 1,000 feet (4.4° C per 1,000 meters) in elevation than they would be otherwise. Temperatures cited later in this article should be considered sea-level equivalents, unless otherwise indicated.

Relief. The topography, or relief, of land has an important effect on climate. Windward mountain slopes, facing moisture-bearing winds, usually receive more precipitation than do either the lower, more level mountain bases or the mountain slopes in the lee (the sheltered side) of the winds. This is because air moving up a mountain slope expands and cools, reducing the amount of moisture needed for saturation (the state in which no more water vapor can be in the air under those conditions). Condensation, clouds, and precipitation are thus frequently produced. Air moving down a mountain slope compresses and warms, increasing the amount of moisture possible in the air, and thus reducing the likelihood of precipitation. This helps explain why the coast of the U.S. states of Oregon and Washington has heavy precipitation while the interior generally has a dry climate.

Mountain ranges may also serve as barriers to outbreaks of cold air. In this way the Alps and other mountain ranges of southern Europe protect much of the Mediterranean coast. Similarly the Himalayas protect the lowlands of India.

Clouds. Clouds exert a significant effect on climate; they are generally associated with humid environment. Temperatures tend to be less extreme in areas with heavy cloud cover. During daylight and in summer, clouds keep temperatures from rising as high as they otherwise might by reducing the amount of heat received from the Sun. At night and in winter, clouds keep temperatures from falling as much as they otherwise might by reducing the amount of heat radiated into space.

Cyclonic activity. Traveling low-pressure centers known as frontal or wave cyclones generally move from west to east and are associated with the systems of cold and warm fronts that produce the variable weather of the middle and higher latitudes. Wave cyclones form along the undulating boundary, or "front" between cold polar air masses and warm tropical air masses. They are stronger in winter, when temperature contrasts in the frontal zones are greater.

Comparing Climates

It is interesting to compare the climates of places that have much in common and yet certain different characteristics, to illustrate the effects of some of the controls of climate. As an example, consider Sydney, in southeastern Australia, and Atlanta, in the southeastern United States. Both are 34° from the equator, though in

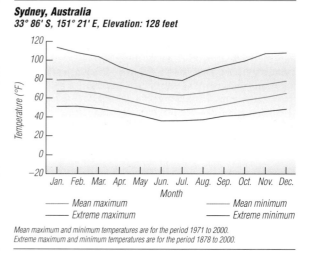

Atlanta, Georgia, U.S.
33° 38' N, 84° 26' W, Elevation: 1,010 feet

Temperature (°F) — Month (Jan. Feb. Mar. Apr. May Jun. Jul. Aug. Sep. Oct. Nov. Dec.)
— Mean maximum   — Mean minimum
— Extreme maximum   — Extreme minimum

Mean maximum and minimum temperatures are for the period 1971 to 2000.
Extreme maximum and minimum temperatures are for the period 1878 to 2000.

Sydney, Australia
33° 86' S, 151° 21' E, Elevation: 128 feet

Temperature (°F) — Month (Jan. Feb. Mar. Apr. May Jun. Jul. Aug. Sep. Oct. Nov. Dec.)
— Mean maximum   — Mean minimum
— Extreme maximum   — Extreme minimum

Mean maximum and minimum temperatures are for the period 1971 to 2000.
Extreme maximum and minimum temperatures are for the period 1878 to 2000.

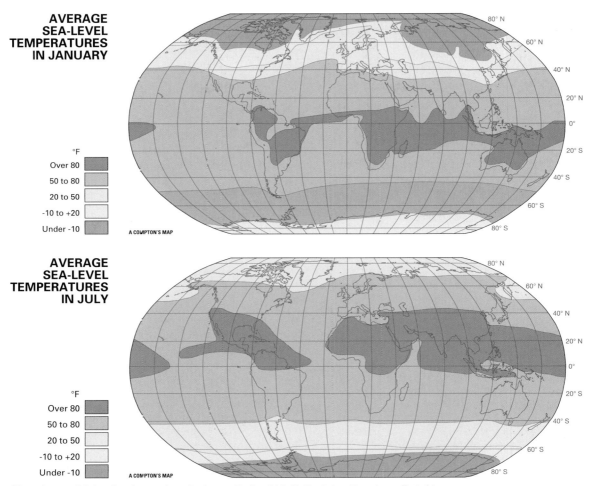

AVERAGE SEA-LEVEL TEMPERATURES IN JANUARY

°F
Over 80
50 to 80
20 to 50
-10 to +20
Under -10

A COMPTON'S MAP

AVERAGE SEA-LEVEL TEMPERATURES IN JULY

°F
Over 80
50 to 80
20 to 50
-10 to +20
Under -10

A COMPTON'S MAP

Maps of mean global surface temperatures for January (top) and July (bottom) show the values adjusted to indicate what the temperatures would be if all the locations were at sea level. (To convert from degrees Fahrenheit to degrees Celsius, subtract 32 and then divide by 1.8.)

opposite hemispheres. As a result, both have about the same mean annual temperature—65° F (18° C) for Sydney and 62° F (17° C) for Atlanta—with the small difference due mainly to Atlanta's elevation being nearly 1,000 feet (300 meters) higher. (The temperatures given in this section are not sea-level equivalents.) However, Sydney's coldest month, July, at 55° F (13° C), is much warmer than Atlanta's coldest month, January, at 43° F (6° C). Sydney's warmest month, February, at 73° F (23° C), is cooler than Atlanta's warmest month, July, at 80° F (27° C). Much of this difference is due to Sydney's almost immediate coastal location, while Atlanta is about 200 miles (320 kilometers) from the nearest water. It is also partly due to Australia being smaller than North America, thus allowing more of a maritime influence.

Extreme temperatures further illustrate differences. Atlanta, with land poleward all the way to the Canadian Arctic, has (rarely) seen temperatures as low as –9° F (–23° C). Sydney, with a great expanse of open sea poleward between Australia and Antarctica, never drops below 35° F (2° C), though it gets almost that cold fairly often. On the other hand, Atlanta's highest recorded temperature, which has been nearly equaled on several occasions, is 105° F (41° C), but Sydney has (rarely) soared to 114° F (46° C) when air has arrived from the hot tropical interior of Australia. In short, Atlanta has cool, quite variable winters and hot, monotonous summers, while Sydney has mild, relatively monotonous winters and warm, but potentially quite variable summers. Thus, there is much more to climate than mere averages.

Classification of Climates

No two locations have precisely the same climate, but there are many useful schemes for classifying climates. The ancient Greeks devised a simple scheme. Noting the relationship between temperature and latitude, they divided Earth into five broad east-west zones, or *klima*: two frigid polar zones, two temperate midlatitude zones, and a torrid tropical zone. One frigid zone lay in the Northern Hemisphere within the Arctic Circle, the

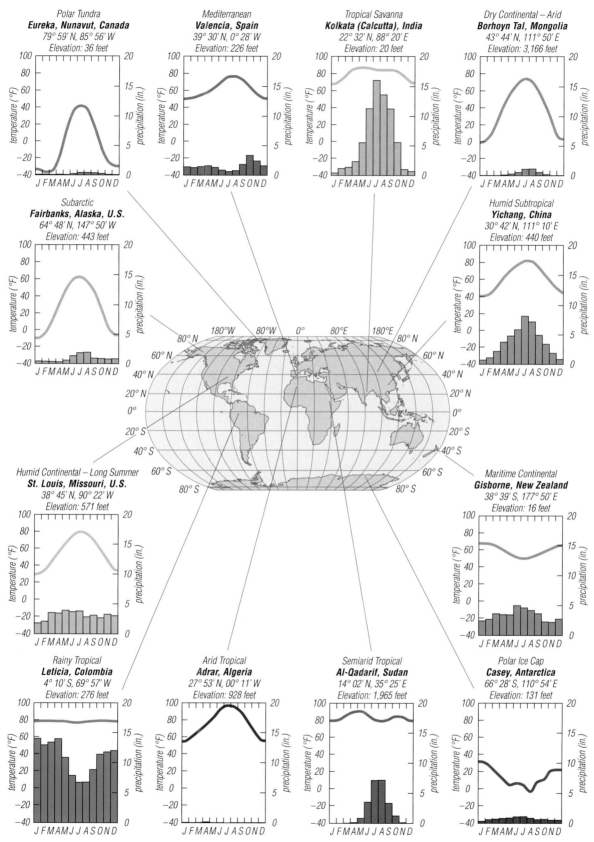

Polar Tundra
Eureka, Nunavut, Canada
79° 59' N, 85° 56' W
Elevation: 36 feet

Mediterranean
Valencia, Spain
39° 30' N, 0° 28' W
Elevation: 226 feet

Tropical Savanna
Kolkata (Calcutta), India
22° 32' N, 88° 20' E
Elevation: 20 feet

Dry Continental – Arid
Borhoyn Tal, Mongolia
43° 44' N, 111° 50' E
Elevation: 3,166 feet

Subarctic
Fairbanks, Alaska, U.S.
64° 48' N, 147° 50' W
Elevation: 443 feet

Humid Subtropical
Yichang, China
30° 42' N, 111° 10' E
Elevation: 440 feet

Humid Continental – Long Summer
St. Louis, Missouri, U.S.
38° 45' N, 90° 22' W
Elevation: 571 feet

Maritime Continental
Gisborne, New Zealand
38° 39' S, 177° 50' E
Elevation: 16 feet

Rainy Tropical
Leticia, Colombia
4° 10' S, 69° 57' W
Elevation: 276 feet

Arid Tropical
Adrar, Algeria
27° 53' N, 00° 11' W
Elevation: 928 feet

Semiarid Tropical
Al-Qadarif, Sudan
14° 02' N, 35° 25' E
Elevation: 1,965 feet

Polar Ice Cap
Casey, Antarctica
66° 28' S, 110° 54' E
Elevation: 131 feet

AVERAGE ANNUAL PRECIPITATION

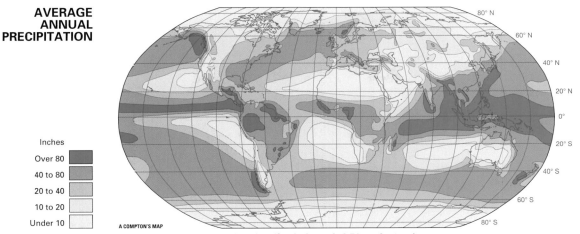

Inches
- Over 80
- 40 to 80
- 20 to 40
- 10 to 20
- Under 10

A COMPTON'S MAP

A map shows the mean global distribution of annual precipitation. (One inch equals 2.54 centimeters.)

other in the Southern Hemisphere within the Antarctic Circle. One temperate zone lay in the Northern Hemisphere between the Arctic Circle and the Tropic of Cancer, the other in the Southern Hemisphere between the Antarctic Circle and the Tropic of Capricorn. The torrid zone straddled the equator between the two tropics. This simple grouping of climates ignored factors affecting temperature and climate other than latitude.

The classification systems most widely used today are based on the one introduced in 1900 by the Russian-German climatologist Wladimir Köppen. Köppen divided Earth's surface into climatic regions that generally coincided with world patterns of vegetation and soils. The boundaries of these climatic regions were defined by using precise temperature and precipitation averages. A unique letter system identified five major climate groups—tropical rainy climates (A), dry climates (B), humid moderate-temperature climates (C), humid low-temperature climates (D), and polar, snow climates (E). The climates were further subdivided by additional letters that referred to seasonal variations and extremes of precipitation and temperature.

A classification of climates introduced by the United States climatologist C. Warren Thornthwaite in 1931 divided the world into five vegetation-humidity zones—wet rainforest, humid forest, subhumid grassland, semiarid steppe, and arid desert—and into six vegetation-temperature zones—tropical, moderate temperature, low temperature, taiga, tundra, and frost. This article uses a modification of Köppen's classification, dividing the world into tropical, subtropical, cyclonic, polar, and highland climates. Oceanic climates are also discussed.

The graphs on the preceding page show climate statistics for 12 cities with different climate types. The line graphs show mean monthly temperatures, corresponding to the scales at left, while the bar graphs show mean monthly precipitation levels, corresponding to the scales at right. The values are long-term averages calculated for the period 1961 to 1990. (To convert from degrees Fahrenheit to degrees Celsius, subtract 32 and then divide by 1.8. To convert from inches to centimeters, multiply by 2.54.)

Each climate classification takes into account the relationship between temperature and precipitation effectiveness, in which the total amount of evaporation is subtracted to determine the amount of precipitation actually available to support plant growth. In order to be classed as humid, for example, a region with high temperatures must have more precipitation than a region with low temperatures because its evaporation rates are greater. Thus a 10-inch (25-centimeter) average annual precipitation might well support a forest of coniferous trees (such as the evergreens spruce, fir, and pine) in a cool climate but only desert shrubs in a warm one.

Tropical climates. The tropical climates lie in the low latitudes and are dominated by tropical and equatorial air masses. They are warm all year with at most a minor cool season. In areas with rainy tropical, or tropical rainforest, climates, precipitation is heavy, usually averaging more than 80 inches (200 centimeters)

With abundant rainfall and warm temperatures year-round, a tropical rainforest in Ecuador is lush with vegetation.

© Victor Englebert

WORLD CLIMATE REGIONS

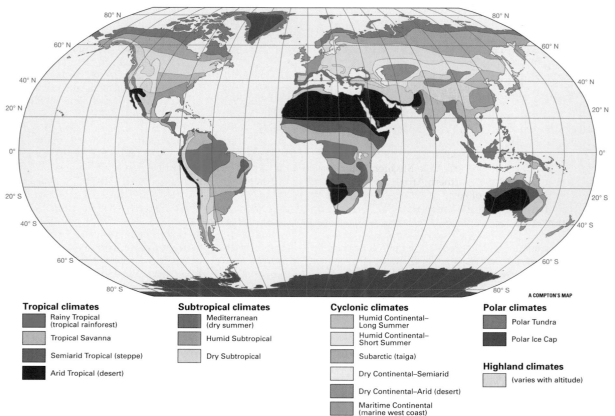

A COMPTON'S MAP

Tropical climates
- Rainy Tropical (tropical rainforest)
- Tropical Savanna
- Semiarid Tropical (steppe)
- Arid Tropical (desert)

Subtropical climates
- Mediterranean (dry summer)
- Humid Subtropical
- Dry Subtropical

Cyclonic climates
- Humid Continental– Long Summer
- Humid Continental– Short Summer
- Subarctic (taiga)
- Dry Continental–Semiarid
- Dry Continental–Arid (desert)
- Maritime Continental (marine west coast)

Polar climates
- Polar Tundra
- Polar Ice Cap

Highland climates
- (varies with altitude)

per year. Humidity is high. Thunderstorms occur almost every day. Every month has a mean temperature close to 80° F (27° C). Temperature variations are small, so that many such locations never experience high temperatures over 100° F (38° C) or lows below 60° F (16° C). Vegetation consists of dense rainforests of broad-leaved evergreen trees. Poorly drained areas have mangrove swamps. Where tree cover is thin and sunlight reaches the ground, there is dense undergrowth known as jungle.

Rainy tropical climates generally occur in the equatorial lowlands and along mountainous tropical coasts exposed to the moist easterly trade winds. The Amazon Basin in South America and the Congo Basin in Africa are the largest continuous areas of rainy tropical climate. Other areas are in the islands of Southeast Asia, the eastern coast of Madagascar, and the windward coasts of Central America. Some rainy tropical areas, such as on the western coast of India and on the northern coast of South America, have a short dry season in "winter," when the noontime Sun is farthest from overhead.

On the poleward side of the rainy tropics, generally between about 5° and 20° latitude, lie the wet-and-dry tropics, which have a tropical savanna climate. Precipitation is not as heavy as in the tropics, and there is a long dry season. As a result, the vegetation is typically tall grasses and scattered trees. The highest

mean monthly temperatures, usually just before the rainy season, may be in the 90s F (30s C). Principal areas with a tropical savanna climate are in Central America, South America, Africa, India, Southeast Asia, and Australia.

The dry season is longer and the wet season is shorter toward the poleward edges of the tropical savanna, where it merges with the tropical steppe, which has a semiarid tropical climate. Farther poleward, generally between 15° and 30° latitude, the steppe merges with the tropical desert, which has an arid tropical climate. Average annual precipitation generally is less than 30 inches (76 centimeters) in the tropical steppe and less than 10 inches (25 centimeters) in the tropical desert. In both these regions, mean monthly temperatures in the summer may reach well into the 90s F (30s C). Temperatures in the tropical deserts are the highest in the world, with extreme afternoon highs of more than 130° F (54° C). Only short grasses and desert shrubs survive there.

The principal tropical deserts are the Sahara and the Kalahari in Africa, the Sonoran in northern Mexico and the southwestern United States, those of Australia, and those of Arabia, Iran, and Pakistan in southwestern Asia. The tropical deserts on continental western coasts result from the influence of the cool ocean currents and dry winds on the eastern sides of the oceanic subtropical high-pressure centers. Examples are the Namib in southwestern Africa, the Atacama in Chile, and those along the coasts of Baja California and Morocco.

Subtropical climates. The area between 20° and 40° latitude is considered subtropical and can be further distinguished by the level of humidity typically found. The dry subtropical and so-called Mediterranean climates are generally found poleward from the arid tropics.

The Mediterranean climate is distinguished by warm to hot, dry summers and cool to mild, fairly wet winters. Areas with this climate generally lie on west-facing coasts at latitudes between about 30° and 40°. There are Mediterranean climates on the coasts of southern California and central Chile, on the Mediterranean coasts of southern Europe and northern Africa, and along parts of the southern coasts of Africa and Australia. Summers typically have mean temperatures near 80° F (27° C), and winters average around 50° F (10° C), with occasional freezing temperatures. Average annual precipitation ranges from less than 15 inches (38 centimeters) on the equatorial side, where the Mediterranean climate region merges with dry regions, to 35 to 40 inches (89 to 101 centimeters) on the poleward side.

Dry subtropical climates exist in such places as central Spain, the Middle East, South Africa, and the interior of eastern Australia. Temperatures are slightly warmer than those of the Mediterranean climate and winter rains are reduced, often by the greater distance from water.

The humid subtropical climate generally occurs between 25° and 35° latitude on the east sides of continents. It is primarily influenced by the warm maritime tropical air masses on the west sides of the subtropical oceanic high-pressure centers. Precipitation, from thunderstorms in summer and cyclonic storms in winter, is moderate and year-round. It averages between 30 and 60 inches (76 and 152 centimeters) per year, enough for the growth of forests. Winters are short and mostly mild, with mean temperatures in the 40s or 50s F (5° to 15° C), but temperatures fall below freezing during occasional

One of the driest areas in the world, the Rub' al-Khali is a vast tropical desert that lies mostly in Saudi Arabia. Vegetation is very scarce there.

Lynn Abercrombie

invasions of polar air. The summer months have mean temperatures in the low 80s F (about 28° C). Humid subtropical climates are found in the southeastern United States, southeastern China and southern Japan, in the southern Brazil–Uruguay–northeastern Argentina area, and along the southeastern coasts of Africa and Australia.

Cyclonic climates. Dominated by the conflict between cold polar and warm tropical air masses and by the movement of frontal cyclones, the cyclonic climate regions lie in a broad belt between about 35° and 70° latitude. Cyclonic climates, at least as experienced on land, are overwhelmingly confined to the Northern Hemisphere, where the landmasses are much larger and extend much farther into the middle and upper latitudes than they do in the Southern Hemisphere. The cyclonic climates can be subdivided into humid continental; subarctic, or taiga; dry continental; and maritime continental.

Humid continental cyclonic climates are found in the northeastern and north-central United States and southeastern Canada; northeastern China; northern Japan; Azerbaijan, Armenia, and Georgia; parts of Central Asia and Russia; and eastern and central Europe. Summers are longest and warmest toward the equator, while winters are longest and coldest toward the poles. Mean monthly temperatures in the north range from the upper 60s F (about 20° C) in the summer to below 0° F (−18° C) in the winter. In the south they range between the upper 70s F (about 26° C) in the summer and the lower 30s F (about 0° C) in the winter.

Precipitation, from both thunderstorms and cyclonic storms, occurs year-round but usually with a summer maximum. The annual average varies between 25 and 60 inches (63 and 152 centimeters). Snow is common, especially in the north. Native vegetation varies from tall prairie grasses in the drier margins to forests of deciduous trees (trees that lose their leaves each fall) in the south and of coniferous trees in the north.

The subarctic cyclonic climate region, or taiga, lies to the north of the humid continental climate regions, between 50° and 70° N. latitude. It covers much of Alaska and northern Canada in North America and much of Scandinavia, Russia, the Baltic countries, Belarus, and Manchuria in Eurasia. In these areas are the source regions of the cold continental polar air masses.

Summers are short and cool—only three months of the year average more than 50° F (10° C). During summer there are occasional nighttime frosts, though temperatures can rise into the 70s F (20s C) during daylight. Winters are long and bitterly cold, with mean January temperatures far below 0° F (−18° C). In northeastern Siberia, minimum temperatures of −90° F (−67° C) have been recorded. The ranges between the January and July mean temperatures reach more than 100° F (56° C), greater than anywhere else in the world.

Precipitation usually averages less than 20 inches (50 centimeters) per year. It is mostly from year-round cyclonic storms, with a maximum during the summer rains. Winter snowfalls are only a small portion of the total precipitation, but snow covers the ground for most of the year. There are large areas of permanently frozen

Ecola State Park, along Oregon's Pacific coast, has a maritime continental, or temperate marine, climate, with mild summers and winters and plentiful precipitation year-round.

subsoil, or permafrost. The subarctic climate generally coincides with a broad belt of coniferous trees known as the boreal forest or taiga.

Dry continental cyclonic climates occur between 35° and 50° latitude, lying either in the lee of mountains or far inland. The three main areas of dry continental climate are the Great Plains and Great Basin of North America; Mongolia, northwestern China, and parts of Central Asia; and northwestern and southern Argentina in South America. Toward the equator, they merge with the dry subtropical and arid tropical regions, differing mainly in having lower winter temperatures. Summers are hot, with mean temperatures in some places rising above 80° F (27° C). Precipitation is low and variable, especially in areas with the dry continental–arid (desert) climate. Annual precipitation in midlatitude deserts such as Death Valley in California and the Taklimakan, the Gobi, and the area around the Aral Sea in Asia averages less than 5 inches (13 centimeters). The semiarid steppes around these deserts average up to 20 inches (50 centimeters) or more.

The maritime continental cyclonic climate is located on the western coasts of the continents between about 35° and 60° latitude. It is also often referred to as the temperate maritime or marine west coast climate. On the equatorial side it merges with the Mediterranean climate. Areas with maritime continental climate are on the Pacific coast of North America from southeastern Alaska to northern California; on the Pacific coast of South America in southern Chile; in northwestern Europe, from Norway and Iceland to Portugal; and in New Zealand and southeastern Australia.

Temperatures are moderated by the prevailing westerly winds moving onshore from the oceanic high-pressure centers. Winters are mild, with mean temperatures in the 40s or 50s F (5° to 15° C). Summers also are mild, with means in the 60s F (10s C). Temperatures seldom fall below 20° F (–7° C) in winter or rise above 85° F (30° C) in summer. Average annual precipitation varies from 20 or 30 inches (50 to 76 centimeters) in low-lying areas and at the equatorial margins to more than 100 inches (250 inches) on windward mountain slopes. Precipitation occurs year-round but is much greater in winter, when cyclonic storm activity increases. Winter fog is common. Where precipitation is heavy, there often are dense forests of coniferous trees.

Polar climates. The polar tundra climate is found just poleward of the subarctic climate, mainly beyond the Arctic Circle on the northern fringes of North America and Eurasia. Winters in the tundra, as in the subarctic, are long and bitterly cold, with temperatures often dropping to –70° F (–57° C). There is no true summer. Temperatures seldom rise above 60° F (15° C), and usually only two or three months have mean temperatures above freezing. Annual precipitation, mostly from cyclonic summer storms, usually averages less than 15 inches (38 centimeters). There are no trees, and permafrost underlies the soil.

The polar ice cap climate has no month with a mean temperature above freezing. Almost all of Antarctica and all but the coast of Greenland have this coldest of all climates. These areas are covered by permanent snow and ice and some bare rock. There is no vegetation. Winter temperatures are most extreme in the interior of Antarctica, reaching world record lows of less than –125° F (–87° C)—partly from the high altitude of the ice cap, which reaches elevations of over 11,000 feet (3,350 meters) in some spots. Even in the summer months temperatures barely rise above freezing and often drop far below 0° F (–18° C). Average annual precipitation—

Like most of Antarctica, Ross Island has a cold, dry polar ice cap climate. Mount Erebus, an active volcano, is visible in the background.

mostly snow—is usually less than 5 inches (13 centimeters).

Highland climates. Highlands are generally cooler than lowlands of the same latitude. Precipitation is much greater on the lower, windward mountain slopes than it is at higher elevations and on the leeward slopes. Great heights often have permanent snow cover. The snow line, or upper limit of summertime melting, is generally highest in the tropics and lowest at high latitudes. The most extensive highland areas are the Rocky Mountains of North America, the Andes Mountains of South America, and the Himalayan mountain–Tibetan plateau area of Asia. Mountain climates are often similar to those near sea level much farther from the equator. For example, above about 6,000 feet (1,800 meters) the mountains in North Carolina and Tennessee have about the same temperatures and vegetation as low-lying areas in eastern Canada, about 700 miles (1,100 kilometers) to the north.

Oceanic climates. People living on small islands or traveling by ship experience climates dominated by the strong moderating influence of large bodies of water. Mean annual temperatures are often similar to those at the same latitude over continents, but the range of temperature is much smaller. For example, the Azores islands, at 39° N. latitude in the eastern Atlantic, have a mean temperature in the coldest months (February and March) of about 57° F (14° C), yet the warmest month (August) is not much warmer, averaging 71° F (22° C).

Rain falls on the oceans, with less obvious effects than on land. Subtropical areas generally get less rain than equatorial or midlatitude places. Some oceanic areas are quite stormy. The seas surrounding Antarctica have frequent cyclonic storms with strong winds and large waves. Tropical oceans often experience tropical storms and tropical cyclones (also called hurricanes or typhoons) in that hemisphere's late summer and autumn. Such storms often strike land, with potentially devastating results.

Climate and the Natural Environment

Of all aspects of the natural landscape, none is affected to a greater degree by climate than is natural vegetation. Each plant species survives only within certain limits of sunlight, temperature, precipitation, humidity, soil moisture, and wind. Variations in these elements are directly reflected in variations in Earth's plant cover. The correspondence between climate and vegetation is so apparent that climate types often are identical with and are given the same names as the dominant natural vegetation in a region. (*See also* Biogeography.)

Climate also affects soils. In warm, wet climates, weathering and formation of soil are more rapid than in cool, dry climates. As a result, soils are generally thicker in the wet tropics than in deserts or polar forest areas. Soils in dry climates, however, tend to be more fertile than those in humid climates. This is mainly because there is less leaching, or removal of plant nutrients from the soil by the downward percolation of water. Soil composition also depends on the effect that climate has in determining the type of vegetation that eventually

Michael Turek—Photonica/Getty Images

Snow covers the slopes of the mountains in Torres del Paine National Park, in the Patagonian Andes of Chile. In areas with highland climates, the temperature is usually cooler than it is at lower elevations of the same latitude.

decays and becomes part of the soil. That is why grassland soils are more fertile than forest soils.

Variations in climate have a marked effect on Earth's landforms. In humid areas, where water is the chief erosional force, landforms tend to have rounded contours. Landforms shaped under arid conditions are more likely to be jagged and angular. This is partly because wind erosion is more dominant. Stream erosion in dry areas, while infrequent, tends to be sudden and torrential, and the runoff of water is not slowed down as much by plant cover.

Climate and Humans

As part of the natural environment, climate greatly affects human activities. Climate is economically most significant in its effect on agriculture. Climatic factors such as the length of growing season, the total amount and seasonal distribution of precipitation, and the daily and seasonal ranges of temperature restrict the kinds of crops and the types of livestock that can be raised.

People have reduced and even overcome climatic restrictions by the use of irrigation in dry climates, drainage in wet climates, and greenhouses in cold climates. New breeds of plants and animals, able to thrive under otherwise adverse climatic conditions, have been developed also. The grazing of livestock, however, still is largely limited to areas where forage crops can be profitably grown. Open-range grazing is particularly sensitive to climate, requiring relatively mild temperatures and adequate water supplies.

Climatic conditions also affect transportation. In areas of frequent storms and recurring fog, transportation movements are frequently slowed or interrupted. Water transportation in many areas is halted by winter ice. Land transportation may be blocked by heavy snowfalls. Air travel especially is affected by stormy climatic conditions.

The major concentrations of population in the world are in the humid middle latitudes and subtropics, where the development of agriculture has been least restricted by adverse climatic conditions. Areas with very dry, very wet, or very cold climates tend to be sparsely populated. However, with technological developments such as refrigeration, air conditioning, and central heating, human settlement has been less and less confined to so-called favorable climates.

Climate Change

While "climate" is intended as a long-term description of weather, there remains the question of just how long a period it should describe. If one adopts a period such as 30 years, one can then describe changes in climate over longer periods, such as thousands or millions of years. Evidence of climate changes includes data from rocks and fossils, tree rings and lake bed sediments, and human historical records. These changes have many causes which operate on many time scales. The drift of continents due to plate tectonics is an important factor over millions of years (*see* Earth). Changes in Earth's orbit and axial tilt are a factor over tens of thousands of years. Varying levels of greenhouse gases, such as carbon dioxide, are important on both long and short time scales. These gases allow sunlight to pass through and warm Earth's surface but impede the flow of infrared energy back into space, thus "trapping" heat and warming the planet. (*See also* Greenhouse Effect.)

In one sense, Earth's overall climate has been rather stable over most of its 4.5-billion-year history—at least enough to have allowed life to persist. While the Sun is believed to have grown about 50 percent brighter during this time, decreasing amounts of greenhouse gases in the past helped keep temperatures from rising much. However, quite different conditions have prevailed at times. For example, there is some evidence that ice may have covered almost the entire planet about 700 million years ago. On the other hand, much of the last 250 million years was quite warm, peaking around 55 million years ago. At that time there was no polar ice and the conditions now called tropical extended almost to the polar regions. After that, worldwide temperatures gradually cooled, eventually resulting in Antarctica and Greenland becoming ice covered.

The last two million years have been a remarkable time of alternating ice ages and somewhat shorter warmer periods called interglacials. The current interglacial, called the Holocene epoch, began a bit more than 10,000 years ago. There have been variations even during the Holocene, including a period around 8,000 years ago when what is now the Sahara was relatively wet and green. In historic times, the period from about AD 1600 through much of the 1800s is known as the

Jim Sugar/Corbis

A scientist displays samples taken from giant sequoias. By studying the trees' growth rings, he can determine the past climatic conditions under which the trees grew. In general, the width of the rings tends to vary according to the amount of available rainfall and the prevailing temperatures.

Little Ice Age, during which temperatures were a bit cooler than today and glaciers were generally growing.

There is currently widespread concern about a rapid phase of climate change, commonly known as global warming. While many complex factors, including slight variations in the Sun's output, can affect climate in general, the large majority of scientists conclude that the chief culprit in the current rapid warming is an increase in greenhouse gases in the atmosphere. The largest contributor is carbon dioxide, the concentration of which increased by about 25 percent during the 20th century, mainly owing to the burning of fossil fuels. In 2007 the Intergovernmental Panel on Climate Change forecast an increase in global mean temperature of between 3.2° and 7.2° F (1.8° and 4.0° C) by 2100 as compared to 1990, depending on various scenarios of future human activity. (*See also* Global Warming.)

FURTHER RESOURCES FOR CLIMATE

Allaby, Michael. Encyclopedia of Weather and Climate, rev. ed. (Facts on File, 2007).

Burroughs, William, ed. Climate: Into the 21st Century (Cambridge Univ. Press, 2003).

Burroughs, W.J. The Climate Revealed (Cambridge Univ. Press, 1999).

Casper, J.K. Water and Atmosphere: The Lifeblood of Natural Systems (Chelsea House, 2007).

Cullen, Katherine. Weather and Climate: The People Behind the Science (Chelsea House, 2006).

Desonie, Dana. Climate: Causes and Effects of Climate Change (Chelsea House, 2007).

The Diagram Group. Weather and Climate: An Illustrated Guide to Science (Chelsea House, 2006).

Human, Katy, ed. Critical Perspectives on World Climate (Rosen, 2007).

Ochoa, George, and others. Climate: The Force that Shapes Our World and the Future of Life on Earth (Rodale, 2005).

Silverstein, Alvin, and others. Weather and Climate (Twenty-First Century Books, 2008).

Unwin, Mike. Climate Change (Heinemann Library, 2007).

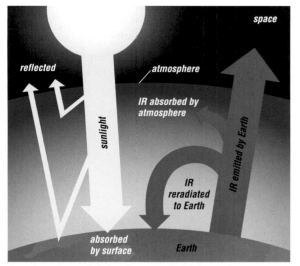

Some incoming sunlight is reflected by Earth's atmosphere and surface, but most is absorbed by the surface, which is warmed. Infrared (IR) radiation is emitted from Earth's surface. Some IR radiation escapes to space, but some is absorbed by greenhouse gases and reradiated toward Earth, where it further warms the surface and lower atmosphere.

GREENHOUSE EFFECT

The warming of Earth's surface and lower atmosphere due to the presence of certain gases in the air is known as the greenhouse effect. The gases involved are collectively termed greenhouse gases; the most significant of these are water vapor, carbon dioxide, methane, and nitrous oxide. The greenhouse effect is so named because it resembles the warming of a botanical greenhouse, but the comparison is not a perfect one. The glass walls of a greenhouse hold heat inside the building by trapping warmed air, preventing heat loss via convection. In contrast, greenhouse gases absorb radiation emitted from the Earth's surface and direct it back to Earth, preventing radiant heat loss.

Natural Occurrence

The greenhouse effect is a natural phenomenon that keeps Earth's temperatures compatible with existing life-forms. As sunlight enters Earth's atmosphere, some of it is reflected back into space. Most of it passes through the atmosphere, however, and heats Earth's surface, which in turn emits some of this energy as infrared radiation. In the atmosphere, some infrared radiation escapes into space but most is absorbed by greenhouse gases and directed back toward Earth, where it further warms Earth's surface and lower atmosphere. Without the

. . . .

This article was critically reviewed by Susan Joy Hassol, author of Impacts of a Warming Arctic, *the synthesis report of the Arctic Climate Impact Assessment, and the global warming documentary* Too Hot Not to Handle *for HBO cable television.*

warming due to the natural greenhouse effect, Earth's surface temperature would be much colder than it is, with an average global temperature around 0° F (−18° C).

As a model of comparison, the planet Venus has a high concentration of carbon dioxide in its atmosphere. The carbon dioxide does not allow the heat from the planet to escape into space, thus causing an extreme greenhouse effect resulting in surface temperatures as high as 840° F (450° C). Mars's atmosphere, on the other hand, contains low concentrations of carbon dioxide and so does not keep nearly as much of the planet's thermal radiation from escaping. In other words, Mars has a weak greenhouse effect, making its surface much colder than it would be if it had a strong one. The average surface temperature of Mars is about −82° F (−63° C).

The most important greenhouse gas that naturally occurs in Earth's atmosphere is water vapor. The amount of water vapor in the air, also called humidity, varies over different parts of Earth. For example, in areas with a cold climate, the water vapor content is lower, while tropical climates are often saturated with water vapor. Water vapor forms clouds, which also have the ability to affect Earth's climate: clouds not only reflect sunlight away, which cools Earth, but also trap infrared radiation coming from Earth, which warms the air near the surface.

Most of the other greenhouse gases also occur naturally in the atmosphere. Carbon dioxide is released when volcanoes erupt, organic materials decay, and organisms exhale. Natural biological processes that occur in environments with low oxygen, such as in swamps, produce and release methane. Nitrous oxide is released from the oceans and from bacteria located within soil. These natural emissions of greenhouse gases are normally balanced by other natural processes that absorb these gases. For example, plants absorb carbon dioxide through the process of photosynthesis. The full complement of processes that release and absorb these gases is known as the carbon cycle.

The concentration of greenhouse gases affects how much heat the atmosphere retains. While the natural

Trees are natural absorbers of carbon dioxide. The loss of massive amounts of trees, including about 99 percent of the forests in Haiti, contributes to the buildup of carbon dioxide in the atmosphere.

AP

Percentages of Human-Induced Greenhouse Gas Emissions

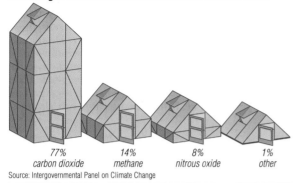

| 77% carbon dioxide | 14% methane | 8% nitrous oxide | 1% other |

Source: Intergovernmental Panel on Climate Change

Human-Induced Carbon Dioxide Emissions

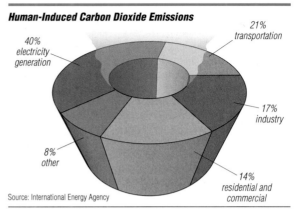

40% electricity generation

21% transportation

17% industry

8% other

14% residential and commercial

Source: International Energy Agency

Globally, about 82% of human-induced carbon dioxide emissions come from the burning of fossil fuels while the other 18% result from deforestation. The chart above breaks down the 82% that come from fossil fuels into the sectors that account for the emissions. The largest single source of carbon dioxide is coal-burning power plants.

greenhouse effect makes life possible on Earth, the intensification of the effect due to human activities prevents the carbon cycle from naturally balancing itself and leads to global warming.

Human-Caused Effects

In 1827 French mathematician Joseph Fourier first discovered that Earth's atmosphere trapped heat much like a greenhouse. It was not until almost 70 years later, in 1896, that Swedish chemist and physicist Svante August Arrhenius first proposed that Earth's average temperature would rise due to the additional carbon dioxide that was accumulating in the atmosphere since the large-scale burning of fossil fuels began with the Industrial Revolution. He hypothesized that as the growth of industry continued, carbon dioxide levels would continue to rise and cause an increase in Earth's average surface air temperature. However, it would take another 50 years before scientists gathered concrete data to prove his theory.

In 1958 Charles David Keeling of the Scripps Institution of Oceanography consistently began to

Charles Keeling's observations of monthly carbon dioxide (CO_2) concentrations at Mauna Loa are charted below. The short dips and spikes are due to summer and winter in the Northern Hemisphere: the majority of Earth's vegetation blooms in summer, thus reducing the CO_2 levels through photosynthesis. During winter the CO_2 levels slightly increase.

The Keeling Curve

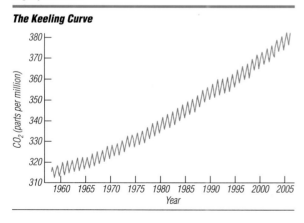

measure the levels of carbon dioxide at Mauna Loa in Hawaii. He charted a steady increase in these gas levels in Earth's atmosphere. Collected data show that the levels of carbon dioxide at present are 35 percent more than what they were before the Industrial Revolution began. This increase in atmospheric carbon dioxide levels is due to human-induced greenhouse gas emissions.

About three fourths of human-caused greenhouse gases come from the burning of fossil fuels, such as coal, oil, and natural gas. When fossil fuels are burned, carbon dioxide is emitted. Coal-burning power plants, automobiles, and factories are the biggest producers of this gas. Methane, an end product of industrial and agricultural processes and the decomposition of landfill wastes, has more than doubled in atmospheric concentration since the Industrial Revolution. Nitrous oxide emissions also increased due to industrial and agricultural activity. Halocarbons, such as the refrigerant perfluorocarbon (PFC), are produced through industrial activity. Although their atmospheric concentration is relatively low, by weight halocarbons trap up to thousands of times more heat than carbon dioxide.

The dramatic increase in greenhouse gases since the Industrial Revolution and their effect on global climate are of great concern to scientists and others. Computer models assessed in the report of the Intergovernmental Panel on Climate Change in 2007 project a 3.2–7.2° F (1.8–4.0° C) rise in average surface temperature during the period from 1990 to 2100. These projections are based on scientific models using scenarios that assume that humans do not make major changes in the energy system to reduce greenhouse gas emissions.

Should present trends in the emissions of greenhouse gases, particularly of carbon dioxide, continue, climatic changes larger than any ever experienced by modern human civilization are expected. This could substantially alter natural and agricultural ecosystems, human and animal health, and climate patterns, increasing the incidence of droughts and major storms and disrupting living things and their interrelationships.

Taxi/Getty Images

The dramatic decrease in the area and thickness of Arctic sea ice due to rising temperatures has been especially hard on polar bears, which depend on ice floes during summer for resting and as platforms for hunting seals, their primary prey. The decreasing summer sea ice is forcing bears to swim greater distances than normal, leaving the animals exhausted, underweight, and vulnerable to drowning.

GLOBAL WARMING

The rise of air temperatures near Earth's surface over the past century is known as global warming. Earth has experienced periods of gradual warming and cooling throughout its existence due to natural causes, such as volcanic eruptions and variations in the Sun's output. However, scientists have attributed the current increase in global temperatures to human causes—primarily the release of certain gases into the atmosphere as a result of industrial activity. These gases—collectively termed greenhouse gases—absorb and trap heat emitted from Earth's surface through a phenomenon known as the greenhouse effect.

In addition to the rise in near-surface air temperatures, global warming encompasses other climatic changes caused by this warming, such as variations in precipitation patterns, winds, and ocean currents. For this reason, the terms global warming and climate change are sometimes used interchangeably.

Causes of Global Warming

The greenhouse effect is a natural process that helps maintain temperatures suitable for life. Without it, Earth

. . . .

This article was critically reviewed by Susan Joy Hassol, author of Impacts of a Warming Arctic, *the synthesis report of the Arctic Climate Impact Assessment, and the global warming documentary* Too Hot Not to Handle *for HBO cable television.*

would be a frozen and likely uninhabitable planet. However, scientists who study climate have determined that increased concentrations of greenhouse gases resulting from human activity have amplified the natural greenhouse effect, causing global warming. The main greenhouse gases with human sources are carbon dioxide, methane, nitrous oxide, and halocarbons.

Carbon dioxide is produced naturally by animals through respiration. The primary human-produced source of carbon dioxide is the burning of fossil fuels: coal, oil, and natural gas. These fuels are widely used in electricity generation, transportation, and industry. Another source of carbon dioxide from human activity is the clearing of forests for agriculture and other purposes (*see* Deforestation).

Atmospheric methane concentrations are much lower than those of carbon dioxide, but they are more potent. By weight, methane is 25 times more powerful at trapping heat than carbon dioxide over a 100-year time period. Methane is produced naturally by, for example, the decay of vegetation in low-oxygen environments such as wetlands. The major human-induced sources of methane include rice cultivation, livestock raising, the use of fossil fuels, and the decomposition of organic matter in landfills.

Nitrous oxide is produced naturally by biological reactions in both soil and water. Human-induced sources include fertilizer use and fossil fuel burning. By

Changes in Greenhouse Gas Concentrations

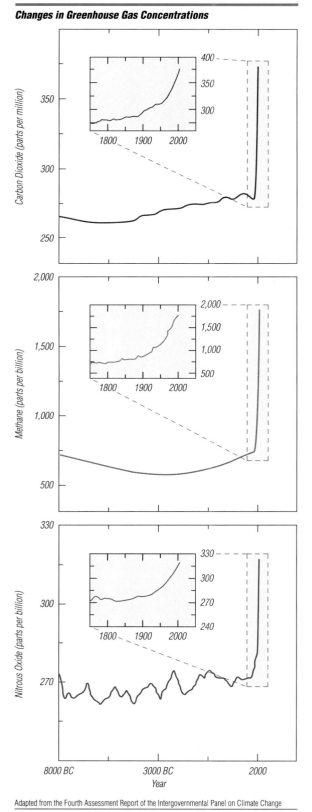

Adapted from the Fourth Assessment Report of the Intergovernmental Panel on Climate Change

weight, its heat-trapping potential is about 300 times that of carbon dioxide over a 100-year time horizon.

Halocarbons are low in concentration but have extremely high potencies—some with more than 10,000 times the warming effect of carbon dioxide by weight. Halocarbons are very rare in nature but have been widely synthesized for industrial applications; they have been used as refrigerants, aerosol propellants, insulation, and cleaning solvents. Halocarbons include chlorofluorocarbons (CFCs), hydrochlorofluorocarbons (HCFCs), and hydrofluorocarbons (HFCs).

In nature, the sources of greenhouse gases are balanced, on average, by physical, chemical, and biological processes called "sinks" that remove the gases from the atmosphere. For example, carbon dioxide sinks include photosynthesis, the process by which green plants use carbon dioxide to make food. However, human activities have produced carbon dioxide in quantities that far exceed the offsetting capacity of natural sinks, leading to its accumulation in the atmosphere. The same is true of other greenhouse gases such as methane and nitrous oxide. (*See also* Greenhouse Effect.)

Studying Global Warming

Scientists use a variety of methods and evidence to study global warming. They analyze data collected by thermometers and other instruments from roughly 1850 to the present. To study climate changes prior to that time, scientists use "paleoclimatic" data from such natural sources as ocean and lake sediments, ice core samples, and tree rings. Finally, they use computers to produce models of Earth's climate that can be used to understand past changes and predict future changes and effects of global warming.

Although some records are available from the 1600s and 1700s, systematic measurements of climate began in the mid-1800s. The data include measurements of surface temperature over land and the oceans, precipitation amounts, sea-ice extents, and global sea levels. Since the 1970s, satellite studies have provided additional data on temperature trends at Earth's surface and through the layers of the atmosphere. In addition, data-collection platforms in the oceans measure temperature and other properties of seawater.

Paleoclimatic data allow scientists to reconstruct climate changes over many thousands of years. Some sources, such as most sediment samples and pollen records, are only detailed enough to describe climate changes on long timescales. Other sources, such as growth measurements from tree rings and gases extracted from ice core samples, can provide a record of yearly or seasonal climate changes. Gas bubbles trapped in ice samples from 10,000 feet (3,000 meters) beneath Antarctica contain gases that were in the atmosphere 900,000 years ago.

Computerized climate models can be used to investigate the climate's natural variability as well as its

Atmospheric concentrations of carbon dioxide, methane, and nitrous oxide remained relatively stable for thousands of years. After the industrial era began in about 1750, the concentrations increased dramatically.

Changes in Temperature and Sea Level

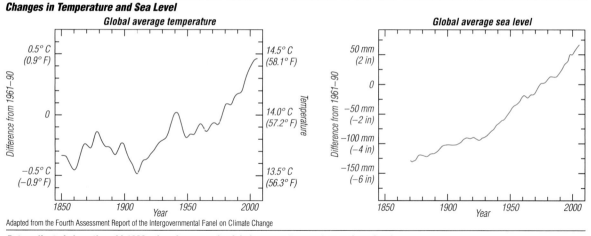

Adapted from the Fourth Assessment Report of the Intergovernmental Panel on Climate Change

Data collected since the mid-1800s show increases in global average temperature and sea level.

response to greenhouse gas emissions. Models vary considerably in their degree of complexity. Even the most detailed models cannot account for all of the processes that affect the atmosphere and oceans. Nevertheless, many models perform very well in reproducing the basic factors that influence climate.

Warming in the 21st century is projected to be greatest over land and in the high northern latitudes. The projections on these maps are based on a midrange emissions scenario and are relative to the period 1980–99.

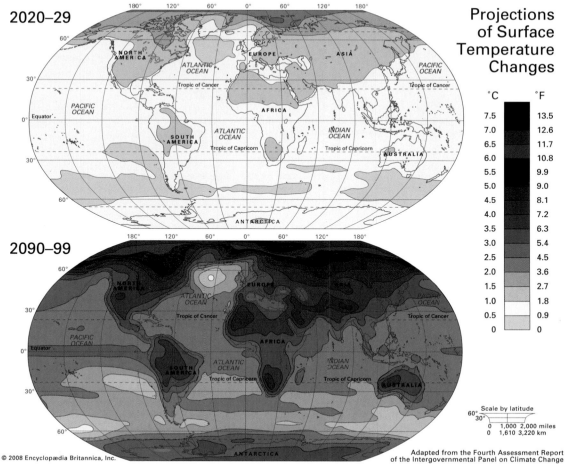

© 2008 Encyclopædia Britannica, Inc.

Adapted from the Fourth Assessment Report of the Intergovernmental Panel on Climate Change

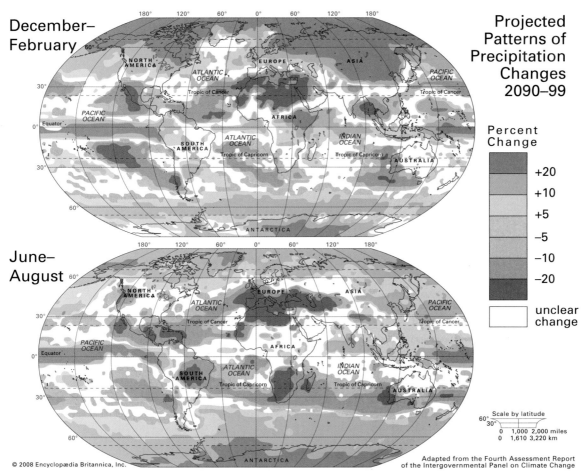

December–February

Projected Patterns of Precipitation Changes 2090–99

Percent Change

+20
+10
+5
−5
−10
−20

unclear change

June–August

Scale by latitude

0   1,000   2,000 miles
0   1,610   3,220 km

© 2008 Encyclopædia Britannica, Inc.

Adapted from the Fourth Assessment Report of the Intergovernmental Panel on Climate Change

Changes in precipitation patterns caused by global warming could lead to drought in some areas and flooding in others. The projections on these maps are based on a midrange emissions scenario and are relative to the period 1980–99.

The leading international organization in the study of global warming is the Intergovernmental Panel on Climate Change (IPCC), which was established in 1988 by the World Meteorological Organization and the United Nations Environment Programme. The IPCC assesses and summarizes the latest scientific, technical, and socioeconomic data on climate change and publishes its findings in reports that are presented to international organizations and policy makers throughout the world. Thousands of the world's leading climate change experts have worked under the IPCC.

The IPCC's reports have documented the progress of global warming and shown a growing consensus on the role of human activity in the phenomenon. The 2007 report stated that the 20th century saw an increase in global average surface temperature of 1.2° F (0.74° C), and it forecasted an additional increase of 3.2° to 7.2° F (1.8° to 4.0° C) by 2100 if measures are not put in place to reduce human-caused emissions of greenhouse gases. The authors of the 2007 report also stated with at least 90 percent certainty that most of the warming since about 1950 had been caused by human activity. The findings of

the IPCC were endorsed by many scientific organizations, including the national science academies of the United States and all the other G-8 (industrialized) countries as well as those of China, India, and Brazil.

Effects of Global Warming

How much temperatures will rise in the future will depend largely on the rate of greenhouse gas emissions. The IPCC based its projected range of temperature increase on a number of emissions scenarios, none of which include policies designed to reduce global warming. Most scientists agree that the effects of global warming will become much more severe if the total increase above pre-industrial temperature exceeds 3.6° F (2° C). Only scenarios that include major reductions in emissions are likely to hold warming below that level.

Warming patterns. The world is not warming uniformly. Surface air temperatures have increased more rapidly over land than over the oceans, a trend that is expected to continue. Thus, the Northern Hemisphere—with less than 40 percent of its surface area covered by water—is expected to warm faster than the Southern

Hemisphere. The greatest increase in surface temperature is projected over the Arctic, due in part to the melting of snow and ice on land and sea. Snow and ice reflect some of the Sun's heat back into space; a reduction in the surface area covered by snow and ice means that more heat will stay in the lower atmosphere, causing more melting, which causes more warming, and so on. The Arctic is already warming twice as fast as the rest of the planet.

Precipitation patterns. Global warming has already led to changes in precipitation patterns across the globe, and these are projected to continue. There has been an observed increase in heavy downpours in most areas. Continued precipitation increases are projected in the polar and subpolar regions, with decreases in the middle latitudes. An increase in rainfall is expected near the equator, and a decrease is expected in the subtropics.

Changes in precipitation patterns are projected to increase further the chances of extreme weather in many areas. Decreased summer precipitation in North America, Europe, and Africa, combined with greater rates of evaporation due to rising temperatures, is predicted to lead to increased droughts. In other regions, greater rates of both evaporation and precipitation will likely cause an increase in very heavy rainfall that can lead to flooding.

Ice melt and sea-level rise. A very visible effect of climate change has been the steady melting of sea ice and glaciers, especially in the Arctic. The IPCC has projected that the Arctic could be virtually free of summer sea ice by 2070, and more recent studies project this could occur several decades sooner. The melting of land-based ice, from glaciers around the world and the large ice sheets on Greenland and Antarctica, has already contributed to sea-level rise, and further increases are projected. Another factor in the sea-level rise, also driven by global warming, is thermal expansion of the oceans—that is, seawater takes up more space as its temperature rises. During the 20th century

the global sea level rose an estimated 7 inches (17 centimeters).

Because heat spreads slowly through water, the oceans are likely to continue to warm for at least several centuries in response to the increases in greenhouse gas concentrations that have already taken place. If greenhouse gas emissions continue at their early-21st-century rate, the combination of thermal expansion and land-based ice melt is predicted to raise the global sea level at least 1 to 3 feet (0.33 to 1 meter) by 2100.

The rise in sea level could be much greater in the longer term. It is probable that the continued warming of Greenland will lead to faster melting of its ice sheet. Paleoclimatic evidence suggests than an additional 3.6° F (2° C) of warming could ultimately cause complete melting of the Greenland ice sheet, which would cause sea level to rise an additional 20 feet (7 meters). Such an increase would submerge many islands and lowland regions. The lowland regions at risk include substantial parts of the United States Gulf coast and Eastern seaboard (including roughly the lower third of Florida), much of The Netherlands and Belgium, and heavily populated tropical areas such as Bangladesh. This level of warming could also accelerate melting of the West Antarctic ice sheet, raising global sea level an additional 15 feet (5 meters).

Tropical cyclones. The impact of global warming on tropical cyclones (including hurricanes and typhoons) is the subject of intense research. It appears likely that rising tropical ocean temperatures will increase the intensity of tropical cyclones. In recent decades scientists have seen a close relationship between warming temperatures in the Atlantic Ocean and an increase in the strength of hurricanes. Trends in the intensities of cyclones in other regions, such as in the tropical Pacific and Indian Oceans, are more uncertain due to a lack of reliable long-term measurements.

Rising sea levels associated with global warming could submerge islands and coastal lowlands throughout the world. Areas at risk include the Gulf coast and Eastern seaboard in the United States and The Netherlands in Europe.

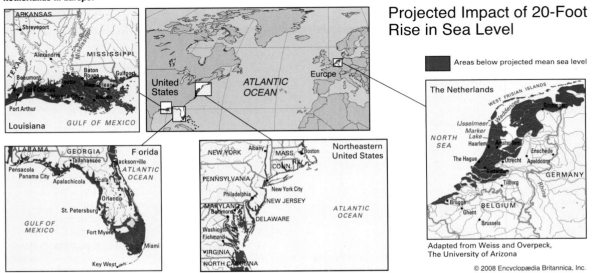

Projected Impact of 20-Foot Rise in Sea Level

Areas below projected mean sea level

Adapted from Weiss and Overpeck, The University of Arizona

© 2008 Encyclopædia Britannica, Inc.

Glaciers around the world are melting as a result of global warming. A series of three photos—taken in 1938, 1981, and 2006—shows the decline of Grinnell Glacier, in Glacier National Park in the U.S. state of Montana. The lake formed by the glacier's meltwater grows each year.

Environmental impact. Global warming is already affecting ecosystems and thus the biodiversity of plants, animals, and other forms of life (*see* Biodiversity). Living things establish their geographic ranges by adapting to their environment, including long-term climate patterns. Relatively sudden climate changes caused by global warming could shrink species habitats, challenging the adaptive abilities of many species, especially those with already restricted ranges. Some plants and animals, both on land and in the sea, have already shifted their ranges in response to warming temperatures. For example, biologists have found that certain species of butterflies and birds in the Northern Hemisphere have moved their ranges northward.

Surface warming has already begun to affect biological processes in some species. For example, trees are producing leaves earlier in the spring, birds are laying eggs earlier, and mammals are ending hibernation earlier. Warming is also influencing the seasonal migration patterns of birds, fishes, and other animals. In the Arctic, continued melting of sea ice threatens such animals as polar bears, seals, and walrus. In western Hudson Bay, Canada, the physical condition and reproductive success of polar bears significantly declined in the 1980s and '90s as sea ice decreased. According to a study by the United States Geological Survey, two thirds of the world's polar bears, including all those in Alaska, could be gone by 2050 due to the ongoing loss of sea ice.

Climate change may also affect marine ecosystems by altering food supplies. The combination of warming waters, decreased sea ice, and other changes to the oceans in the high latitudes could lead to reductions or redistributions of algae and plankton. As a result, fish and other animals that feed on these organisms may be threatened. Near Antarctica, the number of krill has declined as the ocean has warmed. This, in turn, has led to a decline in the numbers of penguins and seals that depend on krill for food.

Ultimately, climate change is expected to play a role in the extinction of certain plants and animals. Biologists have estimated that a warming of between 2.7 and 4.5° F (1.5 and 2.5° C) could put one fifth to one third of all plant and animal species at an increased risk of extinction. This range of temperature increase is possible by the year 2100 in even the lower-end emissions scenarios prepared by the IPCC. Estimates of species loss climb to as much as two fifths for a warming of more than 8.1° F (4.5° C). Average global temperatures could increase to this level in the 21st century according to the IPCC's higher-end emissions scenarios.

Socioeconomic impact. The socioeconomic effects of global warming and climate change could be substantial, especially in the areas of agriculture, forestry, water supply, human health, and infrastructure. In some of these areas the impact of warming temperatures is already evident.

Climate change has so far had a mixed impact on agriculture. Regions in the mid-to-high latitudes have had an earlier spring and a longer growing season, which has modestly boosted crop yields. If warming surpasses 5.4° F (3° C), however, productivity is expected to decrease in these regions. In tropical and subtropical areas, agricultural production has already been affected negatively by global warming. The Sahel region of Africa has seen crop failures, and accompanying famines, due to intense and more frequent droughts. Elsewhere, floods caused by climate change could hurt productivity. In some places farmers have changed their practices in an attempt to adapt to changing conditions—for example, they plant crops earlier in the growing season.

The effect of global warming on forestry has also been mixed. Forests of the Northern Hemisphere have taken advantage of the longer growing season. However, this advantage has been offset in some places by other changes brought on by global warming. In North America, for example, forests from British Columbia to Alaska have suffered from severe beetle infestations and an increase in forest fires encouraged by the warmer weather.

Global warming and climate change are expected to affect water supplies across the globe. At current rates of warming, by the middle of the 21st century, scientists have predicted a 10 to 40 percent decrease in water availability in parts of the tropics and subtropics. In some places water availability is already declining because of drought. Such regions as the African Sahel, western North America, southern Africa, the Middle East, and western Australia are particularly vulnerable. Elsewhere, the reduction of snow pack and shrinking of glaciers will likely cause serious water shortages. Less snow accumulation and earlier seasonal snowmelt will affect places that depend on a long, slow melt for their summer water supply, such as the western United States, which gets 75 percent of its surface water from snow pack. Places that rely on glacial melting for their water—particularly near the Himalayas in Asia and the Andes Mountains in South America—face an even greater risk because glaciers, unlike snow, cannot be replenished.

Human health will be affected by climate change in a number of ways. The spread of infectious diseases will likely change because the ranges of disease carriers, such as insects and rodents, are often determined by climate. Warmer winters in the Korean Peninsula and Southern Europe, for example, have allowed the spread of *Anopheles*, a mosquito that carries the malaria virus. In addition, a warmer winter in New York in 1999 appears to have been partly responsible for the outbreak of West Nile virus, which then spread across the country. Climate change is also expected to increase malnutrition due to food shortages and cause more cases of diarrhea, cardiorespiratory illness, and allergies as a result of rising pollen levels. Rising temperatures could also increase the frequency of killer heat waves, such as the one that killed tens of thousands of people in Europe in 2003.

The heightened risk of severe weather, flooding, and wildfire associated with global warming is expected to threaten the infrastructure of many countries. Homes, dams, transportation networks, and other facets of infrastructure could be affected. Rising sea levels and more intense tropical cyclones (hurricanes) are a particular threat to coastal areas. Poor people in the densely populated, low-lying regions of Africa, Asia, and tropical islands will be the most vulnerable because of their limited ability to adapt.

Responses to Global Warming

Since the 1980s global warming has been the subject of a debate over the extent and seriousness of rising surface temperatures, the possible effects of observed and future warming, and the need for action to reduce warming and deal with its consequences. Some people have stressed the role of natural forces in past climatic variations and argue that the current warming trend is part of a natural cycle. They point to uncertainties in the science of climate change and maintain that predictions of dire consequences are exaggerated. Leading climate scientists now agree, however, that rising concentrations of greenhouse gases in the atmosphere resulting from human activity are primarily responsible for rising temperatures and associated climate changes. They stress that if emissions are left unchecked, the impacts of warming will become much more severe in the 21st century and beyond.

As the scientific consensus on global warming has evolved, governments around the world have begun to develop policies to address the threat. Public policy related to global warming and climate change may be divided into two types: adaptation and mitigation. Experts say that both types will be needed to respond to global warming. The goal of adaptation policy is to improve the ability of communities to face the challenges of a changing climate. For example, some policies encourage farmers to change their practices in response to seasonal changes. Other policies are designed to prepare cities located in coastal areas for elevated sea levels.

Adaptation policy addresses the immediate consequences of climate change. But reducing the impact of climate change requires addressing the fundamental cause—the production of greenhouse gases. This is the goal of mitigation policy. This type of policy focuses mainly on reducing the use of fossil fuels in electricity generation and transportation, which account for most greenhouse gas emissions. One mitigation strategy that most economists consider essential to combating global warming is putting a price on carbon—that is, holding the producers of greenhouse gases economically responsible for their emissions. The idea is to provide a financial incentive for industries to reduce their dependence on fossil fuels and invest in low-carbon technologies. One method of establishing a carbon price is to tax polluting companies for each ton of carbon dioxide they emit. Another method is carbon trading—a system that sets a limit on total carbon dioxide emissions and allows companies to buy and sell emissions permits. In other words, a company that emits more than its share of carbon dioxide has to buy permits from a company whose emissions fall below its target. In 2005 the European Union instituted the world's first multilateral carbon trading system. On an international scale, carbon trading could result in industrialized countries buying permits from developing countries. In addition to encouraging the industrialized countries to reduce their emissions, such a system would give developing countries the resources to invest in alternative energy sources of their own.

The development of energy-efficient and renewable energy technologies is another key to mitigation policy. Some policies encourage using electricity more efficiently—for example, by mandating that appliances use less energy. Others encourage the use of energy sources that do not produce carbon dioxide, such as wind and solar power, and biomass—plant materials that can be used to make fuels and produce electricity. These alternative energy sources have the added advantage of being renewable, or constantly replenished; in contrast, the supply of fossil fuels is limited and dwindling. Other mitigation policies seek to improve the energy efficiency of vehicles. A successful example is the development of cars called hybrids, which cut emissions by using an electric motor along with a small gasoline motor.

An emerging technology with great potential for limiting global warming is carbon sequestration. In this process, carbon dioxide emitted from factories or power stations is captured and stored underground or underwater. The gas is pumped into natural reservoirs, such as depleted oil and natural gas fields. Proponents of carbon sequestration believe that it could store vast quantities of carbon dioxide safely and permanently. However, the technology is still unproven.

International Cooperation on Global Warming

International efforts to address global warming have been complicated by the national interests of various countries. The most divisive issue has been determining the differing responsibilities of developed (industrialized) and developing countries in reducing greenhouse gas emissions. Countries from both groups have claimed that emissions limits could dampen their economies.

The first major multinational agreement aimed at curtailing greenhouse gas emissions was the United Nations Framework Convention on Climate Change (UNFCCC). It was signed by representatives of 154 countries at the United Nations Conference on Environment and Development, or Earth Summit, in Rio de Janeiro in 1992. The stated objective of the convention was the stabilization of greenhouse gas concentrations in the atmosphere at a level that would prevent dangerous human interference with the climate system. The convention called for industrialized countries to reduce their greenhouse gas emissions to 1990 levels, but it set no deadline for this target.

In 1997 representatives from more than 150 countries negotiated the Kyoto Protocol of the UNFCCC at a United Nations conference in Kyoto, Japan. After a long ratification process, the protocol went into force in 2005. The protocol called for industrialized countries to collectively decrease greenhouse gas emissions to approximately 5 percent below 1990 levels by no later than 2012. The protocol set different reduction targets for different countries. For example, it called for an 8 percent decrease among countries of the European Union and a 7 percent decrease in the United States. The protocol did not require developing countries to restrict their emissions at that time. Reasons for this differentiation include the fact that carbon dioxide

remains in the atmosphere for over a century, so the warming to date is primarily the result of a century's worth of emissions from the industrialized world. Per capita emissions are much greater in the industrialized countries, and these countries have more resources with which to make the required changes.

The Kyoto Protocol was widely hailed as an important step in addressing the long-term challenge of global warming. Nevertheless, some critics questioned its effectiveness. One major obstacle to the protocol's success was its rejection by the United States. In 2006 the United States dropped to second place behind China among the world's leading emitters of greenhouse gases. With just one fourth of China's population, however, the United States remains the leading per capita emitter by far. Nevertheless, the United States government refused to back the protocol because of its failure to set mandatory emission reductions for developing countries. Indeed, the lack of restrictions in such rapidly industrializing countries as China and India was another reason why the protocol's success was far from assured.

Countries differ in opinion on how to proceed with international global warming policy after the 2012 target date set by the Kyoto Protocol. The European Union supports the continuation of a legally binding collective approach in the form of another protocol under the UNFCCC. The United States has backed emissions reductions through voluntary action and the encouragement of new energy technologies. However, analyses including the IPCC's reports and the British government's Stern Review have concluded that only aggressive cuts in emissions (on the order of 80 percent reductions globally in the 21st century) have a reasonable chance of keeping global warming below the 3.6° F (2° C) threshold associated with severe consequences.

All countries face the challenge of sustainable development—that is, reducing their greenhouse gas emissions while still promoting economic development. Some opponents of those calling for corrective action maintain that the costs of stemming global warming will be too high. Economists and a growing number of policy makers, however, argue that early action will be much less costly than dealing with severe climatic changes in the future.

FURTHER RESOURCES FOR GLOBAL WARMING

Braasch, Gary. Earth Under Fire: How Global Warming Is Changing the World (Univ. of Calif. Press, 2007).

Chehoski, Robert, ed. Critical Perspectives on Climate Disruption (Rosen, 2006).

Dow, Kirstin, and Downing, T.E. The Atlas of Climate Change (Univ. of Calif. Press, 2006).

Gore, Al. An Inconvenient Truth: The Crisis of Global Warming, rev. ed. (Viking, 2007).

Green, Kenneth. Global Warming: Understanding the Debate (Enslow, 2002).

Houghton, John. Global Warming: The Complete Briefing, 3rd ed. (Cambridge Univ. Press, 2004).

Kolbert, Elizabeth. Field Notes from a Catastrophe (Bloomsbury, 2006).

Weart, Spencer. The Discovery of Global Warming (Harvard Univ. Press, 2003).

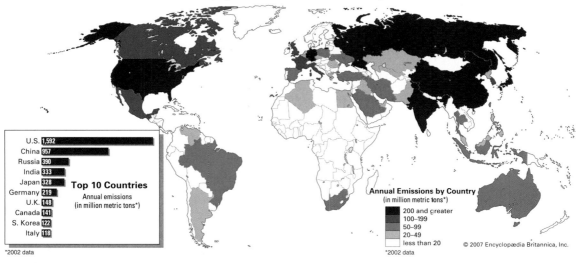

Annual CO₂ Emissions
(expressed in metric tons of carbon)

Top 10 Countries
Annual emissions
(in million metric tons*)

U.S.	1,592
China	957
Russia	390
India	333
Japan	328
Germany	219
U.K.	148
Canada	141
S. Korea	122
Italy	118

*2002 data

Annual Emissions by Country
(in million metric tons*)
200 and greater
100–199
50–99
20–49
less than 20
© 2007 Encyclopædia Britannica, Inc.
*2002 data

KYOTO PROTOCOL

After more than two years of discussions and negotiations, representatives from more than 150 nations in December 1997 forged the landmark Kyoto Protocol at the United Nations Conference on Climate Change in Kyoto, Japan. Following several additional years of negotiations to clarify the protocol, participating countries ratified it in 2005. It calls for participating industrialized countries to reduce their emissions of six greenhouse gases. The overall goal was a reduction of 5.2 percent below 1990 levels between the years 2008 and 2012.

The countries that signed the Kyoto Protocol agreed to develop national programs to reduce their emissions of greenhouse gases. Such gases, including carbon dioxide, methane, and nitrous oxide, affect the atmosphere in ways that lead to an overall warming of Earth's surface and atmosphere, known as global warming (*see* Greenhouse Effect; Global Warming).

In order to combat global warming, scientists determined that reducing the amount of greenhouse gas emissions was essential. The governments of more than 150 countries heeded this warning, eventually producing the Kyoto Protocol. The protocol mandated that the countries signing the document follow emission-reduction targets, which varied depending on the unique circumstances of each country. Countries belonging to the European Union were given a target of an 8 percent decrease in emissions below 1990 levels. Japan received a target of a 6 percent decrease. The United States, solely responsible for 20–25 percent of all greenhouse gas emissions in 2000, was asked to reduce emissions to roughly 7 percent below 1990 levels. Developing countries were not required to restrict their emissions.

The protocol provided several ideas for countries to reach their targets. One approach was to make use of natural processes, such as planting trees, which remove carbon dioxide from the air. Another approach was the international program called the Clean Development Mechanism. This program encouraged developed countries to invest in technology and infrastructure in less-developed countries by allowing the investing country to count its work reducing the emissions in the less-developed country toward meeting its own obligations under the protocol. An example would be investing in a clean-burning natural gas power plant to replace a coal-fired plant. A third approach was emissions trading. This plan allowed participating countries to buy and sell emissions rights. For example, a country that did not use up its allotted emissions would receive a credit. Later the country would be able to sell the credit to another country that was unable to meet its quota.

According to the protocol, countries that failed to meet their emissions targets would be penalized. They would be not only required to make up the difference between their targeted and actual emissions but also pay a penalty amount of 30 percent. The emission targets for periods after 2012 were to be established in future protocols.

Australia and the United States were the only industrialized countries that refused to back the protocol. Both countries expressed concern that they would suffer economic setbacks if they were required to limit emissions but less-developed countries were not. Reports issued in the first two years after the treaty took effect indicated that most participants would fail to meet their emission targets. However, the Kyoto Protocol has been praised as a major step in bringing countries together to fight global warming.

Carlos Navajas—Stone/Getty Images

ECOLOGY

The study of the ways in which organisms interact with their environment is called ecology. The word ecology was coined in 1869 by the German zoologist Ernst Haeckel, who derived it from the Greek *oikos*, which means "household." Economics is derived from the same word. However, economics deals with human "housekeeping," while ecology concerns the "housekeeping" of the natural world.

For many years many people did not consider ecology to be an important or even a real science. By the late 20th century, however, ecology had emerged as one of the most popular and important areas of biology. The effect of the environment on the organisms that inhabit it and vice versa is now acknowledged as a key element in a wide range of issues, from population growth to climate change, environmental pollution, species extinction, and human health and medicine. Many public health specialists are incorporating an ecological component in programs to control infectious diseases.

For example, the rapid spread of West Nile Virus (WNV) in the United States in the early 21st century resulted from the interaction of environmental factors with human and animal populations. Mosquitoes spread the virus by biting infected birds and then biting humans and other animals. One study of WNV in Florida noted that the number of WNV cases was especially high for years in which a dry spring season was followed by an especially wet summer. Further studies of environmental factors suggested that the limited water resources resulting from a dry spring may drive mosquitoes to congregate in isolated patches of dense vegetation where conditions remain humid. These humid patches also serve as nesting sites for an array of wild birds. In the close quarters of this temporary home, mosquitoes feed on and infect more birds than usual. When conditions change and the mosquitoes disperse,

. . . .

This article was contributed in part by E.J. Dyksterhuis, Professor of Range Ecology, Texas A & M University.

more people will be bitten by these mosquitoes and become infected than usual.

Such insights gained from recognizing environmental factors promoting infection and transmission are crucial for fighting not only WNV but many other diseases. If the ecology of the organisms is known, scientists can use an environmental approach to disrupt infection and transmission of infectious diseases, while treating and preventing the disease through medication and vaccination. This is but one example of the numerous ways in which scientists rely on an understanding of the complex interactions and interdependencies of living things and their environments.

Early Studies of the Natural World

Long before the science of ecology was established, people in many occupations were aware of natural events and interactions. Early fishermen knew that gulls hovering over the water marked the position of a school of fish. Before the use of calendars to mark time, humans used natural cues to guide seasonal endeavors: corn (maize) was planted when oak leaves were a certain size; the sight of geese flying south was a warning to prepare for winter.

Until about 1850, the scientific study of such phenomena was called natural history, and a person who studied this was called a naturalist. As natural history became subdivided into special fields, such as geology, zoology, and botany, the naturalist began incorporating laboratory work with field studies. This multidisciplinary approach gradually led to the establishment of ecology as a distinct field of study.

The modern study of ecology encompasses many areas of science. In addition to a solid understanding of biology, ecologists must also have some knowledge of weather and climate patterns, rock and mineral types, soil, and water. Familiarity with mathematics and statistics is essential. Whereas the study of natural history was largely based on observation and record-keeping, today most ecological studies center around a rigorous experimental design requiring testable hypotheses and statistical analysis. Ecologists supplement their study of actual habitats with both computer models and laboratory experiments. In the laboratory, ecologists can construct environmental chambers in which they can control the temperature, humidity, light, and other variables. They can then change one or more of these variables in specific, controlled ways and see how this affects plants, animals, and other organisms they establish in the chambers.

Interdependence in Nature

Ecology emphasizes the dependence of every form of life on other living things and on the natural resources in its environment, such as air, soil, and water. The English biologist Charles Darwin noted this interdependence when he wrote: "It is interesting to contemplate a tangled bank, clothed with many plants of many kinds, with birds singing on the bushes, with various insects flitting about, and with worms crawling through the damp earth, and to reflect that these elaborately constructed forms, so different from each other, and so dependent upon each other in so complex a manner, have all been produced by laws acting around us." Darwin's observations of the relationship between organisms and their environment formed a key element in his theory of evolution by natural selection.

The term environment in ecology refers to both the physical and biological factors affecting organisms. The physical environment consists of abiotic, or nonliving, factors. These include resources such as light, carbon dioxide, oxygen, and soil; physical characteristics such as atmospheric pressure, temperature, and rainfall; and disturbances such as fire or tsunamis. The biological environment is made up of biotic, or living, factors— anything that is living or was living, as well as things that are immediately related to life. For example, the

biotic factors in a forest include all of the organisms living in it—plants, animals, fungi, and microbes—as well as animal droppings, leaf litter, and rotting logs.

Interactions Occur at Different Scales

The interactions between living things and their environment occur at different scales. The most basic of these is the interaction between an individual organism and its environment. The largest scale is the biosphere, which consists of the relatively thin layers of Earth's air, soil, and water that are capable of supporting life together with all the organisms that live there. The biosphere extends from roughly 6 miles (10 kilometers) above Earth's surface to the deep-sea vents of the ocean. The biosphere is divided into large regions called biomes (or major life zones) that are distinguished by climate and vegetation patterns. Most studies in ecology focus on interactions taking place at scales that fall in between the extremes of individuals and the biosphere: populations, communities, and ecosystems.

POPULATIONS

A population consists of all of the individuals of the same species living within a given area. The area can be as small as a city park or as large as an ocean. For

Ecologists study the interconnectedness of organisms with each other and with their physical environment. Some interactions seem obvious: the red-eyed tree frog (left) needs a place to rest; the antelope squirrel gets nutrients (top right) by eating yucca seeds; the woma python needs sunlight to warm its body. Other interactions are less apparent: by preying on desert rodents, snakes control rodent population size (bottom right); this indirectly benefits desert plants that are damaged by rodents.

The wildebeest at the Talek River in Kenya form a population: a group of individuals of the same species occupying the same area.
Lucasseck—ARCO/Nature Picture Library

example, the polar bears that live in the area near Thunder Bay, Ontario, form a population, as do the saguaro cacti inhabiting the Sonoroan desert, the maple trees growing in a particular city, and the *E. coli* bacteria living in a person's large intestine. Ecologists who study populations are interested in how the population members interact with each other and with their environment. Many factors, from the size of the population to its spatial arrangement, play a role in these relationships.

Population Characteristics

Populations are characterized by several attributes. Among these are size, density, distribution, and life-history strategies.

Size. The size of a population is defined simply as the number of individuals in that population at a given time. Population size is determined by four factors: the number of births, the number of deaths, the amount of immigration (the movement of individuals into one population from another), and the amount of emigration (the movement of individuals out of a population) experienced by the population. Most ecologists study these factors as rates—the number of events per unit time. For example, birthrate is generally expressed as the number of births per year.

Births and immigration increase population size, while deaths and emigration lower it. When all of these factors are balanced, population size is at equilibrium. However, most populations in nature are dynamic—that is, they are always increasing or decreasing in size. Changes in population size are connected to many factors, from the availability of resources in the environment to certain innate species characteristics such as life-history strategies.

Density. Population density is a measure of the number of individuals within a given area. Assuming that the population remains within the same area, the density then increases or decreases as the population size grows or falls, respectively. Some organisms, such as bees, are adapted to living in high-density populations. Others, such as brown bears and alley cats, live in low-

density populations. The latter is characteristic of animals that display marked territoriality.

Distribution. The spatial arrangement of population members reveals quite a lot about how they live and interact with their environment. Ecologists have described three distinct distribution patterns based on how key resources are distributed. In a random distribution, individuals are scattered randomly across a landscape without any particular pattern. Random distributions result when resources are distributed evenly or sporadically. They are very uncommon in nature; some examples include tropical fig trees, which are distributed sporadically most likely because their seeds are dispersed by fig-eating bats. Dandelions, which are wind-dispersed, also display a random distribution.

Uniform, or even, distribution patterns are common where there is strong competition for a limited resource. The scarcity of water drives the uniform spacing of desert shrubs, while competition for light produces the uniform spacing of redwood trees. Animals that display strong territorial behavior, such as stray cats, also tend to be distributed uniformly.

Clumped distributions are observed when resources are patchy or because of social structures. For example, the sporadic distribution of watering holes in the African savanna influences the clumped distribution of elephants. The strong social bonds of elephants, bees, and gorillas require that they have a clumped distribution.

Life-history strategies. The life history of a species concerns the relationship between the age at which reproduction occurs and the age at death. Ecologists have observed two major life-history strategies that represent a tradeoff between the amount of energy and resources "invested" in reproduction versus the amount invested in the parent itself. Such investment is not a conscious decision, of course, but rather an adaptation that has evolved over time. Both strategies maximize evolutionary fitness—the number of offspring that survive to have offspring of their own. Which strategy is followed depends on the species and the normal circumstances in which it exists.

Spatial Distribution Patterns

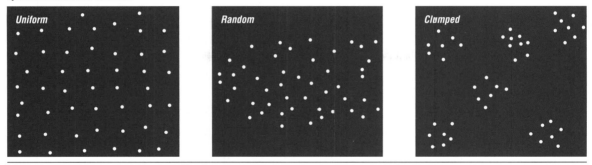

The way a population is spaced across an area is driven largely by food supply and other resources. In uniform distribution, organisms are spread out in a fairly regular pattern. This occurs often where individuals must compete for a limiting resource, such as water or light. Desert shrubs and redwood trees grow in a uniform distribution—shrubs compete for water, while redwoods compete for light. Random distribution occurs where resources are distributed evenly or sporadically. Dandelions grow in a random pattern, as do many other plants whose seeds are distributed by wind. Clumped distributions are found in places where resources are patchy. Mammals in arid environments have a clumped distribution owing to the patchy distribution of watering holes.

At one extreme are opportunistic, or *r*-selected, species (the letter *r* represents the growth rate in statistics). Opportunistic species inhabit highly variable and unstable environments, such as newly burned forests or marine tidepools. Life and death are unpredictable in such settings; it is not as efficient to be good at competing for resources or evading predation as it is to produce as many offspring as possible as early as possible. Little is invested in growth and repair, both for the parent and the offspring: most opportunistic species are small-sized and do not nurture their young. Instead, opportunistic species invest in quantity, not quality, producing many offspring at a relatively early age and then dying soon after. Dandelions, goldenrod, algae, mosquitoes, and bacteria are examples of opportunistic organisms.

At the other extreme are equilibrial, or *K*-selected, species. These organisms tend to remain near their carrying capacity, which is the maximum number of individuals the environment can support, symbolized by the letter *K*. They inhabit relatively stable environments, in which survival depends on the ability to compete successfully for resources. Consequently, equilibrial species invest in quality, not quantity: they are larger than opportunists, live longer, reproduce later, and have fewer offspring. Some familiar equilibrial organisms include gorillas, elephants, trees, and humans.

Limiting Factors Control Populations

Even when birth rates and immigration are high and resources are plentiful, population growth cannot continue unchecked because resources are limited in the natural world. Most populations will increase in size until one or more crucial resources in their habitat are exhausted. At that point, the population size will decrease until it reaches its carrying capacity.

Factors that control population size are called limiting factors. Ecologists divide these into two categories: density-independent and density-dependent factors. Density-independent factors affect the same proportion of

individuals in a population regardless of population size. Forest fires, severe storms, volcanic eruptions, acid rain, and climate changes are examples of density-independent factors. Density-dependent factors intensify as population size increases and become less intense as population size drops. For example, diseases transmitted through the air,

The Canada snowshoe hare population and lynx population show regular cycles of increase and decrease spanning many years. When hares are abundant, they provide a plentiful food source for lynx, causing an increase in the latter's population size. As lynx numbers rise, hare numbers fall until there are too few hares to support the lynx population. Lynx numbers slowly fall as individuals starve or emigrate to other areas. While lynx numbers fall, there is less predation on hares, and the latter increase in number, and the cycle begins again.

Population Fluctuations: Lynx-Hare Cycle

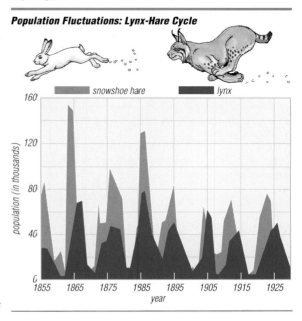

Communities consist of groups of species connected through a network of interactions. The ochre sea stars in this Oregon tide pool prey on mussels and other invertebrates. The bright green color of the green sea anemones comes from algae that live inside these animals in a symbiotic relationship called a mutualism.
Stuart Westmorland/Corbis

such as tuberculosis, spread faster in dense populations than in sparse populations. Competition for food, shelter, mates, and other resources is another density-dependent factor that regulates populations, as is predation.

Population Fluctuations

Populations of some species show regular cycles of increase and decrease over several years. One such example is the fluctuating population cycles of snowshoe hare (*Lepus americanus*) and lynx (*Lynx canadensis*) populations in northern Canada. Hare populations grow steadily, reaching peak numbers roughly every ten years, and then sharply decline. Lynx populations increase at roughly the same annual rate as hares, but with a one- to two-year time lag. Lynx eat larger numbers of hares as the hares become more common. However, the rate of predation quickly overtakes the population growth of the hares—that is, the lynx consume hares faster than the hare population can reproduce to replace its dwindling numbers. The hare population size plummets, thereby decreasing the amount of prey available to the lynx. The lynx begin to starve, and soon their population numbers begin falling. As the lynx population crashes, the hare population begins again to increase, and the cycle repeats itself.

ECOLOGICAL COMMUNITIES

A community is made up of interacting groups of species living in a common location. The members of the community are connected through a network of interactions in which a direct interaction between two species may indirectly affect the community as a whole.

Certain types of plants and animals live together in similar communities regardless of their location on Earth. Antelope and other grazing mammals inhabit dry grasslands; songbirds migrate seasonally from northern temperate woodlands of oak and maple to southern tropical forests; marine tidepools contain algae, crustaceans, and mollusks. Some communities are populated by species unique to that area: American bison (buffalo) and prairie dogs are unique to the grasslands of North America, while platypuses are found only in the waterways of Australia.

Characteristics of Communities

Like populations, communities and the way they function are affected by the presence and interplay of several factors. These include the diversity of the species in the community, the functional roles that the species play, and the presence of dominant species and those that have a disproportionately large impact on the community.

Biodiversity. A high level of biodiversity, or biological diversity, is generally the sign of a healthy well-functioning natural community (*see* Biodiversity). Biodiversity is often measured as the number of species within a given area. Some habitats have a modest amount of biodiversity; others, such as rainforests and coral reefs, are extremely rich in species. Long-term studies have shown that species-rich communities recover faster from disturbances than communities with low diversity. In the midwestern United States, grasslands with higher biodiversity were more drought-resistant compared to species-poor grasslands. Likewise, grasslands in the Serengeti region of eastern Africa that had greater species richness were able to recover better after grazing by animals than grasslands with fewer species.

Low biodiversity is a characteristic of artificial "communities," such as croplands and wide expanses of lawn. Natural communities that have become polluted often exhibit low species diversity (*see* Pollution, Environmental). For example, a lake polluted with industrial and agricultural wastes such as sewage, detergents, and fertilizers may undergo eutrophication, which is an increase in concentrations of phosphorous, nitrogen, and other plant nutrients. The excessive amount of nutrients allows certain species of microscopic organisms or algae to grow on the lake's surface in much greater numbers. "Blooms" of some microbes may release toxins into the water. In addition, the mat of surface organisms blocks out much of the sunlight that would normally penetrate the water and also eventually causes the water to become deficient in oxygen. Species of fish and other underwater organisms may then die.

Niche. In ecology, a niche is the functional role played by a species in the community it inhabits: where it lives, what it eats and recycles, and what preys on it. A community may have millions of different niches, all of which are connected and all of which must be occupied for the community to function effectively. Only one species can occupy a niche. Two species trying to fill the same niche must compete for it, with one species eventually outcompeting the other.

When a species goes extinct, its niche becomes empty, and many species will compete to fill it. Many niches become available following mass extinction events and are rapidly filled by surviving species that have adaptations that allow them to take over the niche.

Just as all niches in a community must be filled, all species in a community must have a niche. If a niche becomes lost or changes because of a disturbance such as an earthquake or fire, the species that had occupied it must emigrate or try to adapt by occupying another niche (for which it has to outcompete the species occupying it). If this fails, the species will probably die out within the community.

Dominance. In most communities, the growth or behavior of one or more species controls the activity and other characteristics of the community. Such species are called dominants. The dominant species in a forest may be a certain tree species whose growth may affect the amount of light available to other species. One of the dominant microbes in the human mouth is *Streptococcus salivarius.* Dominant species influence community diversity as well as stability.

Keystone species. The presence of a keystone species is crucial to maintaining the functioning and diversity of many communities. A keystone species is a species that has an unusually large effect on its neighbors. Through predation or competition it may prevent the overgrowth of a population that would otherwise dominate the community. This is the case in the rocky intertidal pools found on the Pacific Northwest coast in which the sea star *Piaster ochraceus* is the keystone species. *Piaster* preys on the mussel *Mytilus californianus,* keeping the mussel population from getting too large. When ecologists removed *Piaster* experimentally, the *Mytilus* population grew so rapidly that it outcrowded every other species that normally inhabited the community.

In some communities, the keystone species provides critical resources for other members of the community. Because they provide fruit year-round, fig trees (*Ficus* species) in the tropical rainforests of Central and South America provide fruit for many birds and other animals during periods in which other fruits are scarce. Without the fig trees, many animals in these communities would have to emigrate to other habitats, thereby decreasing community diversity.

Abiotic Influences on Communities

The makeup of a community is largely determined by abiotic factors such as climate and rainfall. In terrestrial communities, vegetation patterns are influenced by climate and soil (*see* Climate). Climate has a marked effect on the height of dominant native plants. For instance, the humid climate of the eastern United States supports tall forest trees. Westward from Minnesota and Texas the change in climate from subhumid to semiarid favors the growth of squatty, scattered trees and tall grasses or thickets. As the climate becomes drier, tall-grass prairies dominate. The harsh arid conditions at the eastern base of the Rockies support the dominant short-grass steppe.

An ecologist wades into a vernal pool in the woods to catch tadpoles, salamanders, or other specimens as part of an ecological study. Such wetlands are important breeding grounds for amphibians.

AP

Competition is a characteristic of all communities and one of the most basic interactions in life. The two caribou must compete for food, shelter, and other resources to survive.

Plants compete for water, nutrients from the soil, sunlight, and space in which to grow. A black walnut tree emits a chemical that kills or inhibits the growth of other trees or shrubs nearby. This is actually an example of amensalism, an interaction in which one organism is harmed but the other (the walnut) is not.

Changes in elevation also are reflected in changes of climate and humidity. At very high altitudes in the Rockies, alpine rangelands exist above the timberline. Here, the climatic factor of cold outweighs that of moisture, and tundra vegetation similar to that of the Arctic regions is nurtured. In the basins west of the Rockies, the desert scrub typical of arid climates prevails. The intense moisture and cool climate of the coastal Pacific Northwest supports the lush temperate rainforests typical of the area. (*See also* Biogeography.)

Community Interactions

The organization and stability of a biological community results from the interactions between its member species. Each interaction between two species directly affects each of them. These effects may be beneficial or detrimental, depending on the species and the interaction. Some interactions have a distinct effect on one species but no effect on another.

In addition to their direct effects, some interactions between two species have indirect effects on other members of the community. The connection between all of the direct and indirect effects forms an interactive web that binds the community together. There are four main types of species interactions: competition, predation, commensalism, and mutualism.

Competition. The struggle between two or more individuals or species for a common resource is called competition. It is a characteristic of all communities and one of the most basic interactions in life. Organisms may compete for several resources simultaneously, though usually one of these is the most critical. This is called the limiting resource because it limits the population growth of both competing species.

Competition may be interspecific (between members of different species) or intraspecific (between individuals of the same species). Examples of interspecific competition include hyenas and vultures that compete for carcasses, birds competing for nesting sites, and plant roots in dry rangelands that compete for water.

Intraspecific competition also occurs over resources such as food or water; it also is common during the mating season as individuals compete for mates.

Competition exerts a strong direct effect on the competing individuals or species. Neither side benefits from competition: in competing for the resource, each side is depriving the other of some share of it. Over evolutionary time competition can reshape the community, as some species emigrate or become extinct, while others evolve adaptations that may enable them to utilize a different resource.

Predation and other feeding methods. The capturing, killing, and eating of one living organism by another is called predation. The organism that consumes is called a predator; the organism that is consumed is the prey. Like competition, predation is one of the driving forces that shape communities. By preying on other organisms, predators help to regulate population sizes. Predation also is an important factor in natural selection—prey that can be captured by a predator are less fit in an evolutionary sense. This does not mean they are physically weak or inferior, though sometimes that also plays a role. Evolutionary fitness is equivalent to reproductive success—therefore, an organism that can be captured and destroyed will not survive to reproduce and thus has a lower fitness relative to organisms that evade predation. Predation also helps to move energy and materials such as nitrogen and carbon through the community. Predation exerts a positive direct effect on the predator and a negative direct effect on the prey.

Herbivory, in which an animal consumes and destroys plants, and parasitism, in which a parasite absorbs its nutrients from the host's body, are closely related to predation in principle. These feeding methods also have a positive direct effect on the feeder and a negative direct effect on the organism being fed upon; however, herbivores and parasites usually do not kill outright the organisms upon which they feed. An herbivore typically eats only part of a plant before moving on to another. While a parasite usually weakens its host, thereby negatively affecting its ability to survive, it also usually does not kill the host directly. Herbivores range from large grazing mammals such as sheep and cattle to tiny ants and other insects. Large grazing mammals tend to feed on grasses and shrubs, while insect herbivores feed on and destroy leaves. Other types of grazers feed on fungi. Parasites may be bacteria, fungi, protozoa, or plants or animals. They are very common, perhaps accounting for as many as half of all species on Earth.

Predation, herbivory, and parasitism can coevolve over time as each side in the battle evolves and mounts an effective defense. In this evolutionary "arms race," natural selection progressively escalates the defenses and counterdefenses of the species. The thick shells of mollusks in Lake Tanganyika and the powerful claws of the freshwater crab that preys on them are thought to have coevolved through this process of escalation. Host species develop defenses against infections, and the parasites, in turn, adapt by gradually evolving resistance to these.

Commensalism. In a commensal relationship one species benefits while the other remains unaffected. The commensal organism may depend on its host for food, shelter, support, or transportation. One example involves the tiny oyster crab (*Pinnotheres ostreum*). As a larva, the crab enters the shell of an oyster, receiving shelter while it grows. Once fully grown, however, the crab cannot exit through the narrow opening of the oyster's valves. It remains within the shell, snatching particles of food from the oyster but not harming its unwitting benefactor. Another form of commensalism occurs between small plants called epiphytes and the large tree branches on which they grow. Epiphytes depend on their hosts for structural support but do not derive nourishment from them or harm them in any way.

Mutualism. An interaction between two species that benefits both of them is called a mutualism. Mutualistic interactions can be integral to the organization of biological communities; in some cases, they are among the most important elements of the community structure. Pollination and seed dispersal are two of the best studied mutualisms. In pollination, an animal—usually a bird or insect—feeds on the nectar or the pollen of a flower. As it feeds, some of the flower's pollen sticks to the animal's body. The animal transfers this pollen to the next flower it visits. The flower benefits from this interaction because its pollen is transferred directly to another flower, a more effective strategy than wind pollination. The bird or insect pollinator benefits because the flowers provide it with nutrients.

Seed dispersal is similar to pollination in many respects. The juicy flesh of cherries and other fruits are an adaptation produced by the plant to attract animals. After a bird feeds on a fruit, it flies off and later regurgitates the seed, usually at some distance from the parent plant. The bird benefits from the nutrients in the fruit, while the plant benefits because its seed is carried away from the parent plant. This is adaptive for the plant in that an offspring that germinates from the seed will not be competing with its parent for resources, as it would if it simply fell from a branch on the parent tree to the ground below.

Many mutualisms have coevolved over time to the extent that one species cannot exist without the other. An example of this is the mutualism between termites

Like competition, predation is a key driving force that shapes communities. By preying on salmon, this brown bear (left) helps regulate salmon population size. Without predation by brown bears and other predators, salmon populations would quickly outgrow their carrying capacity and the population would crash. In a commensal relationship, one organism benefits while the other is unaffected. By attaching itself to a leopard shark, the remora (right) is carried along on the shark's power. This allows the remora to "travel" to different areas without having to expend its own energy to swim. The shark is completely unaffected by the remora's presence.

(Left) Hans Christoph Kappel/Nature Picture Library; (right) Douglas Faulkner

John Shaw—Bruce Coleman Inc.

In a mutualism, both sides benefit. Pollen, a grainy substance that contains the flower's sperm cells, is a food source for the bee. As the bee eats the pollen, some grains (white) stick to the bee's body. When the bee flies to another flower, some pollen will fall onto the flower and fertilize it. Thus the flower provides food for the bee, and the bee directly transports pollen to another flower of the same species.

and a protozoan species that lives in their guts. Although termites feed on wood, they cannot digest it, but the protozoa in their guts can. The termites benefit by getting nutrients from a food source that few organisms compete for, while the protozoa get a place to live.

Succession

Communities are constantly changing, not just in response to seasons but also in response to disturbances. In ecology, a disturbance can range from a localized event, such as the loss of a tree that creates a gap in the canopy of a forest, to events of catastrophic consequences, including wildfires, violent storms, or volcanic eruptions. Each new disturbance within a landscape creates an opportunity for new species to colonize that region. In doing so, these new species also alter the character of the community, creating an environment that is suitable to even newer species. This process, in which the structure of the community evolves over time, is called ecological succession.

Two different types of succession have been distinguished: primary succession and secondary succession. Both create a continually changing mix of species within communities as the landscape is altered by different types of disturbances. The progression of species that evolve during both types of succession is not random, however. Both forms of succession proceed in a very ordered, sequential manner. Only a small number of species are capable of colonizing and thriving in a disturbed habitat. As new plant species colonize the habitat, they modify it by altering such things as the amount of shade on the ground or the mineral composition of the soil. These changes allow other species that are adapted to the changed habitat to invade and succeed the old species, which usually cannot live in

the environment they themselves changed. The newer species are superseded, in turn, by still newer species. A similar succession of animal species occurs. Interactions between plants, animals, other living things, and the environment influence the pattern and rate of successional change.

Primary succession. While this general sequence holds true for both primary and secondary succession, the processes are distinguished by several key elements. The process of primary succession begins in essentially barren areas—regions in which the substrate (the surface or material forming the foundation of the area) cannot sustain life. Lava flows, newly formed sand dunes, and rocks exposed by a retreating glacier are typical substrates from which primary succession begins. These barren substrates are colonized by pioneer organisms such as lichens that can live on the barren rocks and physically break them down, extracting minerals and providing organic matter as they die and decompose.

Over hundreds of years, the substrate gradually turns into soil that can support other plants, such as mosses and grasses. These plants in turn modify and stabilize the soil so that it can support shrubs and trees such as cottonwoods that cannot tolerate shade. The presence of the shade-intolerant trees creates shade, however, allowing the colonization by other trees, such as jack pines.

The last stage of primary succession is the climax community, which is relatively stable. In most temperate areas, the climax community is a hardwood forest dominated by trees such as oak and hickory. In contrast to the pioneer community at the onset of succession, the climax community is more complex, composed of many different species occupying many niches.

Secondary succession. The main difference between primary and secondary succession is that the latter occurs on soil that already exists—that is, in areas where a previously existing community has been removed, most often by disturbances that are relatively smaller in scale and that do not eliminate all life and nutrients from the environment. A grassland wildfire or a storm that uproots trees within a forest create patches of habitat that are colonized by early successional species. Depending on the extent of the disturbance, some of these are original species that survived the disturbance; other species may have recolonized the area from nearby habitats. Still other species may actually be released from a dormant condition by the disturbance. Many plant species in fire-prone environments have seeds that remain dormant within the soil until the heat of a fire stimulates them to germinate.

Because soil does not have to be formed, secondary succession is considerably faster than primary succession. For example, the pioneer species colonizing an abandoned field might be weeds such as crabgrass. After a year or so, perennials and tall grasses will invade, followed several years later by pine seedlings. The latter will mature into a pine forest, which may stand for about 100 years before giving way to a climax community of hardwoods.

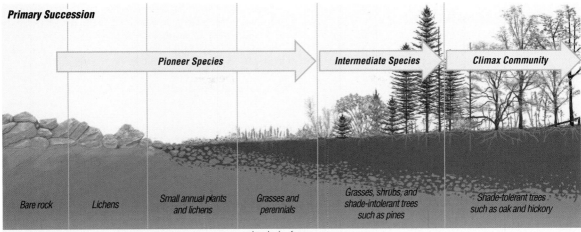

Primary Succession

Pioneer Species → Intermediate Species → Climax Community

| Bare rock | Lichens | Small annual plants and lichens | Grasses and perennials | Grasses, shrubs, and shade-intolerant trees such as pines | Shade-tolerant trees such as oak and hickory |

hundreds of years

Primary succession begins in barren areas, such as the bare rock exposed by a retreating glacier. The first inhabitants are lichens or plants that can grow on bare rock. Over hundreds of years these "pioneer species" convert the rock into soil that can support simple plants such as grasses. These grasses further modify the soil, which is then colonized by other types of plants. Each successive stage modifies the habitat by altering the amount of shade and soil composition. The final stage of succession is a climax community, a very stable stage that can endure for hundreds of years.

ECOSYSTEMS

An ecosystem consists of a biological community and its physical environment. Terrestrial ecosystems include forest, savanna, grassland, scrubland, tundra, and desert. Marine and freshwater aquatic ecosystems include oceans, lakes, rivers, and wetlands. All of Earth's ecosystems together constitute the biosphere.

Ecosystems are categorized into abiotic components—minerals, climate, soil, water, sunlight—and biotic components—all living members and associated entities such as carcasses and wastes. Together these constitute two major forces: the flow of energy through the ecosystem and the cycling of nutrients within the ecosystem.

Trophic Levels and Energy Flow

The fundamental source of energy in almost all ecosystems is radiant energy emitted from the Sun. The biotic components of an ecosystem are classified into three levels: producers, consumers, and decomposers.

Producers are organisms that do not eat other living things to obtain energy and nutrients. They are also called autotrophs, meaning "self-nourishing." Most producers

Secondary succession takes place following a major disturbance, such as a fire or flood. Farmland that has been abandoned also can undergo secondary succession. The stages of secondary succession are similar to those of primary succession with one important difference: primary succession always begins on a barren surface, while secondary succession begins in an area that already has soil.

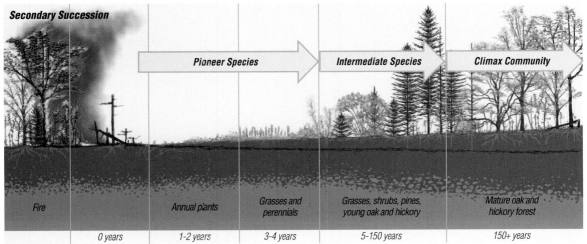

Secondary Succession

Pioneer Species → Intermediate Species → Climax Community

| Fire | Annual plants | Grasses and perennials | Grasses, shrubs, pines, young oak and hickory | Mature oak and hickory forest |

| 0 years | 1-2 years | 3-4 years | 5-150 years | 150+ years |

obtain energy and nutrients through photosynthesis, using energy from the Sun to convert carbon dioxide and water into simple sugars. The producer can then use the energy stored in these sugars to produce more complex compounds. All green plants are producers that undergo photosynthesis, as are algae and certain kinds of microscopic organisms, such as cyanobacteria (formerly called blue-green algae). A second and much rarer kind of producer gets its energy not from sunlight but from chemicals, through a process called chemosynthesis.

These producers include microscopic organisms living at extreme conditions at volcanic vents in the deep-sea floor and in rock deep underground.

All other living things—including all animals, all fungi, and many bacteria and other microorganisms—depend on producers as sources of energy and nutrients, either directly or indirectly. These forms of life are called heterotrophs, meaning "other-nourishing." They include consumers and decomposers. Neither can make their own food. Instead, consumers must feed on other

Organisms in a community are linked through what they eat and what eats them. A food chain is a single pathway connecting a producer with several levels of consumers. In a typical marine food chain, dinoflagellates convert energy from sunlight into food through photosynthesis and store it in their tissues. Copepods feed on dinoflagellates and incorporate this energy into their own tissues. The energy is transferred to sunfish when they feed on copepods, to small sharks that feed on sunfish, and to large sharks that feed on small sharks. The feeding relationships in an ecosystem consist of many food chains interconnected into a network called a food web.

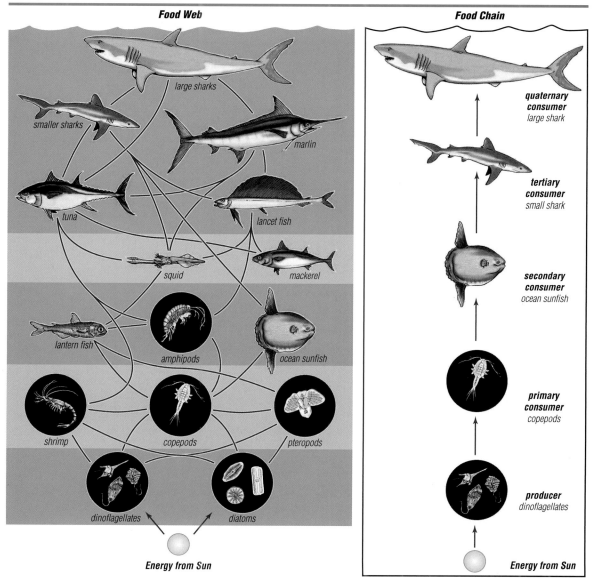

Food Web

large sharks

smaller sharks

marlin

tuna

lancet fish

squid

mackerel

lantern fish

amphipods

ocean sunfish

shrimp

copepods

pteropods

dinoflagellates

diatoms

Energy from Sun

Food Chain

quaternary consumer
large shark

tertiary consumer
small shark

secondary consumer
ocean sunfish

primary consumer
copepods

producer
dinoflagellates

Energy from Sun

Energy Flow and Trophic Levels

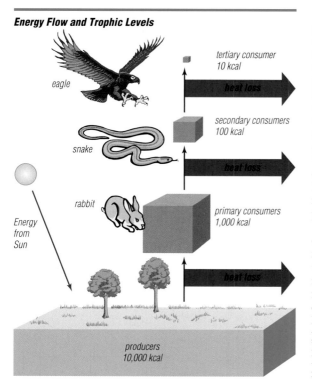

The amount of energy at each trophic level decreases as it moves through an ecosystem. As little as 10 percent of the energy at any trophic level is transferred to the next level; the rest is lost largely through metabolic processes as heat. If a grassland ecosystem has 10,000 kilocalories (kcal) of energy concentrated in vegetation, only about 1,000 kcal will be transferred to primary consumers, and very little (only 10 kcal) will make it to the tertiary level. Energy pyramids such as this help to explain the trophic structure of an ecosystem. The number of consumer trophic levels that can be supported is dependent on the size and energy richness of the producer level.

organisms, including producers and other consumers. Most animals, for example, eat plants or other animals that have fed on plants. Decomposers feed on the tissues of dead or dying producers and consumers. Bacteria and fungi are common decomposers.

The producers, consumers, and decomposers in an ecosystem form several trophic, or feeding, levels in which organisms at one level feed on those from the level below and are themselves consumed by organisms at the level above. At the base of these trophic levels are the producers—by converting light energy or chemical energy into nutrients, producers essentially support the entire ecosystem. The next trophic level above the producers consists of the primary consumers. These generally are herbivores such as cows and other organisms that consume only plants or other producers. The next trophic level contains the secondary consumers—organisms that consume primary consumers as well as producers. Some ecosystems have more consumer levels—tertiary consumers, which feed on secondary consumers, and so on. The final link in all food chains is the decomposers, which break down dead organisms and organic wastes.

The movement of organic matter and energy from the producer level through the trophic levels of an ecosystem makes up a food chain. The levels of a food chain are essentially the same across ecosystems, though the organisms at each level differ. For example, a grassland food chain might include grasses (producers), field mice (primary consumers), snakes (secondary consumers), and hawks (tertiary consumers). A marine aquatic food chain might consist of algae (producers), copepods (primary consumers), sunfish (secondary consumers), mackerel (tertiary consumers), tuna (quaternary consumers), and sharks (quinary consumers). The consumers at the uppermost trophic level of any food chain are called top predators. As their name implies, they have no predators; instead, their population size is controlled through competition.

Most ecosystems have more than one food chain, which overlap and interconnect, forming a food web. As energy moves through the ecosystem, much of it is lost at each trophic level. Only 10 percent of the energy stored in grass is incorporated into the body of the mouse that eats it. The remaining 90 percent is essentially lost, being stored in compounds that cannot be broken down by the mouse or lost as heat during respiration and other metabolic processes. Similar proportions of energy are lost at every level of the food chain. That is, each successive trophic level has less energy than the level below it. This is the main reason that few food chains extend beyond five levels (from producer through decomposer): there is not enough energy available at higher trophic levels to support consumers occupying these.

Nutrient Recycling

Through plant growth and decay, water and carbon, nitrogen, and other elements are circulated in endless cycles through the ecosystem. Nutrients in soil, as well as the carbon and oxygen from carbon dioxide, are incorporated into plant tissues. When the plant is consumed, these nutrients are passed to the consumer, which incorporates them into its tissues and ultimately passes them on to the next trophic level when it is itself consumed. Organisms that are not eaten die and transfer nutrients in their tissues to decomposers, which then recycle these into the ecosystem, where they become available to producers. (*See also* Earth, "Carbon Cycle".)

FURTHER RESOURCES FOR ECOLOGY

Fullick, Ann. Feeding Relationships (Heinemann, 2006).
Gibson, J.P., and Gibson, T.R. Plant Ecology (Chelsea House, 2006).
Krasny, Marianne, and others. Invasion Ecology, student ed. (NSTA Press, 2003).
Leuzzi, Linda. Life Connections: Pioneers in Ecology (Franklin Watts, 2000).
Pollock, S.T. Ecology, rev. ed. (DK, 2005).
Quinlan, S.E. The Case of the Monkeys that Fell from the Trees: And Other Mysteries in Tropical Nature (Boyds Mills, 2003).
Scott, Michael. The Young Oxford Book of Ecology (Oxford Univ. Press, 1998).
Slobodkin, L.B. A Citizen's Guide to Ecology (Oxford Univ. Press, 2003).
Ziegler, Christian, and Leigh, E.G. A Magic Web: The Forest of Barro Colorado Island (Oxford Univ. Press, 2002).

Kim Heacox—Photographer's Choice/Getty Images

The leaves of birch and maple trees change colors before falling in autumn, in a forest in New York State. In such deciduous forests, which are found in many temperate areas in the Northern Hemisphere, the trees lose their leaves for the winter and regrow them in the spring.

BIOGEOGRAPHY

The study of the geographic distribution of living things is called biogeography. Biogeographers use observations from ecology, evolutionary biology, geology, paleontology, and climatology to examine distribution patterns of organisms at local, regional, and global levels. From these studies they learn about past ecological and geologic events that in turn affect present-day biodiversity—the number of species or other grouping of living things relative to a given area. Understanding how and why organisms live where they do allows scientists and conservationists to better manage and protect preserves and wilderness areas.

Although the major patterns of distribution and broad principles of biogeography have been established, many specific questions remain to be answered. These questions relate primarily to the unique distribution of certain organisms. For example, hundreds of species of lungless salamanders are widespread in the Western Hemisphere, but only two species are found in the Eastern Hemisphere. How do such differences in populations occur?

Biogeographers also ask questions about environmental factors such as climate, and physical features such as mountain ranges, that affect the movement of organisms and the colonization of a region. Biogeography also looks at how human

. . . .

This article was contributed in part by J. Whitfield Gibbons, Professor of Ecology and Senior Research Scientist, Savannah River Ecology Laboratory, University of Georgia.

activities have influenced distribution patterns by causing the rapid extinction of some species and the introduction of others to regions where they never occurred before.

Historical Background

The earliest explorers were aware of broad global patterns of animal and plant distribution as they discovered new lands and found unknown varieties of plants and animals. Charles Darwin recognized and reported on the significance of geographic distribution patterns. In his classic book 'On the Origin of the Species' (1859), Darwin devoted two chapters to plant and animal distribution. He noted that each continent or region had representative and distinctive species, yet each species possessed some qualities and characteristics found in other species in similar but distant environments.

Darwin attributed these patterns to several factors. He presumed that the common ancestors of these species were extinct and noted that changes in climate had probably occurred over geologic time. He hypothesized that the extinction of species in the central part of a geographic range would isolate separate populations of the same species at either end of the range, where conditions might be different. Upon all of these ideas Darwin imposed his theory of natural selection, a process that operates on variation within a species. Organisms that have traits allowing them to adapt to changes in their surroundings will thrive and reproduce. Those that cannot adapt will die or emigrate to other areas. Over time, this leads to the evolution of new species.

Alfred Russel Wallace, a contemporary of Darwin, recognized the dynamic aspects of biogeographical patterns. In his book 'The Malay Archipelago' (1869) Wallace discussed the animals of that region. He recognized the fauna (animal life) of Celebes, New Guinea, and Australia as distinctive and separate from the fauna of Borneo, the Sunda Islands, and the Malay Archipelago. The boundary line, from the Philippines southward, that separates the two faunal units is called Wallace's Line by modern biogeographers. Wallace's 'Geographical Distribution of Animals' (1876) was the first thorough presentation of the present distribution of animals throughout the world.

During the 20th century several schemes of biogeographic distribution patterns were developed, and refinements were made on the observations and explorations of regional patterns. Although there is increased knowledge of the global distribution of many species, the general ideas and hypotheses of Darwin and Wallace have withstood more than a century of scientific scrutiny and still apply to modern biogeography.

Continental Drift

A key to the modern distribution of a species is the site of its ancestral origin. The origin of many organisms was a puzzle until the significance of continental drift—the movement of major landmasses over geologic time—to biogeography became apparent.

Pangea. The history of continental drift with respect to living things can be traced back to the breakup of a single enormous landmass, Pangea, over some 200 million years. It formed roughly 270 million years ago, during the early Permian period. The major nonoceanic habitat of the time, Pangea was a compact landmass composed of all of today's continents. Starting about 240 million to 200 million years ago, the landmass fragmented, and its components drifted slowly apart.

Laurasia and Gondwana. By the beginning of the Jurassic period, about 200 million years ago, Pangea had begun to separate into northern (Laurasia) and southern (Gondwana) landmasses. Laurasia comprised what later became North America and Eurasia (Europe and Asia), except for India. Gondwana consisted of all the other land. Antarctica, India, and Australia began to shift away from Gondwana in the middle of the Jurassic period. By the end of the Cretaceous period, about 66 million years ago, Gondwana had separated into South America and Africa, but Australia and Antarctica remained connected to each other. India was joined to Madagascar. North America and Eurasia, which had begun drifting apart during the Jurassic, were still joined at the site of the present Bering Strait.

The drift toward modern continents. During the Paleogene period, about 66 million to 23 million years ago, the continental landmasses drifted to their present locations. South America became connected by Central America to North America. India separated from Madagascar, migrated northward, and crashed into Asia, an event that formed the Himalayas. The Antarctica-Australia landmass split apart: Antarctica moved toward the South Pole, and Australia moved toward the equator. (*See also* Earth, "Continental Drift.")

The effect on species distribution. Understanding the patterns of continental drift has greatly increased scientists' understanding of the modern distribution patterns of living things. Although the geologic changes occurred over about a 200-million-year time frame, some organisms show little evidence of evolutionary change. For example, side-necked turtles (suborder Pleurodira) have changed little since the Jurassic period. Scientists presume they dispersed throughout Gondwana before it broke apart. Today the turtles are found in parts of South America, Africa, Madagascar, Australia, and islands of the Indian Ocean—but in no other parts of the world.

Groups such as the mammals evolved more rapidly in the last 100 million years. Because of this, land areas isolated from each other through the separation of continents may have widely different forms of mammals. For example, the marsupials of Australia are distinct from the mammals of other continents. This is because the Australian marsupials evolved under different conditions than other marsupials after Australia separated from the other continents.

Climatic Life Zones

Although the present distribution of organisms depends on their ancestral distribution and evolution over geologic time, environmental factors have also played a role. The most apparent general environmental factor affecting the distribution of a species is climate. Suitable conditions of temperature and moisture are vital to all organisms.

Certain species are intolerant of cold; other species cannot live in warm climates. Some have evolved to withstand extreme drought; others are adapted to excessively wet conditions. Temperature, rainfall, and other environmental factors such as soil type and day length, determine if a species can survive in a region.

The major recognizable life zones of the continents are called biomes. Because vegetation is usually the dominant and most apparent feature of the landscape, a biome is characterized by its plant community.

Biomes represent the large-scale general patterns of species distribution and do not include regional variations. At least six major terrestrial biomes are generally recognized (plus the marine and freshwater biomes): tundra, taiga, temperate deciduous forest, tropical rainforest, grassland and savanna, and desert. Most of these biomes are subdivided in several ways as a result of regional variability. Each is characterized by organisms that are adapted to the climatic conditions and environment of the biome.

Tundra. The coldest of the six major biomes, and one of the driest, is the tundra of the Arctic regions. Tundra covers much of the land between the North Pole and the taiga, in some places farther south than latitude 60° N. It is so cold that a layer of permanently frozen soil, called permafrost, lies under the rocky topsoil. Although the tundra receives little precipitation, bogs and ponds often form, because little evaporation and drainage take place.

Alaskan tundra abounds with life in the summer.

The number of species in the tundra is low compared to other biomes. Life abounds during the warmer months, but only species specially adapted to the long frozen winters can survive year-round. In the winter most of the organisms become dormant or migrate to warmer regions. Lichens, mosses, and grasses are the dominant ground cover, but some flowering plants are abundant during the short, cool summers. There are some low and dwarf shrubs but no trees. Animals include wolves, foxes, reindeer (caribou), voles, squirrels, and hares, as well as birds, insects, and fish. Amphibians and reptiles are rare.

Taiga. The taiga, or boreal forest, covers a broad region of cold, but not permanently frozen, land south of the tundra. It extends in a belt across North America, Europe, and Asia between about the latitudes 60° N. and

Evergreen trees surround a beaver pond in the taiga, or boreal forest, in Alaska.

50° N. The taiga is warmer than the tundra and also receives more precipitation, mostly in summer. The winters are long and cold, while the summers are short and cool to moderately warm.

Species diversity is higher than in the tundra but lower than in warmer biomes. Evergreen conifers—needle-leaved shrubs and trees such as pines, firs, and spruces—dominate the landscape. Some areas have hardwoods, such as birch and aspen, that are deciduous, meaning that they lose and regrow their leaves seasonally. Many areas of the taiga have dense stands of a few species of tree. As a result of their thick growth, little light reaches the lower levels of the forest and fewer plants grow there. Mosses and lichens form the principal ground cover. Boreal fauna include bears, moose, wolves, lynx, reindeer, shrews, snowshoe hares, and rodents. Birds and insects are plentiful in summer.

Temperate deciduous forest. In some of the milder climates of the Northern Hemisphere, temperate deciduous forests grow. They are found mainly in the temperate regions of eastern North America, western and central Europe, and eastern Asia. Humans have cleared much of the area that the forests originally covered, however. The winters vary from cold to mild, but the warm growing season is several months long, and rainfall is generally high.

The species diversity is also high. Temperate forests are dominated by hardwood broad-leaved trees, most of which lose their leaves each fall and grow new ones each spring. Oaks, beeches, hickories, and maples are common. Sufficient light reaches the forest floor to support the growth of many species of shrubs, herbs, and mosses. Flowering plants are abundant in the spring. Animals include squirrels, rabbits, deer, foxes, wolves, bears, and many other mammals; many kinds of birds, such as owls, pigeons, and migrating songbirds; and some reptiles and amphibians.

Tropical rainforest. Lush with broad-leaved evergreen trees and diverse plant and animal life, tropical rainforests are situated in the wet, warm areas near the equator. Rainforests occupy parts of northern South America, Central America, equatorial Africa, India and Southeast Asia, and northeastern Australia.

Tropical rainforests receive the most rainfall of any terrestrial biome and have warm temperatures year-round. The trees often form a dense canopy, or upper layer, sometimes resulting in daytime semidarkness at the ground level. Many animals live in the canopy and rarely leave. Epiphytes, or air plants, live on tree trunks or branches and never touch the ground during their life cycle. Among them are numerous species of orchids, ferns, and bromeliads. Lianas (woody vines) almost completely cover many of the trees.

Species numbers and interactions among species in tropical rainforests surpass those of any other terrestrial environment. Many species found in rainforests are not found anyplace else on Earth. Among these are mammals such as gorillas, orangutans, and most monkeys; birds such as toucans and many parrots; numerous species of reptiles and of frogs and other amphibians; and countless plants, including trees such

Tropical rainforests are the most biologically diverse places on land.

as mahogany and teak. Sadly, large tracts of rainforest are being lost as land is cleared for human activities such as logging and agriculture. (*See also* Biodiversity; Deforestation.)

Grassland and savanna. In temperate or tropical regions where precipitation is sparse or erratic, grasses are the dominant plants. Trees and shrubs are rare or absent in temperate grasslands, which cover large tracts of central North America, central and eastern Asia, eastern Europe, southern Africa, and southern South America. These grasslands have dry, warm to hot summers and damp, cold winters. Prairies, steppes, and pampas are all types of temperate grasslands.

Tropical grasslands, or savannas, have scattered drought-resistant trees. Savannas are found in northern Australia, southern India, part of Southeast Asia, northern South America, and more than half of sub-Saharan Africa. Savannas are warm year-round, with distinct wet and dry seasons.

Both savannas and grasslands are vast plains that accommodate grasses plus a limited number of other vascular plants. Characteristic animals include small burrowing mammals, large grazing mammals, and the mammals that prey on them. Animals range from the lions, hyenas, baboons, zebras, gazelles, giraffes, warthogs, vultures, and ostriches of Africa's Serengeti Plains, to the coyotes, skunks, badgers, and songbirds of North America's prairies.

Desert. Many people associate deserts with intense heat, but these biomes actually are characterized by their extreme dryness. Deserts typically receive less than 10 inches (25 centimeters) of rain annually. The vegetation is normally very sparse, and both plants and animals are specially adapted to withstand low moisture levels.

Deserts are found on every continent. Hot deserts, where it can be extremely hot during the day but cool at night, are found near the latitudes 30° N. and 30° S. The Sahara in northern Africa is the world's largest hot desert. Other hot deserts include the Kalahari in southern Africa and those in the southwestern United States and in the outback of Australia. Plants and animals are adapted to the harsh environment in many ways. Plants such as cacti and some euphorbias store moisture in their stems and have needlelike leaves that limit water loss. Some plants complete their entire life cycle within just a few weeks after a rain. The kidneys of some desert mammals, such as rodents, are uniquely adapted to retaining water. Many animals are active at night, thereby avoiding the daytime heat.

Temperate, or cold, deserts lie at higher latitudes. Sometimes much of Antarctica is considered a desert. Aside from this, other large cold deserts include the Taklimakan in northwestern China, the Gobi in Mongolia, the Great Basin in the western United States, and the Atacama Desert in Chile. Cold deserts have cold winters but may have fairly warm summers. Scattered small bush vegetation is common.

Burchell's zebra graze on a savanna in Kenya.

Dennis Brokaw

California's Sonoran Desert is a typical hot desert.

Animals in the various deserts include many lizards and snakes, plus burrowing rodents such as gerbils, mice, and gophers. There are also jackrabbits, gazelles, coyotes, foxes, owls, vultures, and hawks. (*See also* Desertification.)

Factors Affecting Distribution

Prehistoric distribution, evolutionary history, and climate are prevalent factors influencing the modern distribution patterns of living things. A variety of other factors also affect regional distribution of species. These factors differ greatly in their impact, depending upon the timing of events and the biology of the species involved.

Environmental barriers. Sometimes environmental barriers can influence the distribution of species by making a region inaccessible to a particular group. For instance, a high mountain range may prevent the migration of ground-dwelling species between two areas. Open ocean is an obvious and significant environmental barrier between landmasses. Biomes themselves can even serve as environmental barriers, one of the most famous being the Sahara, which ecologically separates central from northern Africa. Biogeographers use ecology, geology, and evolutionary biology to determine the impact of environmental barriers on species distribution.

Dispersal mechanisms. Biogeographers are also interested in how species colonize new areas. The study of dispersal patterns in living things involves examining their structure, function, and behavior. Their degree of mobility and the methods for the dispersal of their eggs or seeds are important in understanding how species overcome environmental barriers and spread to new areas. Plant seeds that are carried by wind, water, or

animals can disperse over great distances. For instance, coconut palms are found on most tropical islands because their fruits—coconuts—can float, carrying their seeds to far-flung islands. Many birds and mammals can migrate over long distances to establish new populations.

Evolution and speciation. As populations of living things adapt to new environmental circumstances over geologic time, they may evolve into new species that are considerably different from their ancestors. Information from the fossil record and from affinities between extant (living) species helps biogeographers speculate about where extant species or their ancestors lived in the past. Comparison of DNA sequences from separate populations of extant species has become a vital tool for calculating when these species may have evolved.

Invasion and competition. Competition between species for the same food sources or for the same habitats is significant in the distribution of organisms. Competition is a complex biological phenomenon that many biologists consider to be a key factor in modern biogeographic patterns. A classic example is the case of the many South American marsupials that became extinct between roughly 24 and 15 million years ago. Biologists believe that the South American marsupials could not successfully compete for resources with North American placental mammals, which invaded South America via the Central American land bridge and gradually replaced them. (*See also* Ecology.)

Human influence. Today's distribution patterns are in great part a product of human intervention, whether intentional or accidental. The house sparrow and the common starling, originally species of Eurasia, have become a dominant part of the bird population of the United States and Canada. The European hare, introduced into Australia, has successfully colonized many areas of the continent. The brown tree snake (*Boiga irregularis*), a native of Papua New Guinea, rendered most of the flightless birds of Guam extinct after being transported accidentally to the island in a ship's cargo. The South American water hyacinth and the Asian kudzu vine are considered pests in the southeastern United States because of their invasion of the region following human introduction.

These instances represent some of the thousands of human introductions of plants and animals to new regions. Although most species introduced from one continent to another do not fare well and eventually become extinct without human care, some are extremely successful and may replace native forms to the extent of becoming unwanted pests.

Besides the transcontinental introduction of species, transplants to different regions on the same continent are also common. For example, rainbow trout, native to rivers along the northwestern coast of North America, have been successfully established in cold-water streams of the central and eastern United States. Because of its commercial importance since ancient times, the date palm has been distributed throughout North Africa and the Middle East to places, including isolated oases, where it might never have reached without human assistance.

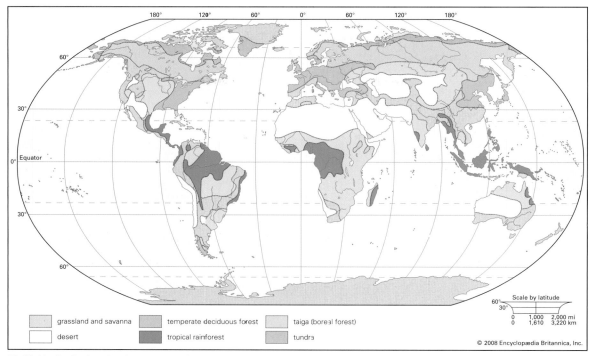

Worldwide distribution of major terrestrial biomes

The extinction of many species has resulted from human activities as well. Over the last several hundred years humans have eliminated countless species—some, such as the dodo bird and the passenger pigeon, through hunting and others, such as the Carolina parakeet, by destroying natural habitat. Hundreds of other species including the Chinese alligator, the lowland and mountain gorillas, the black, Sumatran, and Javan rhinoceroses, and the California condor live at the edge of extinction. Although extinction and the gradual replacement of species by others is a natural phenomenon, the rapid and global impact of human activity has greatly accelerated the process; thus evolutionary replacement has not had time to occur. Many changes incurred by the introduction of species to new areas and the relentless extinction of others are irrevocable. (*See also* Endangered Species.)

Island and Marine Biogeography

Because islands are small geographic units with distinct boundaries, they serve as useful models to illustrate the mechanisms of biogeographic phenomena. Intensive ecological studies on islands have provided key insights into invasion and colonization patterns, dispersal mechanisms, and extinction rates.

Ecologists have documented that the amount of usable habitat on an island determines how many species can be supported. Mathematical formulas show that islands reach an equilibrium, or balance, when the rate at which immigrating species integrate into the island's communities equals the rate at which resident species become extinct. These findings have vital implications for the conservation and management of actual islands,

as well as mainland "islands"—areas of habitat that are isolated from each other by geographic barriers such as highways or shopping malls built in formerly intact habitat. Such construction presents a tremendous barrier to species such as turtles.

Ocean environments have not received the level of attention that terrestrial habitats have from a biogeographic point of view. Environmental barriers in marine systems are seldom as abrupt as in terrestrial systems, so that distinct groups of organisms are not as recognizable. Furthermore, the world's oceans are continuous, so migration between areas and mixing of species are likelier. Because of these differences, isolation of major groups from each other is less likely to occur in marine habitats.

FURTHER RESOURCES FOR BIOGEOGRAPHY

Allaby, Michael. Deserts; Grasslands; Temperate Forests; Tropical Forests (Chelsea House, 2006).

Cox, C.B., and Moore, P.D. Biogeography: An Ecological and Evolutionary Approach, 7th ed. (Blackwell, 2005).

Crisci, J.V., and others. Historical Biogeography (Harvard Univ. Press, 2003).

Day, Trevor. Lakes and Rivers; Oceans; Taiga (Chelsea House, 2006).

MacArthur, R.H., and Wilson, E.O. Theory of Island Biogeography (Princeton Univ. Press, 2001).

MacDonald, G.M. Biogeography: Space, Time, and Life (Wiley, 2003).

Moore, P.D. Agricultural and Urban Areas; Tundra; Wetlands (Chelsea House, 2006).

Quammen, David. The Song of the Dodo: Island Biogeography in an Age of Extinction (Scribner's, 1997).

Warhol, Tom. Chaparral and Scrub; Desert; Forest; Grassland; Tundra; Water (Marshall Cavendish Benchmark, 2006–07).

Brigitte Wilms—Minden Pictures/Getty Images

Fish swim among many species of coral at a reef in the Red Sea off the coast of Egypt. Coral reefs are often called the "rainforests of the sea" because of their great biodiversity.

BIODIVERSITY

The variety of living things in a given place—whether a small stream, an extensive desert, all the forests in the world, the oceans, or the entire planet—is called its biodiversity, which is short for biological diversity. In general, tropical regions, with their long growing seasons, have greater biodiversity than temperate ones, while areas with very harsh conditions, such as Antarctica, are low in biodiversity. Biodiversity is important to the health of the world's ecosystems (different communities of living things and their environments, as well as their many interactions).

Measuring Biodiversity

Scientists use different methods to describe and compare the biodiversity of different areas. A common measurement is species richness, or the number of species in an area. For example, a coral reef off the coast of Australia may be home to 500 species of fish, while only 100 species of fish might live off the rocky coasts of Japan. The world's tropical rainforests are thought to have more than two and a half times as many species of mammals, birds, reptiles, and amphibians than are found in savannas and more than 20 times the number in the Arctic tundra. Species richness is different from species abundance, or the number of individuals of a particular species (which is also an important consideration). A population of lions might include 3,000 individual animals—its abundance—but it represents one species in a count of species richness.

A species count can be a very useful measurement, but it does not alone provide a full picture of an area's biological richness. For one thing, the data on species numbers are far from complete and are not uniformly available for all areas. Roughly 1.5 million species of living things (excluding bacteria) have been discovered and scientifically described, but scientists believe there

may be a total of some 10 million species on Earth (again excluding bacteria).

Besides, the kinds of different species in an area and how similar they are to one another are also key factors. Consider two areas that each include five species of birds. In one area, all five may be closely related sparrows from the same genus. The other may be home to more distantly related birds from five different orders, such as a woodpecker, an owl, a pigeon, a songbird, and a nightjar. The second area might be considered to have a greater biodiversity.

Biologists also pay special attention to organisms that are unique or unusual. Some places are home to species, genera, families, or even larger groups that have no close relatives or that are found in few, if any, other places. The communities that live around vents in the deep sea, for instance, including microbes that produce energy from sulfur (instead of sunlight), are extremely unusual. So far, scientists have discovered at least 200 species, 75 genera, 15 families, an order, a class, and even a phylum of organisms around these vents that have been found nowhere else. Likewise, the world's only egg-laying mammals are found only in parts of Australia and New Guinea. Such species are called endemic, meaning that their range is restricted to a relatively small area.

In some places, nearly all the native species are endemic. Nearly three quarters of Australia's mammals are endemic. The Hawaiian Islands have about 1,000 species of plants, almost all of which are found only there. Biologists sometimes call such places hotspots, because of their exceptional biodiversity and to prioritize their conservation.

Other factors that biologists consider when assessing biodiversity are the various kinds of ecosystems that organisms form and the genetic variability within a particular species. In a plant species, for instance, different genes in different individual plants may provide resistance to different diseases.

Loss of Biodiversity

As living things evolve, some species become extinct, or die out completely. Extinction is a natural phenomenon. It is clear, however, that humans have been greatly accelerating this process, especially since the mid-20th century. Scientists estimate that human activities have been causing species to become extinct at hundreds to perhaps a thousand times the background, or natural, rate. The genetic diversity within species, especially domesticated animals and crops, has also decreased.

A major factor leading to a loss of biodiversity is the destruction and fragmentation of habitats, as land is cleared for lumber or to make room for agriculture, settlement, and other human activities. Other factors include global warming, pollution, overfishing and overhunting, and the introduction of species into new habitats. Many scientists believe that habitat destruction will put a quarter to a half of all species on a relentless path to extinction in the next few decades. If that comes to pass, by the mid-21st century, extinction rates would be several thousand times the background rate. (*See also* Conservation; Endangered Species.)

Some Biodiversity Hotspots That Have Lost Large Areas of Habitat*

Hotspot	Original Extent (sq mi)	Percent Remaining	Number of Known Endemic Species				
			Plants	Birds	Mammals	Reptiles	Amphibians
North America							
California Floristic Province	113,438	25	2,124	8	18	4	25
Caribbean Islands	88,629	10	6,550	163	41	469	170
Madrean Pine-Oak Woodlands (Mexico)	178,095	20	3,975	22	6	37	50
Mesoamerica	436,303	20	2,941	208	66	240	358
South America							
Atlantic Forest (Brazil)	476,402	8	8,000	144	72	94	282
Cerrado (Brazil)	784,556	22	4,400	17	14	33	28
Tropical Andes	595,618	25	15,000	579	75	275	673
Tumbes/Chocó/Magdalena (northwest coast)	106,022	24	2,750	110	11	98	30
Eurasia							
Himalaya	286,374	25	3,160	15	12	48	42
Indo-Burma	916,242	5	7,000	64	73	204	154
Irano-Anatolian	347,404	15	2,500	0	10	12	2
Japan	144,205	20	1,950	13	46	28	44
Mediterranean Basin	805,136	5	11,700	25	25	77	27
Mountains of Central Asia	333,346	20	1,500	0	6	1	4
Mountains of Southwest China	101,331	8	3,500	2	5	15	8
Philippines	114,741	7	6,091	186	102	160	76
Sundaland (Southeast Asia)	579,564	7	15,000	142	172	243	196
Wallacea (Indonesia)	130,693	15	1,500	262	127	99	33
Western Ghats/Sri Lanka	73,209	23	3,049	35	18	174	130
Africa							
Cape Floristic Region (S.Afr.)	30,330	20	6,210	6	4	22	16
Coastal Forests of Eastern Africa	112,452	10	1,750	11	11	53	6
Eastern Afromontane	392,977	11	2,356	106	104	93	68
Guinean Forests of West Africa	239,505	15	1,800	75	67	52	85
Horn of Africa	640,684	5	2,750	24	20	93	6
Madagascar/Indian Ocean Islands	231,839	10	11,600	181	144	367	229
Maputaland/Pondoland/Albany (S.Afr.)	105,845	24	1,900	0	4	30	11
Oceania							
New Zealand	104,324	22	1,865	86	3	37	4
Polynesia/Micronesia	18,239	21	3,074	163	12	31	3

*Terrestrial areas that have at least 1,500 species of endemic vascular plants and that have lost at least 75 percent of their original habitat. Country names given in parentheses do not necessarily include all the countries in which the hotspot occurs.
Source: Conservation International.

Why Is Biodiversity Important?

Ecological communities with a high biodiversity are generally more stable and healthy than others. Biological variety buffers communities from environmental stresses and allows them to recover more quickly after disturbances. To take a very simple example, a forest that contains many different kinds of tree would not suffer many losses if there were an outbreak of Dutch elm disease, while a planted stand that contained mostly elm trees would be devastated.

Humans depend on living things in various ecosystems in a myriad of ways. Some are fairly obvious, such as using wood as a building material and fuel, eating fish as a food, and relying on certain insects to pollinate crops. A loss of biodiversity could lead to a loss of resources. Species richness provides a "safety net," so that if one food source or other resource becomes unavailable, another can be used in its place. This has been especially important to people in some rural areas and developing countries. In addition, reduced biodiversity could lead to a loss of future opportunities. Scientists continue to discover chemicals produced by living things in rainforests and other ecosystems that can be made into effective medicines. Compounds from the rosy periwinkle, a flowering plant of Madagascar, are used to make cancer-fighting drugs, to name just one example. The loss of species lessens the chance that similar discoveries may be made in the future.

Biodiversity is also important in other, less obvious ways. Living things in various ecosystems perform such vital functions as helping to form the soil and maintain its fertility, purifying the water, cycling nutrients through the environment, and regulating the climate. All the many organisms in an ecosystem form a complex web of interactions and interdependencies, and biodiversity is essential to keeping ecosystems functioning well. Finally, many people also believe that biological richness is important in its own right, aside from the material benefits it provides. (*See also* Ecology.)

A black rhinoceros roams the Ngorongoro Conservation Area in Tanzania. The black rhinoceros is one of the species considered critically endangered by the International Union for Conservation of Nature and Natural Resources.
Staffan Widstrand/Corbis

ENDANGERED SPECIES

Although there were about 65,000 black rhinoceroses in the world in 1970, at the start of the 21st century there were fewer than 3,000 left. Even rarer was the mandrinette, a shrub from Mauritius with bright red flowers. Fewer than 50 of the plants were known in the wild. The black rhinoceros and the mandrinette are endangered species—they face a high risk of extinction throughout all or a significant portion of their range. An extinct species is one that has completely died out; living individuals of its kind no longer exist. By 2006 the International Union for Conservation of Nature and Natural Resources (IUCN) estimated that more than 16,000 species of animals and plants around the world were threatened with extinction.

History

Plants and animals have become extinct and new species have evolved since life on Earth began. Preliterate human cultures may have caused the extinction of some species, but the primary causes for species to become extinct were natural ones. Major environmental changes resulted in the eventual disappearance of species unable to adapt to new conditions. Well-known natural extinctions include that of the dinosaurs and many other species represented in the fossil record.

. . . .

This article was originally contributed by J. Whitfield Gibbons, Senior Research Ecologist and Professor of Zoology, Savannah River Ecology Laboratory, University of Georgia; author of 'Their Blood Runs Cold: Adventures with Reptiles and Amphibians' (1983).

Natural forces are still at work, but human activities cause most of the rapid and widespread environmental changes that affect plants and animals today. Many species have been unable to make the biological adjustments necessary for survival. Thus more species than ever before are threatened with extinction.

Destruction of forests, draining of wetlands, and pollution are environmental changes that may eliminate species in an area. Some herbicides and pesticides can have severe effects on certain species. Many species have small geographic ranges, so habitat alteration may eliminate them entirely. The logging of tropical forests, with their tremendous diversity of species having specialized requirements, has caused a steady increase in the extinction rate. Excessive hunting and trapping for commercial purposes also cause major problems. Elephants have been reduced to critically low numbers because of uncontrolled killing for their tusks, used to make ivory piano keys, jewelry, and other art objects. Plants also can be reduced to near extinction levels by extensive collecting. Many cactus species of the arid southwestern United States are now legally protected by state laws to prevent their removal.

The planned or accidental introduction of exotic species to a region can also lead to extinction. An introduced species often has no natural enemies to control its spread, and native species may have no natural protection against it. The introduction of the fungus that causes Dutch elm disease to North America, mongooses to Jamaica, and pigs to Hawaii resulted in the loss of native species that had inadequate defenses.

Twilight for Tigers?

At the beginning of the 20th century, the world's tiger population was estimated at 100,000, even though they had been hunted for at least a thousand years. Tigers were prized as trophies and as a source of skins for expensive coats. They were also killed on the grounds that they posed a danger to humans. As the century drew to a close, only 5,000 to 7,500 were left in the wild, and captive tigers may now outnumber wild ones. The South China tiger is the most endangered, with only a few dozen animals remaining. The Siberian and Sumatran subspecies number less than 500 each, and the Indo-Chinese population is estimated at about 1,500. Three subspecies have gone extinct within the past century: the Caspian of central Asia, the Javan, and the Bali tigers. Because the tiger is so closely related to the lion, they can be crossbred in captivity. The offspring of such matings are called tigons when the male (sire) is a tiger, and ligers when the sire is a lion.

Serious concern for the declining number of tigers was expressed during the latter half of the 20th century, and gradually all countries in the tiger's range took measures to protect the animal, but with varying degrees of success. The tiger is now legally protected throughout its range, but law enforcement is not universally effective. India, which accounts for half the world's tiger population, declared it the national animal and launched Project Tiger in 1973, a successful program under which selected tiger reserves received special conservation efforts and status. Nepal, Malaysia, and Indonesia have set up a string of national parks and sanctuaries where the animal is effectively protected; Thailand, Cambodia, and Vietnam are pursuing the same course. China, the only country with three subspecies of tigers, is also giving special attention to conservation. In Russia, where poaching seriously endangered the Siberian tiger, concentrated effort and effective patrolling have resulted in a revival of the subspecies.

Poaching and the underground trade in tiger parts continue despite seizures and destruction of the confiscated parts. Although poaching has been responsible for keeping the number of tigers low during the past three decades, wild tigers would still be threatened even if all poaching ceased. In countries such as India, the needs of rapidly growing human populations over the last two centuries have reduced both the quantity and the quality of habitat. Forests and grasslands so favored by the tiger are cleared for agriculture. Reduction in prey populations results in greater dependence on livestock and the consequent retribution from man.

Fortunately, the status of the tiger has aroused widespread empathy, and its cause has received substantial international support. The World Wide Fund for Nature has been a pioneer and the largest contributor, along with corporate donors and nongovernmental organizations. The Convention on International Trade in Endangered Species is entrusted with the task of controlling illegal trade in tiger parts.

Protection

Only since the 19th century has there been international concern about the plight of species in their natural environments. In earlier times, when human population sizes were small and modern technology was developing, the effects of human activities on natural populations seldom seemed significant. Protection of animal species on an international scale was initiated as early as 1916 with the Migratory Bird Treaty between

A family of Asian elephants gathers around a salt lick. At the beginning of the 21st century, fewer than 50,000 Asian elephants remained in the wild.
Manoj Shah—Riser/Getty Images

the United States, Great Britain, Canada, and later Mexico.

A far-reaching wildlife conservation measure came from a United States–hosted conference in 1973 that resulted in an international treaty known as CITES—the Convention on International Trade in Endangered Species of Wild Fauna and Flora. This program involves more than 150 nations working together to protect endangered species through worldwide control of exports and imports. The United States Fish and Wildlife Service (FWS) of the Department of the Interior is authorized to assist in the development and management of endangered species programs in foreign countries.

The IUCN, founded in 1948, is the world's largest conservation organization. It is headquartered in Gland, Switzerland. The goal of the IUCN is to promote the protection of endangered and threatened "living resources." It publishes information on endangered species worldwide in the *IUCN Red List of Threatened Species*.

Government Involvement in the United States

One of the earliest official recognitions of an endangered species problem in the United States was the Buffalo Protection Act of 1894. The enormous herds of buffalo that roamed through North America had been reduced to just a few individuals by the late 1800s. The law to protect the few remaining in Yellowstone National Park was the first federal legislation that focused on conserving a once-vast wildlife resource. Other national laws and regulations followed. In 1900 the Lacey Act made it illegal to import certain birds and mammals that other countries had identified as requiring protection. The National Wildlife Refuge System was started in 1903 to protect habitats that harbored fast-disappearing wildlife species. In 1940 Congress enacted the Bald Eagle Act to protect the national bird.

The Endangered Species Preservation Act of 1966 and the Endangered Species Conservation Act of 1969 demonstrated concern for disappearing species on a worldwide scale, but the laws did not directly protect the species themselves. The 1973 Endangered Species Act was the most effective and far-reaching law ever passed in the United States to protect plants and animals

---

IUCN Categories of Extinction Threat

The International Union for the Conservation of Nature and Natural Resources (IUCN) evaluates the extinction risk of thousands of plant and animal species around the world. The IUCN groups species and subspecies into various categories depending on their conservation status. The organization's three "threatened" categories include:

Critically endangered: Considered to be facing an extremely high risk of extinction in the wild.

Endangered: Considered to be facing a very high risk of extinction in the wild.

Vulnerable: Considered to be facing a high risk of extinction in the wild.

Other categories include:

Extinct: There is no reasonable doubt that the last individual has died.

Extinct in the wild: Known only to survive in cultivation, in captivity, or as a naturalized population (or populations) well outside the past range.

Near threatened: Does not qualify as critically endangered, endangered, or vulnerable now but is likely to qualify for a threatened category in the near future.

Least concern: Widespread and abundant species and subspecies of plants and animals are included in this category.

---

in natural ecosystems. The act obligates the government to protect all animal and plant life threatened with extinction, defining as threatened any species "which is likely to become endangered in the foreseeable future throughout all or a significant portion of its range." It also provides for the drawing up of lists of such species and promotes the protection of critical habitats (areas designated as critical to the survival of a species).

The Endangered Species Act is administered by the FWS and the National Marine Fisheries Service (NMFS) of the Department of Commerce. Species are officially added to the endangered list through an established administrative process. A proposed listing of a species is published in the *Federal Register*. Scientists, conservationists, and government officials are asked to provide information about the biological status of the species. The FWS or NMFS accumulates the data and makes a decision about the species within the guidelines

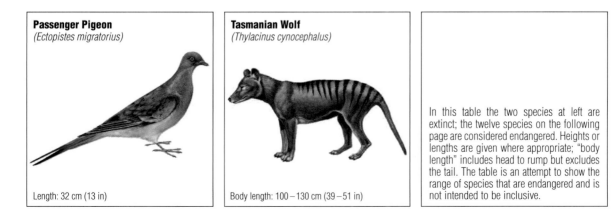

Passenger Pigeon
(Ectopistes migratorius)

Length: 32 cm (13 in)

Tasmanian Wolf
(Thylacinus cynocephalus)

Body length: 100–130 cm (39–51 in)

In this table the two species at left are extinct; the twelve species on the following page are considered endangered. Heights or lengths are given where appropriate; "body length" includes head to rump but excludes the tail. The table is an attempt to show the range of species that are endangered and is not intended to be inclusive.

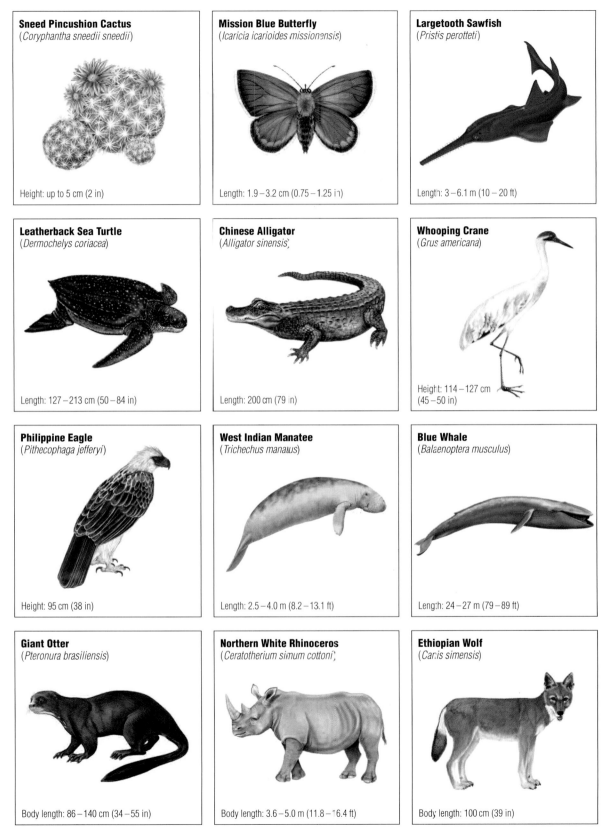

Sneed Pincushion Cactus
(*Coryphantha sneedii sneedii*)

Height: up to 5 cm (2 in)

Mission Blue Butterfly
(*Icaricia icarioides missionensis*)

Length: 1.9 – 3.2 cm (0.75 – 1.25 in)

Largetooth Sawfish
(*Pristis perotteti*)

Length: 3 – 6.1 m (10 – 20 ft)

Leatherback Sea Turtle
(*Dermochelys coriacea*)

Length: 127 – 213 cm (50 – 84 in)

Chinese Alligator
(*Alligator sinensis*)

Length: 200 cm (79 in)

Whooping Crane
(*Grus americana*)

Height: 114 – 127 cm
(45 – 50 in)

Philippine Eagle
(*Pithecophaga jefferyi*)

Height: 95 cm (38 in)

West Indian Manatee
(*Trichechus manatus*)

Length: 2.5 – 4.0 m (8.2 – 13.1 ft)

Blue Whale
(*Balaenoptera musculus*)

Length: 24 – 27 m (79 – 89 ft)

Giant Otter
(*Pteronura brasiliensis*)

Body length: 86 – 140 cm (34 – 55 in)

Northern White Rhinoceros
(*Ceratotherium simum cottoni*)

Body length: 3.6 – 5.0 m (11.8 – 16.4 ft)

Ethiopian Wolf
(*Canis simensis*)

Body length: 100 cm (39 in)

specified in the Endangered Species Act. A species may be listed as endangered or threatened, it may be removed from consideration, or more information may be required. Once a species has been listed, the FWS and NMFS develop programs to protect the remaining members of the species and to return it to a point at which it can function in a natural manner. Programs for raising some species in captivity have been carried out in attempts to restore population levels.

Private Organizations

Further aid for vanishing species comes from private organizations involved in educating the public about environmental issues. Many organizations promote species preservation through magazines, lecture series, World Wide Web sites, and television programs. In addition, many groups lobby legislators to support protection laws. Some also take more direct action. The Nature Conservancy, for example, buys and preserves tracts of habitat vital to endangered species. The World Wildlife Fund monitors the illegal trade in endangered animals and helps establish reserves for threatened wildlife, among many other projects. The primary tactic of Greenpeace has been "direct, nonviolent actions," such as steering small inflatable craft between the harpoon guns of whalers and their endangered prey.

Examples

The list of plant and animal species recognized as endangered or threatened is too long for discussion of each. Selected examples, however, serve to indicate the problems faced and solutions being applied.

Birds. The IUCN lists more than 500 bird species as endangered (or critically endangered) worldwide, and

The dusky seaside sparrow became extinct in 1987.

U.S. Fish and Wildlife Service

the FWS lists more than 75 in the United States. Birds provide several modern examples of how extinction can occur. One of the best known is the passenger pigeon, a species said to have occurred in greater numbers than any other bird or mammal for which there are records. Passenger pigeons looked very similar to mourning doves, a close relative that is still common. One distinction—a requirement for nesting in colonies—ultimately led to the downfall of the passenger pigeon. The birds, concentrated at nesting sites, were slaughtered for food by the millions. The extinction of the passenger pigeon is a commentary on the erroneous belief that if a species occurs in large numbers it is not necessary to be concerned about its welfare. Although John James Audubon reported seeing more than 1 billion of these birds in Kentucky in 1813, the last member of the species died in 1914.

The ivory-billed woodpecker, the largest woodpecker to inhabit North America, was believed to be on the verge of extinction, if not already extinct. There were unconfirmed sightings of the bird in the southern United States in the late 1990s. In 2005 a team of researchers announced that the ivory-billed woodpecker had indeed been sighted in eastern Arkansas, though skepticism over the rediscovery persisted among some scientists. The species' decline coincided with the logging of virgin forest, where it had subsisted on deadwood insects.

The world's last dusky seaside sparrow died in Florida in June 1987 because its habitat, Florida's coastal salt marsh, was severely depleted. Among birds outside of the United States, the Philippine eagle, the Chinese crested tern, and the Siberian crane are just a few examples of species considered critically endangered.

Insects. According to the IUCN, nearly 200 of the world's insect species are endangered. The FWS identifies more than 50 in the United States that are endangered or threatened, including two butterfly species—the San Bruno elfin and the mission blue—whose populations have been reduced in size or eliminated because of urban development in the San Francisco area. The FWS recovery plan focuses primarily on conserving the few remaining habitats where the species occur. Threats to the species and their habitats include new urban development, herbicides that destroy plants on which the species depend, insecticides that kill butterflies as well as pests, off-road vehicles that destroy vegetation, and the introduction of nonnative plants that compete with native species required by butterflies. The recovery plan also provides for research programs designed to understand the requirements of each species so that proper habitat management decisions can be made.

Fishes. Worldwide nearly 1,200 species of fish have been identified as threatened with extinction. Examples of fish deemed endangered include the Asian arowana, the Chinese paddlefish, and the Nassau grouper. In the United States, many species of desert fishes became extinct before protective measures were taken. Despite laws for protection, many of the desert aquatic habitats

Saving the Giant Panda: Still at a Critical Stage

With its striking black-and-white coat, round black ears, circular black eye patches set against a large white face, bulky body, and waddling gait, the giant panda is one of the world's most beloved animals. Unfortunately, it also is one of the most endangered.

Its challenges come from more than human sources, however. Despite adaptations to facilitate the consumption of bamboo, its dietary staple, the giant panda still retains the digestive system of its carnivore past and is unable to digest cellulose, a primary component of bamboo. To deal with this problem, the giant panda rapidly passes large quantities of bamboo grass through its digestive tract every day, but as a consequence it can be susceptible to a variety of digestive disorders.

Giant pandas are also afflicted by reproductive problems and low birth rates. The female breeds only once a year, for two or three days, and may not mate successfully within that time.

The panda's most serious problems, however, and the ones most responsible for its near extinction, are poaching and deforestation of its natural habitat. Fossils from northern Myanmar (Burma), Vietnam, and much of China as far north as Beijing reveal that the giant panda existed throughout much of eastern Asia during the Pleistocene Epoch (1,800,000 to 10,000 years ago). In modern times, human destruction of its forest habitat has restricted the species to remote mountain areas in Sichuan, Shaanxi, and Gansu provinces in China. In addition, periodic mass flowering and die-offs of bamboo have caused starvation for some populations. (Bamboo forests require 5 to 10 years to recover from such events.)

AP

A male panda raised at the China Research and Conservation Center for the Giant Panda in Wolong, Sichuan province, is released into the wild.

The good news is that efforts to save the giant panda, though still at a critical stage, have been meeting with success. Since the 1990s China has greatly expanded its conservation efforts and now regards the giant panda as a national treasure. The country's reserve system has grown from 14 to more than 40 sites, and it has cooperated internationally to provide training in reserve-management and captive-breeding programs.

The focal point of China's preservation efforts is the China Research and Conservation Center for the Giant Panda in the Wolong Nature Reserve, about a three-hour drive from Chengdu in Sichuan province. Established in 1963, the Wolong Nature Reserve consists of some 5,000 square miles (13,000 square km) of forest. The center, founded in 1980, is home now to about 100 pandas. The first panda birth at the center took place in 1986; in 2006, 18 cubs were born there. Altogether, about 180 pandas live in China's breeding facilities, with a combined total of 30 cubs born in 2006. The first release into the wild of a panda raised in captivity took place at the Wolong Nature Reserve, also in 2006.

Estimates of the total giant panda population range from about 1,300 to as many as 3,000, but the higher figure may reflect recent improved counting methods, not an actual increase in the number of pandas. In the wild the panda's life span is about 20 years, but captive pandas may live more than 30 years.

The future of the giant panda is brighter than it was 20 years ago but still very precarious. Only continued vigilance on the part of China and the international community will save it finally from extinction.

and their associated species are still in danger. Numerous conservation groups and concerned individuals are working in cooperation with the FWS to assure more lasting protection for desert fishes through land acquisition and the passage and enforcement of stricter laws.

Reptiles and amphibians. More than 1,300 species of reptiles and amphibians are recognized by the IUCN as endangered, including certain crocodiles and sea turtles. Many species have been depleted by overhunting and by damage to their nesting grounds. Among the United States amphibian species listed as endangered or threatened by the FWS are the Red Hills salamander, confined to a few streamside habitats in Alabama, and the Houston toad of Texas. Listed reptile species in the United States include the desert tortoise in the Southwest, the blunt-nosed leopard lizard in California, and the eastern indigo snake in the Southeast. Outside of the United States, the Venezuelan yellow frog, the Cuban pine toad, and the Baw Baw frog of Australia number among the endangered amphibians, while endangered reptiles include the Chinese alligator and the Asian three-striped box turtle.

Mammals. More than 1,000 mammals of the world are threatened with extinction. These include both

Can These Birds Be Saved?

Birds that have become extremely rare are the ivory-billed woodpecker, the California condor, the whooping crane, and the trumpeter swan. The ivory-billed woodpecker may already be extinct, though there have been a number of reported sightings in recent years. The big woodpecker depended for its existence upon stands of virgin timber in Cuba and the southern United States, where the dead and rotting trees provided it with insect food. Following the clean sweep of the southern forests by lumber companies, it has all but vanished.

The California condor, a large vulture, at one time nested in the Sierra Nevada and fed in the valleys on the carcasses of wild animals and livestock. Poisoned meat set out by livestock owners for bears and coyotes was once a major factor in the high death rate of the condor. A continuing decrease in numbers was caused by the settlement of the condor's nesting area and the loss of its natural food supply. Captive breeding programs in zoos in the United States have proved successful in raising young California condors and then releasing them into the wild.

The trumpeter swan and the whooping crane have suffered in part because of damage to their breeding and wintering ranges. These beautiful large white birds have also been sport targets for the thoughtless human with a rifle. Now under rigid protection, the trumpeter swan has increased in numbers beyond the danger point, but the fate of the whooping crane is still very much in question.

During the summer, whooping cranes nest in Wood Buffalo Park in northern

(Top) John Borneman—The National Audubon Society;
(bottom) International Crane Foundation, Baraboo, WI.

By 1982 fewer than 25 California condors (top) remained in the wild. Conservation efforts, including captive breeding, enabled the total California condor population to reach 305 by 2007. At the beginning of the 21st century fewer than 350 whooping cranes (bottom) remained in the wild.

Canada. They overwinter in the Aransas National Wildlife Refuge on the Gulf coast of Texas. The birds lay only one or two eggs a year. In 1939 there were 18 whooping cranes left in the world. Since then the number of these wild birds has risen slowly.

Canada and the United States have made strenuous efforts over the years to protect this magnificent bird. The education of hunters along the birds' flyway is important. The cranes are impressive in flight—great white birds with a 7-foot (2-meter) spread between their black wing tips. There are other large white birds with black wing tips, however—the white pelican, wood ibis, and snow goose. And the young birds, mottled with rusty brown, could be mistaken for the more common sandhill cranes. The federal authorities, therefore, are urging hunters to adopt the slogan, "Don't Shoot Any Large White Bird."

Several other government measures have been taken to protect the whooping crane and its environment. The Canadian government has forbidden aircraft to fly lower than 2,000 feet (610 meters) over the birds' nesting grounds or to land in the area during the breeding season. A proposal by the United States Air Force to set up a photoflash bombing range near the Aransas refuge was defeated because of public protest. In addition, captive flocks in both countries were bred, raised, and reintroduced into the wild. In a few more years, the graceful whooping cranes may become an inspiring example of what can be achieved for wildlife when conservationists, good sportsmen, and an alert public work together.

Johnny Johnson

A mother grizzly bear is flanked by her two cubs in Alaska's Katmai National Park. Although grizzly bears may be legally hunted in Alaska, they are protected by law in the continental United States.

species of elephant, eight species of whale, and some 65 primates, as well as deer, leopards, tigers, and other large mammals whose numbers have been severely reduced by overhunting and habitat destruction. Included among United States mammals that are protected to some degree are the gray wolf, the Florida panther, and the grizzly bear. Many other countries around the world have increased their protection of mammals. Since the 1990s, for instance, China has greatly expanded its efforts to protect the giant panda, and it now regards this endangered species as a national treasure.

Why Preservation?

The 1973 Endangered Species Act addressed the issue of why an endangered species of plant or animal should be offered formal protection. As stated in the act, such species "are of esthetic, ecological, educational, historical, recreational, and scientific value to the Nation and its people." Numerous species are medically or agriculturally significant because of their unique properties or traits. It cannot be predicted when a species might be discovered to be of direct value to humans. Once a species becomes extinct, any benefits it might have provided are lost forever.

As scientists unravel the intricate network of plant-animal relationships in the natural world, more and more species are discovered to have a vital, and often unsuspected, dependence on other species. Obviously, if the extinction of one species is permitted through rapid, human-caused activities that do not permit natural adaptations and evolution to occur, certain other species may also be affected. This can result in a "domino effect" of potential extinctions.

Through breeding programs and reintroduction of animals into their natural habitats, several species have been brought back from the brink of extinction, including the black-footed ferret and the California condor, though both are still endangered. Several more species are undergoing such programs, and they will eventually be reintroduced into the wild.

FURTHER RESOURCES FOR ENDANGERED SPECIES

Asimov, Isaac. Why Are Animals Endangered? (Gareth Stevens, 1993).
Barnes, Simon. Planet Zoo: One Hundred Animals We Can't Afford to Lose (Orion Children's, 2000).
Bright, Michael. The Encyclopedia of Endangered and Extinct Animals (Copper Beech Books, 2001).
Goodnough, David. Endangered Animals of North America: A Hot Issue (Enslow Publishers, 2001).
Miles, Victoria. Wild Science: Amazing Encounters Between Animals and the People Who Study Them (Raincoast Books, 2004).
U.S. Dept. of the Interior. Endangered and Threatened Wildlife and Plants (U.S. Fish and Wildlife Service, annual).

H. John Maier Jr.—Image Works/Time Life Pictures/Getty Images

In an example of slash-and-burn agriculture, land in the Amazon Basin has been burned and cleared for planting. This method of cultivation has been shown to contribute to soil infertility and erosion.

DEFORESTATION

Deforestation is the clearing or thinning of forests, the cause of which is normally implied to be human activity. As such, deforestation represents one of the largest issues in global land use in the early 21st century. Estimates of deforestation traditionally are based on the area of forest cleared for human use, including removal of the trees for wood products and for croplands and grazing lands. In the practice of clear-cutting, all the trees are removed from the land, which completely destroys the forest. In some cases, however, even partial logging and accidental fires thin out the trees enough to change the forest structure dramatically.

Conversion of forests to land used for other purposes has a long history. The Earth's croplands, which cover about 6 million square miles (15 million square kilometers), are mostly deforested land. More than 4 million square miles (11 million square kilometers) of present-day croplands receive enough rain and are warm enough to have once supported forests of one kind or another. Of these 4 million square miles, only 400,000 square miles (1 million square kilometers) are in areas that would have been cool boreal forests, as in Scandinavia and northern Canada. Some 800,000 square miles (2 million square kilometers) were once moist

tropical forests. The rest were once temperate forests or subtropical forests including forests in eastern North America, western Europe, and eastern China. About another 1.2 million square miles (3 million square kilometers) of forests have been cleared for grazing lands.

Although most of the areas cleared for crops and grazing represent permanent deforestation, deforestation can be transient. About half of eastern North America lay deforested in the 1870s, almost all of it having been deforested at least once since European colonization in the early 1600s. Since the 1870s the region's forest cover has increased, though most of the trees are relatively young. Few places exist in eastern North America that retain stands of uncut old-growth forests.

Elsewhere, forests are shrinking, the greatest deforestation occurring in the tropics. A wide variety of tropical forests exists. They range from rainforests that are hot and wet year-round to forests that are merely humid and moist, to those in which trees in varying proportions lose their leaves in the dry season, to dry, open woodlands. Because boundaries between these categories are inevitably arbitrary, estimates differ in how much deforestation has occurred in the tropics.

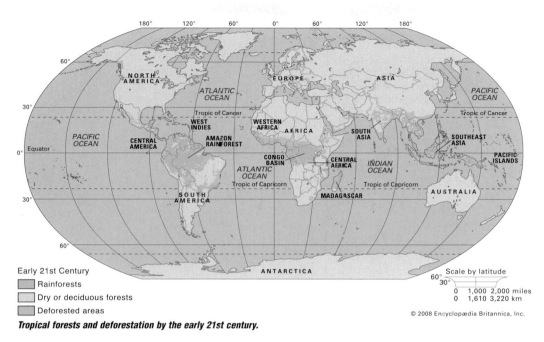

© 2008 Encyclopædia Britannica, Inc.

Tropical forests and deforestation by the early 21st century.

Nevertheless, it can be safely said that about 90 percent of the dry forests in the Caribbean, Central America, and the *cerrado* (savanna and scrub) of Brazil have been cleared. (The drier *cerrado* lies between the humid Amazon Rainforest and the humid forests along the Atlantic coast.) Dry forests in general are easier to deforest and occupy than moist forests and so are particularly targeted by human actions. Worldwide, humid forests once covered an area of about 7 million square miles (18 million square kilometers). Of this, about 4 million square miles (10 million square kilometers) remained in the early 21st century. It is estimated that about 620,000 square miles (1.6 million square kilometers) of tropical forest are cleared each decade. If deforestation continues at that rate, all tropical forests on Earth will be gone in less than a century.

The human activities that contribute to tropical deforestation include commercial logging and land clearing for cattle ranches and plantations of rubber trees, oil palms, and other economically valuable trees. Another major contributor is the practice of slash-and-burn agriculture, or swidden agriculture. Small-scale farmers clear forests by burning them and then grow their crops in the soils fertilized by the ashes. Typically, the land produces for a only few years. After several years of cultivation, fertility declines and weeds increase; the area is left fallow and reverts to secondary forest of bush. Cultivation then shifts to a new plot.

The Amazon Rainforest (*see* Sidebar) is the largest remaining block of humid tropical forest, and about two-thirds of it is in Brazil. (The rest lies along that country's borders to the west and to the north.) Detailed studies of Amazon deforestation show that the rate of forest clearing has varied from a low of

about 4,200 square miles (11,000 square kilometers) per year in 1991 to a high of about 12,000 square miles (30,000 square kilometers) per year in 1995. The high figure immediately followed an El Niño, a repeatedly occurring global weather anomaly that causes the Amazon basin to receive relatively little rain and so makes its forests unusually susceptible to fires. Studies in the Amazon also reveal that 4,000–6,000 square miles (10,000–15,000 square kilometers) are partially logged each year, a rate roughly equal to the low end of the forest clearing estimates cited above. In addition, each year fires burn an area about half as large as the areas that are cleared. Even when the forest is not entirely cleared, what remains is often a patchwork of forests and fields or, in the event of more intensive deforestation, "islands" of forest surrounded by a "sea" of deforested areas.

The effects of forest clearing, selective logging, and fires interact. Selective logging increases the flammability of the forest because it converts a closed, wetter forest into a more open, drier one. This leaves the forest vulnerable to the accidental movement of fires from cleared adjacent agricultural lands and to the killing effects of natural droughts. As fires, logging, and droughts continue, the forest can become progressively more open until all the trees are lost.

Although forests may recover after being cleared, this is not always the case. About 150,000 square miles (400,000 square kilometers) of tropical deforested land exists in the form of steep mountain hillsides. The combination of steep slopes, high rainfall, and the lack of tree roots to bind the soil can lead to disastrous landslides that destroy fields, homes, and human lives. Steep slopes aside, only about one-fourth of the humid forests that have been cleared are exploited as croplands.

One of the animals most threatened by deforestation, the jaguar survives in reduced numbers only in remote areas of Central and South America.

The rest are abandoned or used for grazing land that often can support only low densities of animals, because the soils underlying much of this land are extremely poor in nutrients.

Deforestation has important global consequences. Forests sequester carbon in the form of wood and other biomass as the trees grow, taking up carbon dioxide from the atmosphere. When forests are burned, their carbon is returned to the atmosphere as carbon dioxide, a greenhouse gas that has the potential to alter global climate (*see* greenhouse effect; global warming), and the trees are no longer present to sequester more carbon. In addition, most of the planet's valuable biodiversity is within forests, particularly tropical ones. Moist tropical forests such as the Amazon have the greatest concentrations of animal and plant species of any terrestrial ecosystem. Perhaps two-thirds of Earth's species live only in these forests. As deforestation proceeds, it has the potential to cause the extinction of increasing numbers of these species.

Saving the Amazon Rainforest: An Interview with Dr. Rosalía Arteaga of the Amazon Cooperation Treaty Organization

Dr. Rosalía Arteaga served (2004–07) as the secretary-general of ACTO (Amazon Cooperation Treaty Organization), or OTCA (Organización del Tratado de Cooperación Amazónica). She is an attorney, an author, and since 2004 a member of Encyclopædia Britannica's Editorial Board of Advisors. In 1996–97 Dr. Arteaga served as vice president and, briefly, as president of Ecuador.

In April 2007 Britannica's Advocacy for Animals (see http://advocacy.britannica.com/blog/advocacy) published an interview with Dr. Arteaga, in which she talked about ACTO, the challenges facing the Amazon River and basin, and her own views on the most diverse biological reservoir in the world. The following is excerpted from that interview:

EB: *What is ACTO, and what are its major activities?*

RA: ACTO is an intergovernmental organization made up of the eight countries of the Amazon basin (Bolivia, Brazil, Colombia, Ecuador, Guyana, Peru, Suriname, and Venezuela). Its origins date to the Amazon Cooperation Treaty, signed in 1978. Since 2002 and early 2003, ACTO has had a permanent secretariat in Brasília. We have the support of the eight governments as well as that of other countries and international organizations in other parts of the world.

© OTCA (Amazon Cooperation Treaty Organization)

Dr. Rosalía Arteaga (right) is shown with Brazilian Minister for the Environment Marina Silva.

One of our major issues is how to maintain the Amazon and its sustainable development. The Amazon is not an empty space, as many people think it is. There are about 30 million human inhabitants, including the indigenous peoples and others who live there. Many live in big cities, like Manaus and Belém in Brazil, Iquitos in Peru, and Santa Cruz in Bolivia—with more than a million people each.

When the Amazon Cooperation Treaty was signed in 1978, the signers emphasized the need for solidarity in defending the Amazon. They were also devoted to fighting poverty and finding ways to improve the quality of life for people.

ACTO is still concerned with these same big issues, but we are also concerned with how science and technology can help promote sustainable development in the Amazon and how we can solve the problems of the Amazon together. In the past, each country saw its part of the Amazon by itself, without a link to the other parts.

Two other big issues for us are water and biodiversity. Scientists say that 20% of the sweet [drinkable] water resources in the world are in the Amazon. Going by the amount of water it deposits into the Atlantic, the Amazon has more water than the nine other largest rivers of the world combined. When it comes to biodiversity, the Amazon has the greatest in the world. . . .

EB: *The things that affect the Amazon are global issues and very much of the moment, like water resources and biodiversity. In the last couple decades, everything seems to be moving toward globalization and creating products for market, and the concerns of the environment can seem overwhelming. Can these two things coexist? Is it hard to get people to care enough about what is threatening the Amazon?*

RA: In a certain way, I think knowledge and concerns about environmental issues are growing in the whole world, and not just regarding the Amazon. And I think the knowledge that globalization affects everyone is a fact in the world. This is borne out by studies of ordinary people on the streets, maybe less in the United States, I have to say, because recent studies show that Chinese and Brazilians are more conscious of environmental issues than people in other parts of the world. The United States is not very high on that scale. But probably the new reports on climate change and some big developments in the U.S., for example, the growing number of hurricanes and extremes of weather in general, will help people focus on what is happening in the Amazon.

EB: *Your organization sponsors an expedition for young people. Can you say more about this? Is the purpose to educate and get them to appreciate the Amazon?*

RA: We started last year with an expedition of young people from the eight countries and French Guiana (because French Guiana shares the same biome with the Amazon basin). It was a very good experience. We chose young people from 15 to 18 years old who had done projects in their own countries and were chosen by their ministers of education. Last year we followed the route of Francisco de Orellana, the first Spaniard to discover the Amazon, in the 16th century (1541–42). Its purpose was to sensitize them to environmental issues, especially in the Amazon. They were from different parts of our countries. Maybe in the U.S. you think of the Amazon as a very distant place. But even kids from large cities in our countries, such as Rio de Janeiro or Quito, wonder what they have in common with the Amazon. Maybe they have nothing. They hear about it and think it is a very distant and exotic place.

This expedition put them in contact with the Amazon for 34 days. They shared the experience with scientists from all over the countries; we had journalists too because we wanted media coverage. If you could have seen the transformation from when they started in Quito to when they finished in Brasília with a visit to President Lula. They were completely different. You can't imagine how they changed their minds, how they engaged with the issues, and how they want to change the bad things that happen to the Amazon.

The next expedition will follow a route from Machu Picchu to the Pantanal in Brazil. And the third one will be comprehensive of Venezuela and the Guyanas [Guyana, Suriname, and French Guiana]. All the trips will end in Brazil because our headquarters is there and because the largest part of the Amazon is there. We want to mobilize a big force of students to be concerned about the Amazon, talk about the Amazon, and work for the Amazon.

EB: *Obviously you work every day to bring governments together to preserve the Amazon and to make people's livelihoods there better and sustainable without damaging the environment. Are you generally hopeful for the Amazon and the world?*

Gervásio Baptista/AEr

Dr. Arteaga and students from the 2006 ACTO (OTCA) Amazon expedition.

RA: It's a hard question. I am an optimistic person who always thinks we'll find ways to go ahead. We are making our best efforts to do our part of the work in the Amazon. But we do need the support and views of other parts of the world to reach our objectives of better quality of life for people, animals, plants, the biome, and biodiversity. Most of the time I am very optimistic, but some days you read reports about burning of the Amazon and you can't be very optimistic. I remember that 2004 was a really bad year. We have reports that 25,000 square kilometers [10,000 square miles], the size of Belgium, of the Brazilian Amazon were lost by burning in that one year. Of course, I can't be optimistic when I go to Santa Cruz in Bolivia or Acre in Brazil and the plane can't land because of the fog from burning. It is terrible. On the other hand, when you think about the efforts that a lot of people are making—NGOs, governments, ordinary people trying to preserve the forest and life there—you have to be optimistic. I think that we can use the best techniques of science and technology to preserve the Amazon. I think people are sensitive around the world. We have a lot of support from governments, such as Germany and The Netherlands and others that are trying to help us save the Amazon.

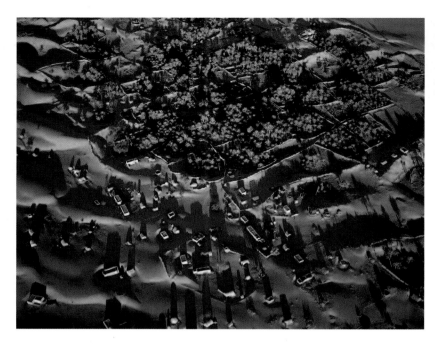

A grid of fencing slows the advance of migrating sand dunes on a Saharan oasis in Mauritania. Around the world, desertification threatens the livelihoods of an estimated one billion people.

George Steinmetz/Corbis

DESERTIFICATION

Desert environments are expanding in many areas of the world. The spread or encroachment of a desert environment into a nondesert region is a process known as desertification. This process results from a number of factors, including changes in climate and the influence of human activities.

Climatic factors include periods of temporary but severe drought as well as long-term climatic changes toward aridity. For example, in areas where vegetation is already under stress from natural factors, periods of drier than average weather may cause degradation of the vegetation. If the pressures are maintained, soil loss and irreversible change in the ecosystem may ensue, so that areas formerly under savanna or scrubland vegetation are reduced to desert.

There is some evidence that removal of vegetation can also affect climate, causing it to become drier. Bare ground reflects more incoming solar energy and does not heat up as much as ground containing vegetation. Thus, the air that is near the ground does not warm up as much and its vertical movement is reduced, as is atmospheric cooling necessary for condensation and ultimately precipitation to occur.

Human activities often play a major role in desertification. The biological environment of a nondesert region may be degraded by removing vegetation (which can lead to unnaturally high erosion), excessive cultivation, and the exhaustion of surface-water or groundwater supplies for irrigation, industry, or domestic use.

Desertification drains an arid or semiarid land of its life-supporting capabilities. The process of desertification is extremely difficult to reverse. It is characterized by a declining groundwater table, salinization of topsoil and water, diminution of surface water, increasing erosion, and the disappearance of native vegetation. Areas undergoing desertification may show all of these symptoms, but the existence of only one usually provides sufficient evidence that the process is taking place. Desertification usually begins in areas made susceptible by drought or overuse by human populations and spreads into arid and semiarid regions.

The main regions currently threatened by desertification are the Sahel region lying to the south of the Sahara desert in Africa, parts of eastern, southern, and northwestern Africa, and large areas of Australia, south-central Asia, and central North America. The arid regions with the longest history of agriculture—from North Africa to China—have generally less well-vegetated deserts. The present extent of certain of these deserts is thought to be significantly greater than it would be had human impact not occurred. Support for this view is found in various places, such as the several-thousand-year-old rock art from the central Sahara that illustrates cattle and wildlife in regions now unable to support these creatures.

Desertification is not limited to nondesert regions. The process can also occur in areas within deserts where the delicate ecological balance is disturbed. The Sonoran and Chihuahuan deserts of the American Southwest, for example, have become observably more barren as the wildlife and plant populations have diminished.

Public awareness of desertification increased during the severe drought in the Sahel (1968–73) that

AP

In an effort to control desertification, farmers plant trees on a slope near Yudushan, China.

accelerated the southward movement of the Sahara. Persistent drought conditions, coupled with substantial growth of both the human and livestock populations in the Sahel, resulted in a gradual desertification of the region. While climatic variations played a major role in this process, economic and social priorities were involved as well. The introduction of Western technology made it possible for the inhabitants of the Sahel to drill deep water wells. This situation encouraged the herdsmen not only to give up their nomadic way of life and remain near the wells but also to raise more livestock. Overgrazing resulted and, as

drought conditions persisted, competition for forage became more and more intense. Herds of goats tore up the remaining indigenous plants by their roots, thereby destroying the ability of the plants to reproduce by themselves. At the same time, the increasing human population led to the cultivating of more and more marginal, ecologically fragile lands for subsistence farming. (The most fertile lands were frequently used to grow cash crops—namely, cotton and peanuts for foreign markets.) Furthermore, Sahelian farmers began reworking the marginal land within one to five years, whereas they had traditionally allowed these lands to remain fallow for 15 to 20 years, giving them ample time to recover. In changing their farming practices, the Sahelians contributed to the destruction of their lands.

As the Sahara moved southward, so did the Sahelians and their livestock. This resulted in further denudation and deforestation. Desertification had set in by the late 1960s, followed by widespread famine. A major international project was undertaken to keep millions of Sahelians alive. Normal rains returned briefly to the Sahel during the mid-1970s; however, since no effective, long-term remedies were applied in animal, agricultural, and human control, outside aid again became necessary in the mid-1980s as drought conditions prevailed once more for a prolonged period (especially in the eastern sections of the sub-Sahara in Ethiopia), causing widespread famine and death. What caused these droughts is still debated, but one of the theories involves unusual or anomalous temperature patterns in certain parts of the ocean.

In 1977 the worldwide consequences of desertification were the subject of a UN Conference on Desertification (UNCOD), held in Nairobi, Kenya.

In the early 21st century, the UN again highlighted the problem by designating 2006 the International Year of Deserts and Desertification. The UN General Assembly warned that desertification threatened the livelihoods of about one billion people.

Signs of desertification are apparent in an area on the outskirts of Ségou, Mali.

Remi Benali/Corbis

A barrier of trees, planted in a desert area of Inner Mongolia, makes up part of China's "Green Great Wall"—a shelter belt of trees designed to protect Beijing from sandstorms.

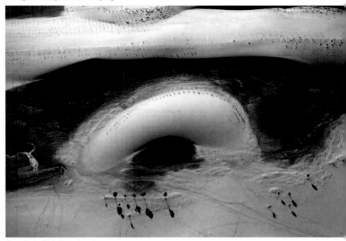

Georg Gerster/Photo Researchers, Inc.

Photos.com/Jupiterimages

PART III

ENVIRONMENTAL POLLUTION

Efforts to improve the standard of living for humans—through the control of nature and the development of new products—have also resulted in the pollution, or contamination, of the environment. Much of the world's air, water, and land is now partially poisoned by chemical wastes. Some places have become uninhabitable. This pollution exposes people all around the globe to new risks from disease. Many species of plants and animals have become endangered or are now extinct. As a result of these developments, governments have passed laws to limit or reverse the threat of environmental pollution.

All living things exert some pressure on the environment. Predatory animals, for example, reduce the population of their prey, and animal herds may trample vast stretches of prairie or tundra. The weather could be said to cause pollution when a hurricane deposits tons of silt from flooded rivers into an estuary or bay. These are temporary dislocations that nature balances and accommodates to. Modern economic development, however, sometimes disrupts nature's delicate balance. The extent of environmental pollution caused by humans is already so great that some scientists question whether the Earth can continue to support life unless immediate corrective action is taken.

Ecology and Environmental Deterioration

The branch of science that deals with how living things, including humans, are related to their surroundings is called ecology (*see* Ecology). The Earth supports some 5 million species of plants, animals, and microorganisms. These interact and influence their surroundings, forming a vast network of interrelated environmental systems called ecosystems. The arctic tundra is an ecosystem and so is a Brazilian rainforest. If left undisturbed, natural

. . . .

This article was contributed in part by John H. Thomas, professor of biology at Stanford University, and Paul J. Allen, Director of Communications at the Natural Resources Defense Council, Washington, D.C.

environmental systems tend to achieve balance or stability among the various species of plants and animals. Complex ecosystems are able to compensate for changes caused by weather or intrusions from migrating animals and are therefore usually said to be more stable than simple ecosystems. A field of corn has only one dominant species, the corn plant, and is a very simple ecosystem. It is easily destroyed by drought, insects, disease, or overuse. A forest may remain relatively unchanged by weather that would destroy a nearby field of corn, because the forest is characterized by greater diversity of plants and animals. Its complexity gives it stability.

Every environmental system has a carrying capacity for an optimum, or most desirable, population of any particular species within it. Sudden changes in the relative population of a particular species can begin a kind of chain reaction among other elements of the ecosystem. For example, eliminating a species of insect by using massive quantities of a chemical pesticide also may eliminate a bird species that depends upon the insect as a source of food.

Such human activities have caused the extinction of a number of plant and animal species. For example, overhunting caused the extinction of the passenger pigeon. The last known survivor of the species died at the Cincinnati Zoo in 1914. Less than a century earlier, the passenger pigeon population had totaled at least 3 billion. Excessive hunting or infringement upon natural habitats is endangering many other species. The great whales, the California condor, the black-footed ferret, and the Atlantic salmon are among the endangered animals. Endangered plants include snakeroot, the western lily, and the green pitcher plant. (*See also* Endangered Species.)

The Exxon Valdez *oil spill of March 24, 1990, in Prince William Sound, Alaska, released about 200,000 barrels of oil into the water. The accident happened when the tanker ran aground on Bligh Reef. Within a month more than 1,400 square miles of water were contaminated. Cleanup efforts, including animal rescue, took months of tireless effort.*
Photri

Population Growth and Environmental Abuse

The reduction of the Earth's resources has been closely linked to the rise in human population. For many thousands of years people lived in relative harmony with their surroundings. Population sizes were small, and life-supporting tools were simple. Most of the energy needed for work was provided by the worker and animals. Since about 1650, however, the human population has increased dramatically. The problems of overcrowding multiply as an ever-increasing number of people are added to the world's population each year.

The rate of growth of the world's population has finally begun to slow to slightly more than 1 percent, after reaching an all-time high of more than 2 percent in the early 1960s. In 2007 there were more than 6.6 billion people on the planet. The United Nations predicts that by the year 2050 almost 9.2 billion people will be living on Earth—almost four times the number of people living on Earth in 1950.

The booming human population is concentrated more and more in large urban areas. Many cities now have millions of inhabitants. In less developed countries of Asia, Africa, and Latin America, many of these cities are overpopulated because of an influx of people who have left rural homes in search of food, shelter, and employment. Some farmers have been forced off their land by drought and famine.

Environmental pollution has existed since people began to congregate in towns and cities. Ancient Athenians removed their refuse to dumps outside the main part of the city. The Romans dug trenches outside the city to hold garbage and wastes (including human corpses), a practice which may have contributed to outbreaks of viral diseases.

The adverse effects of pollution became more noticeable as cities grew during the Middle Ages. In Europe, medieval cities passed ordinances against throwing garbage into the streets and canals, but those laws were largely ignored. In 16th-century England, efforts were made to curb the use of coal in order to reduce the amount of smoke in the air—again with little effect.

In the 19th century, the Industrial Revolution placed greater pressures on the environment, and pollution

Automobiles and buses, such as these stuck in a traffic jam in Beijing, China, emit a high concentration of air pollutants from their exhausts.

AP

changed and increased dramatically. Although industrial development improved the standard of living, there was a great environmental cost.

Air Pollution

Factories and transportation depend on huge amounts of fuel—billions of tons of coal and oil are consumed around the world every year. When these fuels burn they introduce smoke and other, less visible, by-products into the atmosphere. Although wind and rain occasionally wash away the smoke given off by power plants and automobiles, the cumulative effect of air pollution poses a grave threat to humans and the environment.

In many places smoke from factories and cars combines with naturally occurring fog to form smog. For centuries, London, England, has been subjected to the danger of smog, long recognized as a potential cause of death, especially for elderly persons and those with severe respiratory ailments. Air pollution in London originally resulted from large-scale use of heating fuels.

A widespread awareness of air pollution dates from about 1950. It was initially associated with the Los Angeles area. The Los Angeles Basin is ringed for the most part by high mountains. As air sinks from these mountains it is heated until it accumulates as a warm layer that rises above the cooler air from the Pacific Ocean. This results in a temperature inversion, with the heavier cool air confined to the surface. Pollutants also become trapped at surface levels. Because of air-circulation patterns in the Los Angeles Basin, polluted air merely moves from one part of the basin to another part.

Scientists believe that all cities with populations exceeding 50,000 have some degree of air pollution. Burning garbage in open dumps, which still takes place in some countries, causes air pollution. Other sources include emissions of sulfur dioxide and other noxious gases by electric power plants that burn high-sulfur coal or oil. Industrial boilers at factories also send large quantities of smoke into the air. The process of making steel and plastic generates large amounts of smoke containing metal dust or microscopic particles of complex and sometimes even deadly chemicals.

The single major cause of air pollution is the internal-combustion engine of automobiles. Gasoline is never completely burned in the engine of a car, just as coal is never completely burned in the furnace of a steel mill. Once they are released into the air, the products of incomplete combustion—particulate matter (soot, ash, and other solids), unburned hydrocarbons, carbon monoxide, sulfur dioxide, various nitrogen oxides, ozone, and lead—undergo a series of chemical reactions in the presence of sunlight. The result is the dense haze characteristic of smog. Smog may appear brownish in color when it contains high concentrations of nitrogen dioxide, or it may look blue-grey when it contains large amounts of ozone. In either case, prolonged exposure will damage lung tissue.

Air pollution has enormous consequences for the health and well-being of people worldwide. Contaminants in the air have been implicated in the rising incidence of asthma, bronchitis, and emphysema, a serious and debilitating disease of the lung's air sacs. In addition, current studies suggest that air pollution may be linked to heart disease.

The pollution from a coal-fired power station races across the sky in Nottinghamshire, England. Chemical emissions from such plants can cause acid rain.

Reuters/Corbis

Children in Manila, Philippines, pick through a smoldering garbage dump, one of many that have cropped up on the outskirts of the city in the past few years.

In the mid-1970s, people became aware of the phenomenon called acid rain. When fossil fuels such as coal, gasoline, and fuel oils are burned, they emit sulfur, carbon, and nitrogen oxides into the air. These oxides combine with particles of water in the atmosphere and reach the Earth as acid rain, snow, hail, sleet, or fog. A special scale, called the pH scale, measures whether a liquid (including rain and snow) is acidic or basic (alkaline). The pH scale is used to describe the concentration of electrically charged hydrogen atoms in a water solution. The scale rates a substance from 0 to 14. A pH of 7, as in distilled water, means that the solution is neutral. A pH above 7 means the solution is basic; below 7 means the solution is acidic. Normal rainwater has a pH around 5.6.

Although the National Center for Atmospheric Research has recorded storms in the northeastern United States with a pH of 2.1, which is the acidity of lemon juice or vinegar, by the early 21st century the most acidic precipitation in the United States had an average pH of 4.3. In Canada, Scandinavia, and the northeastern United States, acid rain is blamed for the deaths of thousands of lakes and streams. These lakes have absorbed so much acid rain that they can no longer support the algae, plankton, and other aquatic life that provide food and nutrients for fish. Acid rain also damages buildings and monuments, including centuries-old relics such as Rome's Colosseum. Scientists are concerned that the deaths of thousands of trees in the forests of Europe, Canada, and the United States may be the result of acid rain. Although many industrialized nations have sought to make changes that will help reduce sulfur dioxide and other air pollutants, less developed countries do not always have the funds to implement such technologically advanced solutions.

Another troubling form of air pollution comes from a variety of man-made chemicals called chlorofluorocarbons, also known as CFCs. These chemicals are used for many industrial purposes, ranging from solvents used to clean computer chips to the refrigerant gases found in air conditioners and refrigerators. CFCs combine with other molecules in the Earth's upper atmosphere and then, by attaching themselves to molecules of ozone, transform and destroy the protective ozone layer. The result has been a sharp decline in the amount of ozone in the stratosphere. At ground level, ozone is a threat to our lungs, but in the upper atmosphere ozone works as a shield to protect against ultraviolet radiation from the sun. If the ozone shield gets too thin or disappears, exposure to ultraviolet radiation can cause crop failures and the spread of epidemic diseases, skin cancer, and other disasters. In late 1987, more than 20 nations signed the Montreal Protocol to limit the production of CFCs and to work toward their eventual elimination; by 2007 more than 190 countries had joined the agreement. The production of CFCs in developed countries ended in 1996, and now amendments to the pact call for reducing and eliminating the use of hydrochlorofluorocarbons, which replaced CFCs.

Air pollution has been the target of some of the most complicated and far-reaching legislation ever enacted in the United States. In 1970, Congress passed legislation aimed at curbing sources of air pollution and setting standards for air quality. A few years later, Congress passed laws designed to phase out the use of lead as an additive in gasoline. By 1990 the Clean Air Act had been amended to regulate automobile emissions and to promote alternative fuels. Further action to reduce acid rain and greenhouse gas emissions is continually debated in North America and throughout Europe and the rest of the world.

Although the release of toxic chemicals into the atmosphere is against the law in most countries, accidents can happen, often with tragic results. In 1984, in Bhopal, India, a pesticide manufacturing plant released a toxic gas into the air that within a few hours caused the deaths of more than 2,000 people.

Acid rain has killed some of the trees in the Great Smoky Mountains National Park in eastern Tennessee and western North Carolina.

Robert Juneit—Taxi/Getty Images

Pollution Speeds the Death of a Lake

1. *Pollution tinges the cold, oxygen-rich waters of a lake in which trout had been thriving.*

☒ pollutants

▦ algae

▤ silt

2. *Pollutants dumped into the lake carry plant nutrients (phosphates and nitrates), causing the growth of algae and other water plants. The warmer water now supports bass and perch. Silt from eroded uplands begins to displace the lake water.*

3. *Algae and vegetation multiply as city sewage and factory wastes pour into the lake. Carnivorous fish are replaced by such plant eaters as bluegills and minnows.*

4. *In the later stages of a lake's death, algal accumulation becomes dense. Scavengers, such as catfish and carp, feed on decomposed algae and other waste in the silty lake bottom.*

5. *Pollution finally generates so much plant life that most of the lake's oxygen is consumed in plant decay. Fish cannot live in the oxygenless water. Rooted plants extend further into the lake, continually reducing its borders. The lake is considered dead and will continue to fill with silt until entirely dry.*

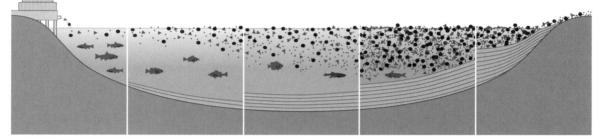

Water Pollution

Since the beginning of civilization, water has been used to carry away unwanted refuse. Rivers, streams, canals, lakes, and oceans are currently used as receptacles for every imaginable kind of pollution. Water has the capacity to break down or dissolve many materials, especially organic compounds, which decompose during prolonged contact with bacteria and enzymes. Waste materials that can eventually decompose in this way are called biodegradable. They are less of a long-term threat to the environment than are more persistent pollutants such as metals, plastics, and some chlorinated hydrocarbons. These substances remain in the water and can make it poisonous for most forms of life. Even

Garbage completely covers the surface of this river in Jakarta, Indonesia, harming both the water and the organisms that live within it.

Jurnasyanto Sukarno—epa/Corbis

biodegradable pollutants can damage a water supply for long periods of time. As any form of contamination accumulates, life within the water starts to suffer. Lakes are especially vulnerable to pollution because they cannot cleanse themselves as rapidly as rivers or oceans.

A common kind of water pollution is the effect caused by heavy concentrations of nitrogen and phosphorus, which are used by plants for growth. The widespread use of agricultural fertilizers and household detergents containing these elements has added large amounts of plant nutrients to many bodies of water. In large quantities, nitrogen and phosphorus cause tiny water algae to bloom, or grow rapidly. When the algae die, oxygen is needed to decompose them. This creates an oxygen deficiency in the water, which causes the death of many aquatic animals. Plant life soon reduces the amount of open water. These events speed up the process of eutrophication, the aging and eventual drying up of a lake.

Sedimentation also pollutes water. It is the result of poor soil conservation practices. Sediment fills water-supply reservoirs and fouls power turbines and irrigation pumps. It also diminishes the amount of sunlight that can penetrate the water. In the absence of sufficient sunlight, the aquatic plants that normally furnish the water with oxygen fail to grow.

Factories sometimes turn waterways into open sewers by dumping oils, toxic chemicals, and other harmful industrial wastes into them. In mining and oil-drilling operations, corrosive acid wastes are poured into the water. In recent years, municipal waste treatment plants have been built to contend with water contamination. Some towns, however, still foul streams by pouring raw sewage into them. Septic tanks, used where sewers are not available, and large farm lagoons filled with animal waste may also pollute the groundwater and adjacent streams, sometimes with disease-causing organisms.

Even the purified effluent from sewage plants can cause water pollution if it contains high concentrations of nitrogen and phosphorus. Farm fertilizers in some regions fill groundwater with nitrates, making the water unfit to drink. Agricultural runoff containing dangerous pesticides and the oil, grime, and chemicals used to melt ice from city streets also pollute waterways.

Land and Soil Pollution

In order to sustain the continually growing human population, current agricultural methods are designed to maximize yields from croplands. In many areas, the overuse of land results in the erosion of topsoil. This soil erosion, in turn, causes the over-silting or sedimentation of rivers and streams.

One of the most hazardous forms of pollution comes from agricultural pesticides. These chemicals are designed to deter or kill insects, weeds, fungi, or rodents that pose a threat to crops. When airborne pesticides drift with the wind or become absorbed into the fruits and vegetables they are meant to protect, they can become a source of many illnesses, including cancer and birth defects.

Pesticides are often designed to withstand rain, which means they are not always water-soluble, and therefore they may persist in the environment for long periods of time. Some pests have developed a genetic resistance to these chemicals, forcing farmers to increase the amounts or types of pesticide.

The pesticide DDT provides a well-known example of the dangers of introducing synthetic chemical compounds into the environment. Chemically a chlorinated hydrocarbon, DDT was widely used for many years after World War II. At first it was highly regarded because it killed mosquitoes, which in turn reduced the incidence of malaria throughout the world. Then, evidence began to show that DDT might be doing more harm than good. DDT, like other chemically stable pesticides, is not readily biodegradable. In addition, many species of insects rapidly develop populations resistant to DDT. The chemical accumulates in insects that then become the diet of other animals, with toxic effects on them, especially certain birds and fishes. While the accumulation of DDT may not kill a bird immediately, it can lead to metabolic disturbances. In some cases, as with the peregrine falcon in the eastern United States, the chemical interfered with the calcium in the eggshells, causing the shells to be abnormally thin and prone to breakage.

Although DDT has been banned in the United States and most other countries, it is still manufactured and used in some parts of the world. Many other pesticides also have been banned. Thousands of pesticides remain in use and, in some cases, their agricultural value may balance out their risks.

Some urban areas are beginning to experience a serious problem regarding the disposal of garbage and hazardous wastes, such as solvents and industrial dyes and inks. In many areas landfill sites are approaching their full capacity and many municipalities are turning to incineration as a solution. Giant high-temperature incinerators have become another source of air pollution, however, because incineration ashes sometimes contain

An unprotected worker sprays tea leaves with pesticide. Pesticides can travel through the air or get into an area's groundwater and adversely affect humans.

very high concentrations of metals as well as dioxins, a dangerous family of chemical poisons.

One answer to the garbage problem is recycling. Most towns in the United States encourage or require residents to separate glass and aluminum cans and bottles from other refuse so that these substances can be melted down and reused. According to the Environmental Protection Agency, the United States recycles more than 30 percent of its garbage. This rate has about doubled over the last 15 years.

The European Union, composed of 27 countries, sets recycling requirements that are met with varying degrees of success. Studies from 2004 show that Greece recycles only 10 percent of its waste while putting 90 percent in landfills. On the opposite side of the spectrum, Denmark recycles about 30 percent, incinerates about 60 percent, and sends a mere 10 percent to landfills.

Radioactive Pollutants

Radioactivity has always been part of the natural environment. An example of natural radioactivity is the cosmic radiation that constantly strikes the Earth. This so-called background radiation has little effect on most people. Some scientists are concerned, however, that humans have introduced a considerable amount of additional radiation into the environment.

Since the first atomic bomb was dropped on Hiroshima, Japan, on Aug. 6, 1945, there has been an increased awareness of the environmental threat posed by nuclear weapons and radioactive fallout. Many scientists are concerned about the long-term environmental impacts of full-scale nuclear war. Some suggest that the large amounts of smoke and dust thrown into the atmosphere during a nuclear explosion would block out the sun's light and heat, causing global temperatures to drop.

Even the testing of nuclear weapons directly affects the environment. Such tests are rarely conducted above

Tass/Sovfoto

A Soviet scientist measures the radiation level outside Unit 4 of the Chernobyl Atomic plant after the April 1986 disaster.

ground or in the ocean. International concern over the effects of these tests led the United States, Great Britain, and the Soviet Union to sign the Nuclear Test-Ban Treaty in 1963, which prohibited all nuclear testing except for that conducted underground. In 1977 negotiations began on a Comprehensive Test-Ban Treaty, which would extend the ban to underground tests. To enter into force, this treaty has to be ratified by all the nuclear powers and by 44 members of the Conference on Disarmament that possess nuclear reactors. By 2007 all but three countries had signed; in addition, 10 of those that had signed the treaty had not ratified it.

On April 26, 1986, the Chernobyl nuclear power plant in the Soviet Union malfunctioned creating the worst peacetime nuclear disaster. Many details of the Chernobyl accident remain undisclosed, but it is known that the radioactive core of the power plant became exposed, and there was a partial meltdown, releasing large amounts of radioactive materials. Because the medical effects of exposure to nuclear radiation can take years to become apparent, it is not yet known how many additional cases of cancer, birth defects, and skin disease will have been caused by the Chernobyl accident; however, it is estimated that thousands of premature deaths will occur as a direct consequence of nuclear radiation poisoning from Chernobyl.

Another immediate environmental problem is the disposal of nuclear wastes. Some radioactive substances have a half-life of more than 10,000 years, which means they remain radioactive and highly dangerous for many thousands of years. In nuclear physics, a half-life is the period of time required for the disintegration of half of the atoms in a sample of a radioactive substance. Science has not yet found a safe method of permanent disposal of high level radioactive wastes. Even temporary storage of these wastes is a dangerous and expensive problem. In the United States steps are being taken to build a containment area inside Yucca Mountain in Nevada that would hold 70,000 metric tons of nuclear waste. This

facility, however, will not be available before 2017. Currently small sites containing nuclear waste are scattered throughout the United States.

Thermal, or Heat, Pollution

While the concept of heat as a pollutant may seem improbable on a cold winter day, at any time of year an increase in water temperature has an effect on water life. Heat can be unnaturally added to streams and lakes in a number of ways. One is to cut down a forest completely. The brooks and streams that flowed through it are then exposed to the sun. Their temperatures begin to rise. As they flow into larger bodies of water, these in turn are warmed. This can kill fish and other water animals incapable of tolerating the higher temperatures.

Heat pollution is a consequence of the rising energy needs of man. As electric power plants burn fossil fuels or nuclear fuel to provide this energy, they release considerable amounts of heat. Power plants are usually located near bodies of water, which the plants use for heat-dissipation purposes. Some stretches of the Hudson River in New York no longer freeze in winter because of the flow of hot water into the river from adjacent power plants. Living things—especially such cold-blooded animals as fish—are very sensitive to even small changes in the average temperature. Because of the added heat in waters affected by power plants, many aquatic habitats may be undergoing drastic change. In some instances, the warmer water may cause fish eggs to hatch before their natural food supply is available. In other instances, it may prevent fish eggs from hatching at all.

Gases such as carbon dioxide, methane, nitrous oxide, and water vapor occur in the environment naturally. These so-called greenhouse gases absorb radiation emitted from Earth's surface and direct it back to Earth, preventing radiant heat loss. This process is known as the greenhouse effect. However, since the Industrial Revolution began to prosper in the 19th century, people have aggressively added more of these gases into the atmosphere through the burning of fossil fuels, the widespread decimation of forests, the raising of large herds of cattle, and other methods. The increase of these gases means that more heat is trapped within Earth's atmosphere, leading to rising global temperatures.

Scientists at the National Aeronautics and Space Administration's Goddard Institute for Space Studies confirm that the five warmest years worldwide since the late 1880s have all taken place since 1998. Four of the last five have taken place in the 21st century. Scientific data suggests that this trend is likely to continue.

Increased global temperatures have resulted in the steady melting of glaciers and ice caps in the Arctic. Scientific evidence suggests that if polar ice and glaciers continue melting at the current rate of 8 percent per decade, they may disappear completely by 2060. In addition, the melting ice contributes to higher sea levels, currently rising at about 0.08 inch (2 millimeters) per year. If this trend continues, low-lying islands will be completely flooded. (*See also* Greenhouse Effect; Global Warming.)

Noise Pollution

The hearing apparatus of living things is sensitive to certain frequency ranges and sound intensities. Sound intensities are measured in decibels. For example, a clap of thunder has an intensity of about 100 decibels. A sound at or above the 120-decibel level is painful and can injure the ear. Likewise, a steady noise at just 75 decibels over numerous hours has the potential to harm hearing. Noise pollution is becoming an unpleasant fact of life in cities, where the combination of sounds from traffic and building construction reverberates among high-rise buildings, creating a constant din.

In addition, the intense volume at which some popular music, especially heavy metal rock and hip-hop music, is played has resulted in the loss of some or all of the hearing of a few musicians and members of their audiences. There is some evidence that extreme levels of noise can cause stress and produce other deleterious effects on human health and on work performance.

Efforts to Halt Pollution

The solution of some pollution problems requires cooperation at regional, national, and international levels. For example, some of the acid rain that falls in Canada is caused by smokestacks of coal-burning power plants in the United States. Thus, rejuvenating the lakes of eastern Canada requires the cooperation of electric utilities in Indiana and Ohio.

In the United States laws have been passed to regulate the discharge of pollutants into the environment. The Environmental Protection Agency (EPA), formed in 1970, oversees most federal antipollution activity. The National Environmental Policy Act also mandated the use of environmental impact statements, which require that businesses or governments examine alternatives and acknowledge the possible harmful effects of such activities as opening new factories, building dams, and developing new oil wells. With the advent of massive oil spills from supertankers, the washing up of medical wastes on shores in New York and New Jersey, and an increased buildup of toxic wastes, such international organizations as Greenpeace have become ever more dedicated to preventing environmental abuses and heightening public awareness of environmental issues.

The 1970s were a time of great public awareness of the environment. The Clean Air Act, the Safe Drinking Water Act, and the Comprehensive Environmental Response, Compensation, and Liability Act (known as Superfund) are among the laws that set standards for healthy air and water and the safe disposal of toxic chemicals. In 1990 President George Bush signed the Clean Air Act of 1990, the second amending legislation since the original Clean Air Act of 1970. The new law called for reductions in emissions of sulfur dioxide and nitrogen oxide by half, carbon monoxide from vehicles by 70 percent, and other emissions by 20 percent. The number of toxic chemicals monitored by the EPA would increase from 7 to about 250, and industry would be required to control their waste release by means of the best technology available. By 2007 the EPA had moved

Construction Photography/Corbis

Recycling plants prepare materials such as plastic for reuse. They have been set up in countries throughout the world in order to help reduce the amount of waste in landfills.

to reduce mercury emissions from power plants and were installing new regulations for exhaust from buses, trucks, and other diesel-powered vehicles.

Internationally, the United Nations Framework Convention on Climate Change adopted the Kyoto Protocol in 2005, a treaty that committed its signatories to develop national programs to reduce their emissions of greenhouse gases. Although the treaty was mired in political debates and most participating countries were not able to meet their goals, the protocol was heralded as a step in the right direction toward an international agreement on environmental policy.

**FURTHER RESOURCES FOR
ENVIRONMENTAL POLLUTION**

Bowden, Rob. Transportation: Our Impact on the Planet (Raintree, 2004).

Calhoun, Yael, ed. Water Pollution (Chelsea, 2005).

Carson, Rachel. Silent Spring, 40th anniversary ed. (Houghton, 2002).

De Rothschild, David. The Global Warming Survival Handbook (Rodale, 2007).

Hill, M.K. Understanding Environmental Pollution, 2nd ed. (Cambridge Univ. Press, 2004).

Kidd, J.S., and Kidd, R.A. Air Pollution (Chelsea, 2006).

Morgan, Sally. Acid Rain (Sea to Sea, 2007).

(*See also* bibliographies for **Conservation; Ecology.**)

Both water and wildlife conservation benefit from the protection of seasonal wetlands that can prevent local flooding during heavy rainfall and retain water during short-term droughts. Isolated wetlands are responsible for the highest productivity of aquatic invertebrates, amphibians, and reptiles in most regions of the temperate zone.

CONSERVATION

Conservation is the responsible stewardship of the environment to preserve natural ecosystems while insuring that balanced consideration is also given to human needs for production and recreation. People vary in their opinions on the levels of importance of the various components and on how much emphasis should be placed on each. Thus, some people view the primary function of conservation as a mechanism to preserve natural habitats and wildlife, whereas others view conservation as the means to assure the persistence of economically important natural resources that are of direct benefit to humans. However, most agree that a major goal of conservation today is reasonable use of Earth's natural resources in the broadest sense, which includes water, soil, wildlife, forests, minerals, and fossil fuels.

Freshwater habitats must be kept clean for drinking and for recreational activities. Soils must be kept fertile, without the accumulation of toxic chemicals from pesticides or herbicides, to provide fruits and vegetables and to prevent poisoning of wildlife. Forests must be managed to provide not only lumber and pulpwood for paper products but also homes and food for native wildlife. The use of oil, coal, and minerals important for an industrial society must be carefully monitored to be certain that the supply does not dwindle too rapidly and that natural habitats are not degraded in the process of producing and using them.

Conservationists work to preserve the natural heritage for future generations. People concerned with conservation seek not only to maintain a high-quality environment suitable for both wildlife and humans but also to preserve the natural biological, genetic, and habitat diversity of ecosystems (*see* Biodiversity). This often involves preventing or minimizing environmental pollution from industrial, agricultural, urban, and domestic sources, including toxic chemicals, radioactive wastes, and elevated water temperatures. Conservationists also seek to prevent the waste of natural resources of any sort, to reduce consumption of energy and unnecessary commercial products, and to support recycling efforts.

This article was contributed by J. Whitfield Gibbons, Professor of Ecology and Senior Research Scientist, Savannah River Ecology Laboratory, University of Georgia, and Herbert A. Smith, Associate Dean for Education, Colorado State University.

Natural resources are sometimes classified as renewable or nonrenewable. Forests, grasslands, wildlife, and soil are examples of renewable resources. They can be regenerated through natural processes, and prudent management can maintain them at steady levels. The consumption of the limited supplies of nonrenewable fossil fuels such as coal, petroleum, and natural gas, whether wasteful or not, speeds their depletion. Conservation measures for fossil fuels involve reduced usage. Likewise, certain nonrenewable critical ores and metals, such as iron, aluminum (bauxite), and copper, have finite supplies and controlled accessibility that sometimes call for conservation measures, such as appropriate recycling programs, to assure continued production.

Another goal of conservation is to preserve the natural beauty of a community. When land is mistreated, the countryside can become aesthetically unpleasant. Vacant lots covered with trash, bare roadsides, garbage-laden streams, and the unregulated sprawl of strip malls are ugly. Conservation also helps to preserve areas suitable for recreation. As cities grow crowded, natural areas are needed for people enjoying leisure time. People need city parks, wildlife preserves, and national parks; grass and trees bordering roads and highways; and clear streams.

Natural resources are a vital part of sustaining human life, and conservation measures are designed to control, manage, and preserve them so that they can be used and appreciated to the fullest. A proper conservation program incorporates effective measures so that all natural resources are managed in the best interest of everyone.

Abuses of Natural Resources

The settlement of the United States provides a dramatic example of unsustainable depletion of resources. When the first European settlers arrived in North America, they found a continent rich in natural resources. Much of the land was covered with forests where wild animals abounded. Great herds of bison roamed the grasslands. The soil was deep and fertile. Clean lakes and streams, unpolluted with silt and chemical wastes, held a wealth of fish.

Surrounded by what seemed to be inexhaustible supplies of natural resources, and in the struggle to obtain food, clothing, and shelter, the settlers cut down millions of acres of the Eastern forests. As they moved westward, they plowed up the native grasslands and prairies to plant corn (maize) and wheat. Their growing cities dumped sewage and waste materials from factories and homes into the lakes and streams.

Much of the spring and summer rain in the United States falls in torrential thunderstorms, especially in the vast Missouri, Mississippi, and Ohio river basins. The farmers who settled the country were mainly Europeans who had been used to gentle rains. The methods of tilling and planting that they brought with them and with which they were familiar were not suited to the new climate.

The land's capacity for water storage was diminished by the loss of the grasses that hold soil in place and prevent the escape of rainwater. With the blotter-like plant cover gone, many rivers flooded at unprecedented levels when the winter snows melted. During natural drought periods, wells ran dry and crops died in the fields Dust storms blew the topsoil away. Birds, fish, and other wildlife that once thrived in the forests, fields, and streams became scarce. Some kinds became extinct, vanishing forever. These negative experiences gradually led the growing nation to recognize some of its environmental problems, ultimately leading to some of the world's strongest and most effective conservation programs.

Factors Involved in Conservation

Worldwide, the abuses of the past, many of which continue into the present, have showed the need for a more sensible use of natural resources. The logging company that cuts down too many trees without replanting for the future or without regard for the welfare of all native wildlife that are affected; the industrial plant that fouls a river or pollutes the air with its wastes; the agriculturists who use pesticides and herbicides without concern for their environmental impacts, injuring not only their own natural communities but also those downstream—all are abusing natural resources.

Conservation groups have promoted corrective legislation and instituted legal proceedings against violators. People have been made increasingly aware that their continued existence depends on these efforts to stop environmental deterioration. However, all members of society are seldom in agreement on what the proper path for conservation is because of special interests and differing personal goals and backgrounds. Although most people would agree that individuals have no right to destroy nature's wealth for personal profit, not all people agree with this view.

Conservation is everyone's responsibility, but a few individuals or companies can cause major setbacks in conservation programs. In many instances stringent laws and regulations must be passed and effectively enforced to stop the degradation and destruction of natural resources that bring gain to particular individuals or corporations but no environmental benefits to society.

However, public pressure can often be brought to bear, as is shown by surveys in the early part of the 21st century revealing that Americans were more concerned about the environment than ever before and that corporate strategies of tracking and responding to public attitudes were economically the most prudent approach. When society collectively expresses the view that conservation of natural resources is important, the corporate industrial world that can affect those resources will respond appropriately. An example of how public attitude could have a measurable direct effect on conservation efforts is that the surveys revealed that more than 60 percent of citizens purchase recyclable products when given a choice. Such information will ultimately lead to companies supporting recycling because it has become more economically profitable to do so

WATER CONSERVATION

Water is undeniably an essential natural resource and is a frequent focus of conservation efforts. Everyone uses it. Water is needed in homes for drinking, cooking, washing clothes, and bathing, and it is used for non-vital activities such as filling home swimming pools, watering lawns, and washing vehicles. Communities must have water for fire protection and also use it for recreational activities such as swimming, boating, and fishing. Industries use water to produce electricity, to cool machinery, and to perform a large number of manufacturing processes. Some agricultural systems use vast quantities of water for crops during the growing season.

Water has been recognized since Babylonian times as one of the most valuable and vital resources for all living things, including humans. Ancient Mesopotamian laws about water use during drought periods designated who got to use water and how they could use it. Such laws were a form of conservation in that they were designed to assure the preservation of a limited environmental resource. Conflicts over water started long ago, and predictions are that they are going to get even worse in the near future as human populations increase in many parts of the world.

To minimize such conflicts, water conservation measures are likely to become commonplace in many regions, even in some places where water is now taken for granted. A dilemma for conservationists is how to deal with the wants and needs of humans for water during long periods of drought. Critical levels of water are required in lakes, streams, and rivers of a region for the basic needs of populated areas. But choices involving water diversion from one region to another involve balancing not only the competing needs of different communities but also options of using the water for power production, recreational activities, and the survival of some species of fish and other wildlife.

Watersheds and Their Importance

A watershed is the area drained by a river or a stream in a region. Such an area slopes toward a common land trough. Some rain runs off, or drains, over the ground surface. Runoff water forms small streams, which flow into larger ones. These eventually join to form a river, which may lead to a lake, reservoir, or ocean.

A natural watershed conserves water. It has clear streams and an ample cover of trees, grasses, and other plants. Plants help contribute to form a part of the topsoil called humus. Humus consists of decaying leaves and wood, bacteria, dead insects, and other plant and animal remains. It provides some of the nutrients for new plant life and many soil invertebrates. Together with a network of roots, it acts as a blotter that soaks up rain. Plants break the force of falling rain and scatter the drops over leaves and branches. Some of the water returns to the air by evaporation. Part of the water used by plants is passed through their leaves into the air again by transpiration.

Any remaining water that does not flow to streams sinks into the earth through countless tiny channels. Some of the spaces in the soil through which water percolates are caused by natural features of the geology or soil itself. Others are made by plant roots and burrowing animals such as earthworms, insects, and moles.

The level at which the earth is permanently saturated is known as the water table. This vast underground water supply fluctuates with the seasons and the amount of rainfall. During long, heavy rains the soil may not be able to soak up all the water. Some of it runs off the surface, but in a forested watershed it moves slowly. Deep snow that melts slowly allows water to soak into the soil gradually. When all trees in an area have been cut down (clear-cut) owing to poor forestry practices, or when grasses and other plants have been stripped off by fire, overgrazing, or poor farming practices, the watershed suffers. The water from rainfall flows over the ground's surface

A great egret wades amid cypress trees in Florida's Everglades National Park, which preserves the largest subtropical wilderness left in the United States. Roughly half of the original natural Everglades area has been destroyed, mainly for land development.
National Park Service

instead of being absorbed by the vegetation and organic materials that would be present on a natural forest floor.

When there are no leaves, branches, or grasses to break the force of falling rain and the blotter of roots and humus is gone, mud closes the channels through which water sinks into the soil. If the land is level, the water stands in stagnant pools; if it slopes, the water runs downhill into the rivers. Streams in a mismanaged watershed become brown with silt, or suspended soil, because the racing water carries soil along with it.

A mismanaged, unvegetated watershed can result in destructive floods in the spring because heavy rains and melting snows reach rivers too quickly and overflow the banks downstream. In the summer, streams, springs, and wells can dry up because little or no water has sunk into the underground reservoirs.

Water Pollution

The silting of streams is a form of water pollution. Heavy siltation in streams and rivers kills fish and other aquatic animals including tadpoles, mollusks, and larval insects indirectly by reducing the amount of oxygen in the water. As the flowing water slows, silt is deposited on streambeds, and the natural flow patterns of waterways become altered. Reservoirs behind dams eventually fill with silt unless erosion is stopped in watersheds above.

Other kinds of water pollution have created other problems. Many waterways are used as dumps for household and industrial wastes. Some communities dump untreated sewage and garbage into the nearest streams. Industries contaminate the waterways when they discharge acids, chemicals, greases, oils, and organic matter into them. Such materials foul drinking water and endanger public health. They destroy commercial fisheries. They also make waterways unusable for recreational purposes. Leaks and spills from offshore oil wells and wrecked or damaged oil tankers have caused the widespread destruction of marine life.

The large-scale use of organic insecticides, herbicides, toxic metals, and pesticides has polluted streams and destroyed wildlife. Some pesticides tend to concentrate in the tissues of plants and animals in nature's food chains. Thus organisms at the ends of these chains, including humans, may take in harmful amounts of pesticides deposited in their food supply.

SOIL CONSERVATION

Whenever land is stripped of its plant cover, soil is inevitably lost by erosion, the so-called silent thief. A single rainstorm can wash away centuries-old accumulations of soil from neglected or badly managed fields. Topsoil is an extremely valuable natural resource. Under this thin blanket of rich soil and humus, in which plants grow best, is a less fertile material called subsoil. If the surface layer of topsoil is blown or washed away, the remaining subsoil often cannot support plant life. The submarginal farms must eventually be abandoned.

Types of Soil Erosion

In the late 1900s more than 700 million acres (283 million hectares) of agricultural land in the United States were subject to erosion. Some 230 million acres (93 million hectares) of cropland required constant supervision to control erosion caused by wind and water.

Dust storms are the evidence of wind erosion. Soil unprotected by plant cover simply blows away. During the 1930s millions of acres of farmlands were badly damaged by wind. Many fields lost from 2 to 12 inches (5 to 30 centimeters) of vital topsoil during this period. As a result, the entire southern Great Plains area was called the Dust Bowl.

One of the several kinds of water erosion is sheet erosion—the wasting away of level land in thin layers. The deterioration may go on for years without being noticed, though the land yields successively smaller crops. A patch of subsoil showing through on some slight rise of ground may be the first sign that the land is nearly finished as a food producer.

Splash erosion is the washing away of soil by the direct battering of rain. In rill erosion, runoff digs small channels called rills in the soil. The little rills run together, form a network of larger rills, and then develop into gullies. When gully erosion occurs, the land can become as unproductive as a desert.

Conservationists also recognize that livestock can overgraze a plot of land until severe soil erosion occurs. In the late 1900s about 4 million acres (1.6 million hectares) of topsoil were lost every year through erosion, of which about 85 percent was estimated to be the result of overgrazing by livestock.

Although major losses of productive agricultural lands occurred in the first half of the 20th century because of erosion, a major concern in the 21st century is the loss of natural soils and habitats as a result of commercial development. Large tracts of productive land—estimated as high as 1 million acres (400,000 hectares) each year—continue to be lost through the building of roads, suburban housing, and industrial and other commercial site developments, including airport expansion.

Soil Conservation in Agriculture

Government agencies in many countries have developed soil and land classification systems. In the United States the Soil Erosion Service (soon renamed the Soil Conservation Service) was created in 1933 as a major division of the United States Department of Agriculture. The Soil Conservation Service (now called the Natural Resources Conservation Service [NRCS]) devised a land classification system that offered guidance in the proper use of land. Such factors as slope, type of soil, amount of rainfall, humidity, and vegetation type were considered when determining land use for maximum productivity. Of the eight land classifications, classes I, II, III, and IV were considered appropriate for cultivated crops; however, classes III and IV required skillful management to avoid serious erosion. Classes V through VII could be used for forests and for grazing. Class VIII land, which included sandy shores and extremely rocky places, was considered suitable only for wildlife or for scenic and recreational purposes. The NRCS uses a modification of the same system today.

Contoured and strip-cropped fields hold water and prevent it from washing away soil. Conservation helps ensure productive fields, adequate and clean water, and a wholesome environment.
Georg Gerster—Comstock

Covering the ground with plants is one of the key elements in soil conservation. To test this, the Department of Agriculture experimented with two steep plots of adjacent land—one planted with crops and the other thickly covered with grass. The cultivated plot lost 7 inches (18 centimeters) of topsoil in 11 years. By contrast, it was estimated that it would take 34,000 years to lose the same amount of topsoil from the grass-covered plot.

Plant cover tends to reduce raindrop energy and hold rainwater where it falls, thus preventing the soil from blowing or washing away. Gullies can be healed in many cases by planting new plants. They provide a tangle of leaves and stems that trap and hold in place part of the soil carried by runoff. Another way to heal gullies is to build brush dams across them at regular intervals. Then soil and water running down the gully are caught behind the dams and held in place.

To help prevent the start of erosion, farmers have used a variety of conservation measures. The effectiveness of each depends on the climate, topography, and soil type.

Contouring and terracing. This practice involves plowing, planting, and cultivating sloping fields around hillsides, with curving furrows horizontal to the hill, instead of furrows running straight uphill and downhill. The curved furrows catch rainfall and allow much of it to soak into the ground. They also catch soil washing down from higher levels. On long slopes a low ridge, or terrace, thrown along the outer side of the slope catches soil and rainwater and retards runoff. Encouraging plant growth on a terrace will help hold soil.

Strip-cropping. Strips of close-growing plants, such as grasses or clover, are alternated between strips of clean-tilled row crops, such as corn and soybeans. The strips of close-growing plants hold water and keep it from eroding the cultivated strip below. These strips are planted on the contour.

Listing. In dry regions a lister plow can be used to throw a ridge of dirt to each side, creating a trough about 18 inches (46 centimeters) wide and 7 inches (18 centimeters) deep. Crops are planted in the bottom of the trough.

Windrows and shelterbelts. On treeless plains, rows of trees planted at the edges of fields break the force of winds across the fields and reduce wind erosion.

Deep tillage, or stubble mulching. Instead of turning over the soil with a moldboard or no-till plow, a deep-tillage plow breaks the soil below the surface. It leaves the surface vegetation or harvest remains from the previous crop to act as a cover.

Crop rotation. Planting different crops each year on a piece of land keeps the soil productive. One crop can benefit the next. For example, nitrogen is essential for plant growth and is added to the soil by nitrogen-producing legumes, such as clover, alfalfa, soybeans, and cowpeas. These combine nitrogen from the air with other elements and store it in the soil through their roots. In a year or two the plants can be plowed under. This is called green manuring.

After the roots have rotted, other plants that need nitrogen but cannot use nitrogen in the air—for example, corn and potatoes—can use the nitrogen stored in the soil for growth. Rotations are programmed with strip-cropping by shifting the close-growing strips and the tilled strips at fixed intervals.

Cover crops. Land is kept covered in winter and summer with either a growing crop or the residue, such as corn stalks, from the crop previously grown. When cover crops are plowed under for green manuring, the plant foods added to the soil improve its water-holding capacity and increase its fertility.

Erosion on Urban Land

Cropland is not the only land with soil subject to erosion. The land on which housing and other urban projects are built is particularly susceptible because its protective cover is generally removed.

To prevent erosion on construction sites, builders should take corrective action. For example, mulches placed on steeply excavated slopes usually prevent soil from washing or blowing away. Straw or fiber netting may be used as mulches. On sites where erosion control is more difficult, hydroseeding can be used. Grass seed, fertilizer, and mulch are power-sprayed on excavated slopes. The quick-growing grass then stabilizes the soil against erosion. Many bridge and highway construction projects use silt fences below the disturbed areas to trap loose soil and prevent runoff into nearby streams.

WILDLIFE CONSERVATION

The preservation of wildlife greatly depends upon water and soil conservation. The native plants and animals constitute the wildlife of a region and are a product of the land resources and habitat conditions. But, like humans, wild animals must have food, water, and shelter. Destroying the forests, marshes, ponds, and grasslands alters their food and water supplies and the places in which they live, hibernate, and reproduce.

Environmental Impact

Wildlife conservationists generally recognize five distinct but interacting categories of environmental impact that need to be considered in regard to how human activities affect native wildlife in the broadest sense (all wild animals and plants). They are habitat loss and degradation, introduced species, pollution, disease and parasitism, and unsustainable use.

Habitat loss and degradation. The loss and degradation of natural habitat is the single most important factor contributing to declines and extirpation of populations and species in most regions of the world. Although examples of other specific causes can be given, the destruction of terrestrial and aquatic habitat through agricultural, urban, and industrial development is generally agreed to be the main cause of declines in native wildlife species. Highway construction and traffic

A wildlife specialist holds a brown tree snake that was captured on a military base in Guam as part of a program to prevent the species from spreading to Hawaii. After the snake was accidentally introduced to Guam in the mid-20th century, it colonized the island and preyed relentlessly on native species, causing the decline, local elimination, or extinction of several species of birds, fruit bats, and lizards.

have caused immeasurable loss of natural habitat and direct wildlife mortality, especially in the United States. For example, the cumulative surface area of paved U.S. highways is more than the area of the state of Indiana.

Introduced exotic and invasive species. Scientists have documented that introductions of nonnative species of plants and animals has resulted in the declines and elimination of native species in some regions. An example in the early 2000s is the destruction of North American hemlock trees by the Asian woolly adelgid insect. Tropical exotic lizards introduced into southern Florida have established populations that outcompete or prey on native species. Numbers of native lizards have declined noticeably, especially in areas where natural habitat has been replaced by houses and other man-made structures.

Environmental pollution. Numerous toxic chemicals and metals that are by-products of industry and agriculture have direct and indirect negative effects on wildlife. Agricultural areas release contaminants such as fertilizers, pesticides, and herbicides into waterways upon which fish and terrestrial wildlife depend. Other environmental contaminants detrimental to aquatic wildlife include runoff of petroleum products from highways and domestic effluents from urban and suburban areas.

For example, many coastal salt marshes and estuaries of the Atlantic Ocean and Gulf of Mexico have become dumping grounds for litter and industrial effluents. Too many coastal areas have been used for commercial developments including resort housing, golf courses, and boat marinas. Continued exploitation of the coastal salt marshes will further reduce the number of wildlife species, including diamondback terrapins, salt marsh snakes, and marsh wrens. (*See also* Environmental Pollution.)

Disease and parasitism. A wide variety of parasites and diseases are known or suspected to be responsible for debilitating illnesses in many plant and animal wildlife species. Wildlife conservation biologists have concluded that the levels of resistance of many species are lower than normal because the species are already stressed from other environmental impacts such as natural habitat destruction or chemical pollution.

Unsustainable use. All human cultures have used wild plants and animals as an integral part of their existence, not only for the necessities of food, clothing, and shelter but also for recreation and leisure activities. However, irresponsible timbering at unsustainable levels and overharvesting for food and for the commercial pet trade has plagued numerous species of plants and animals on a global scale. The dramatic loss of millions of acres of tropical rainforest in the Americas, Africa, and Asia has unquestionably driven hundreds of species to extinction. In the early 21st century the unregulated commercial trade in edible Asian freshwater turtles as delicacies was documented by conservation biologists to exceed any possible sustainable levels. Many of the species were already recognized as endangered, and their extinction in the wild is expected early in the century unless such activities are curtailed.

A worker in a zoo in India takes care of star tortoises that were seized from traders. The tortoises will later be released back into the wild. The large illegal trade in Asian turtles for their meat or for use as pets has put the survival of many species in jeopardy.

An additional category of concern for wildlife conservationists, despite political debates about the issue, is global climatic change. Many climatologists predict major alterations in temperature and rainfall patterns in many regions. Such changes will result in habitat modifications that could affect most wildlife in minor or major ways and will become the focus of many wildlife conservation efforts.

Another area that needs to be considered is unexplained declines such as the disappearance of populations or reduction in numbers of species that are not directly related to any of the above causes but that may be natural in occurrence. Of course, an unexplained decline of a species may have been exacerbated in an indirect or undetectable manner by human activities or may be a cumulative effect of several unidentified causes. The role of wildlife conservation is to identify and minimize the impacts of human-caused activities that are controllable through a combination of regulation, management, and education.

Endangered Species

Of the original native wildlife of the United States many species are now extinct. These include the passenger pigeon, the Carolina parakeet, the great auk, the Labrador duck, the Pallas cormorant, the dusky seaside sparrow, and the heath hen. Mammals gone forever include the Eastern elk, the Plains wolf, the sea mink, and the Badlands bighorn. Many smaller birds and mammals have also become extinct in the wild. Several species of mountaintop salamanders with small geographic ranges in the Appalachian Mountains are assumed to have been extirpated during strip mining activities of the past. The number of certain United States reptiles, including bog turtles, indigo snakes, southern hognose snakes, and northern cricket frogs, grows smaller every year. Many game species are now protected by law from overhunting and overfishing.

The United States Fish and Wildlife Service maintains a list of endangered and threatened species of the United States. Environmental concerns for a variety of nongame species of reptiles, amphibians, small fishes, insects, and mollusks, as well as other animals and plants, is reflected in the number of species classed as threatened or endangered. Some states also have laws and regulations that protect many of these species. However, many continue to be threatened by habitat destruction.

In the United States the Endangered Species Act has been effective for preserving some species that seemed destined for extinction. For example, the American alligator had been reduced to a relatively small number by the early 1960s because of overhunting for hides and meat. After 20 years of protection, the species recovered to a large extent. By the early 2000s, coastal states where alligators are abundant allowed limited hunting of the species.

Worldwide, the World Conservation Union (also called the IUCN) keeps track of species threatened with extinction. Endangered species include many of the world's great cats, whales, rhinoceroses, tapirs, and many other mammals, birds, and reptiles. However, housing and other facilities needed by an expanding human population are encroaching on their habitats. In addition, many species are the victims of the illegal pet trade and of the trade in exotic pelts and skins.

The African elephant, once common throughout the sub-Saharan region of the African continent, has been greatly reduced in numbers because of illegal poaching for the ivory trade. (*See also* Endangered Species.)

Many nonprofit conservation organizations have been formed to protect nongame species. Some focus on single species, and others on natural groupings of organisms. Two successful programs established in the 1990s are Partners in Flight (PIF) and Partners in Amphibian and Reptile Conservation (PARC); PIF emphasizes conservation of land birds, while PARC is the largest program addressing conservation of both amphibians and reptiles. Both organizations have a U.S. focus but are international in scope. Other major conservation organizations that protect wildlife and their ecosystems worldwide include WWF (also called the World Wildlife Fund or the World Wide Fund for Nature), Conservation International, the Wildlife Conservation Society, and the International Crane Foundation, and, in the United States, Defenders of Wildlife and the National Wildlife Federation. (*See also* Some Prominent Environmental Organizations on page 81).

A lioness carries her cub in the grasslands of the Maasai Mara National Reserve, a large wildlife refuge in Kenya.
Joe McDonald/Corbis

Refuges for Wildlife

Some governments have established national wildlife reservations and game refuges. Many refuges are established in places to which animals, especially migratory birds, have long been attracted. In the United States, many of these are administered by the Fish and Wildlife Service. All United States national parks and national monuments, operated by the National Park Service, serve as wildlife refuges.

Individuals can help restore wildlife to the countryside simply by providing birds, fish, and other animals with natural feeding, breeding, and refuge sites. They can do even more by encouraging their state and federal governments to provide effective laws for habitat protection.

Brush piles scattered through a woodlot provide retreats for cottontails, weasels, mink, and woodchucks. Small wetlands, whether natural or man-made, without fish provide breeding habitat for frogs and salamanders and feeding areas for turtles, snakes, and aquatic insects. Fencerows can provide a haven for many kinds of birds.

FOREST CONSERVATION

Among the most valuable of nature's resources are forests. They play a key role in the maintenance of the watersheds that are essential to water and soil conservation. They shelter many forms of wildlife. They supply lumber for construction, cordwood for fuel, and pulp for paper. Forests also provide the raw materials used in many synthetic products considered essential for modern life, including fibers, plastics, and medicines.

Fire can be a major scourge of a forest, especially if natural fires have been suppressed in a region. Although lightning is sometimes responsible for kindling forest fires, human carelessness is most often the cause. Ground fires can destroy the organic soil of the forest and render it incapable of supporting tree life. Also,

elimination of the understory leaves bare soil, making it more susceptible to water and wind erosion. When crown fires rage through the leafy tops of trees, they destroy timber and its resident wildlife. However, fire is a natural occurrence in many regions, and most forests

A fire manager starts a prescribed burn in Yellowstone National Park, in the northwestern United States. Such fires are intentionally set to mimic the natural burn cycles of forests and to prevent the buildup of dead plant matter on the ground, which can fuel dangerous crown fires.

Bryan Harry/NPS

Grant Heilman—Grant Heilman Photography

Loggers planted new saplings on a hillside to replace the trees they cut down.

rebound quickly from occasional fires and the wildlife returns.

A common tool of foresters is the use of prescribed burning (sometimes known as controlled burning) to attempt to imitate the natural burning cycle of forests in a region. The purpose is to burn off leaf or pine needle litter and fallen twigs on the ground's surface to return nutrients to the soil. Occasional burning also prevents the buildup of such organic fuels, which can result in major forest fires that cannot be controlled. Prescribed burning presents a dilemma for forest managers and timber companies in some areas. Prescribed burns in populated areas near forests can send smoke into nearby homes, resulting in complaints from homeowners. However, foresters receive worse criticism when a forest fire becomes a completely unmanageable crown fire that burns down houses because prescribed burning was not done and natural burning cycles were suppressed.

Insect infestation can also threaten the life of a forest. In the United States, the Forest Pest Control Act of 1947 and later laws authorized surveys of public and private forests so that insect-borne diseases of trees could be detected and suppressed before they became epidemic.

A more serious threat than fire or insects is indiscriminate logging. When every tree of a stand is cut without any provision for natural reseeding or manual replanting, as is still common in many parts of the world, particularly the tropics, no canopy is left to protect the soil against the splash erosion of rainfall. The loose soil soon becomes deposited as silt in nearby streams. Timber must be treated as a renewable crop, carefully harvested to ensure a sustained yield of trees. In this way, a balance is struck between the cutting of mature trees and the growth of saplings. A major problem with forest removal in tropical areas is that no topsoil layer is present to promote natural reseeding. In the tropics, most of the nutrients are aboveground in the

vegetation itself, rather than stored in the soil as is typical of temperate-zone forests. Thus, different forestry techniques must be used to assure conservation of tropical forests. (*See also* Deforestation.)

MINERAL AND FOSSIL-FUEL CONSERVATION

Minerals and fossil fuels are nonrenewable resources. Once exhausted, they can never be replaced. The United States has valuable stores of coal, oil, natural gas, and minerals. Until the United States Mineral Leasing Act was passed in 1920, the resources on public lands were transferred to private individuals, who sometimes overexploited them for personal gain. Today, in many countries worldwide, including the United States, government regulation attempts to assure that private industry make proper use of these resources. In some countries, the government itself operates key mining industries.

Limited Supply

For years coal was mined as though it were inexhaustible—about one ton wasted for each ton mined. Various government agencies have promoted more efficient mining methods. In addition, the use of other sources of energy in home construction and in industry, and to generate electricity, has greatly extended the life of the coal supply. Natural gas and petroleum were once carelessly wasted also. In earlier days, for example, because no use for natural gas had been found, it was burned off or allowed to escape into the air.

Like other conservation needs, the wise management of mineral resources has become more pressing because of the growing number of consumers. As the human population increases, the demand increases for more consumer goods, such as household appliances and automobiles. Manufacturers meet these rising demands from already dwindling deposits of metal ore and fuels.

Some mineral resources, particularly metals, may be recycled so that they can be salvaged and reused. The recycling of waste metals is an important conservation practice that has become a major business. It is known as secondary production. Conservation programs for fossil fuels include replacing them with more abundant and cleaner sources of energy.

Effects on the Environment

Conservation programs also call for curtailing environmental pollution, habitat degradation, and erosion caused by mining, processing, and using mineral products. Mining wastes are often rich in sulfuric acid, for example, and their runoff into streams can devastate communities of plants and animals living in the water and nearby. Without proper land reclamation programs, surface mining for coal and other minerals can strip off the fertile topsoil in an area and leave behind an abandoned wasteland in which few, if any, plants can grow. Coal burning can create pollution problems, not only in the atmosphere but also for organisms, especially amphibians and fish, living in aquatic systems. In addition, the burning of coal, oil, and natural gas, such as in power plants, factories, and motor vehicles, also

Renewable Energy Sources

Energy produced from such sources as the Sun, the wind, and the carbohydrates in plants is considered renewable because it can be replenished easily and within a short time period: sunshine and wind are exceedingly abundant, and plants can be regrown quickly. Other major sources of renewable energy include hydropower, in which the force of flowing water is used to generate electricity, and geothermal power, in which hot water and steam from Earth's interior, captured from natural hot springs and geysers or drilled wells, is used to heat buildings or run generators that produce electricity. In addition to being renewable, such energy sources emit either virtually no pollutants or far fewer pollutants during their use than fossil fuels do.

Solar power. Enormous amounts of energy reach Earth each day in the form of sunshine. Solar energy systems capture radiation from the Sun and convert it into thermal energy (heat) or electricity, without emitting pollution. In common home and business systems, flat-plate collectors—typically blackened metal plates covered with one or two sheets of glass—are mounted on the roof, where they absorb heat from sunlight. The intensity of the solar radiation at Earth's surface is low, however, so the collectors need to be fairly large. Small pipes carry water, an antifreeze solution, or another fluid (or sometimes air) through the collectors. This heats the fluid, which is then carried into the building to heat water in a hot-water tank or, by being passed through radiators, to heat the living space. Water heated during sunny periods is commonly stored in a tank for use on cloudy days and at night.

Concentrating collectors, or solar furnaces, produce heat at very high temperatures for use in industry or to generate electricity. These collectors consist of an array of lenses or mirrors that focus the solar radiation received from a large area onto a small receiver. In power plants, the resulting intense heat is used to run a boiler that produces steam; the steam in turn drives a generator that produces electricity.

In addition, solar cells convert solar energy directly into electricity. Light striking the cells, which are usually made mostly of silicon, knocks electrons out of their atoms to produce an electric voltage. Since solar cells operate at low efficiencies, they are used mainly in low-power or remote applications; however, researchers continue to develop more efficient cells.

Wind power. People have used wind power to grind grain, pump water, and perform other work for hundreds of years. Today, it is more often used to produce electricity from an inexhaustible and readily available source of energy without causing pollution. In the early 21st century, wind power was one of the fastest growing sources of electricity worldwide, though it still only accounted for a small share of electricity production. Germany, Spain, the United States, India, and Denmark were leaders in the total amount of wind power produced, and Denmark obtained about 20 percent of its electricity from wind power.

A wind energy system is fairly simple: wind spins the propeller-like blades of a wind turbine, which looks like a fan mounted on top of a tower. This motion turns a central shaft and a series of connected gears, which drive a generator that converts the mechanical energy into electricity. Some homes, businesses, and farms use individual wind turbines as a source of electricity. At commercial wind farms, many wind turbines, sometimes as many as several hundred, are grouped in rows and are connected to a central utility power grid. Of course, wind power is only generated when winds blow fast enough to turn the blades, and much more energy is produced by fast winds than by moderate ones—if the wind speed doubles, eight times as much power can be generated. Because of this, wind farms are built in areas with reliably strong and steady winds.

Biomass energy. People have long burned wood for heat. Plant matter, an abundant resource, can be used in several ways to generate power. Most commonly it is burned to produce heat or electricity or is made into biofuels for use in motor vehicles. Animal wastes are also used. Biomass power plants burn wastes from agriculture, forestry, and manufacturing, including wood, sawdust, tree bark, and crop residues, and even city garbage containing plant and animal products (such as food scraps, lawn trimmings, paper, and leather). This burning yields heat, which is used to produce steam; the steam in turn drives a generator that produces electricity. Biomass can also replace some of the coal used in conventional coal-burning plants to reduce the emissions of pollutants.

Plant matter is also fermented to make alcohols used as transportation fuels, such as ethanol. Some vehicles, called flexible-fuel vehicles, can use E85, a mixture of up to 85 percent ethanol and as little as 15 percent gasoline, while conventional vehicles can use gasohol, which contains up to 10 percent ethanol with the remainder gasoline. Ethanol is commonly made from the starches and sugars in corn and other grains and in sugarcane and sugar beets. Using the entire plant, including the cellulose, of such plants as switchgrass and fast-growing trees has the potential to provide high yields of biomass energy more efficiently, while also enriching the soil and providing habitat for wildlife.

Using biomass energy typically causes less air pollution, such as of sulfur dioxide and nitrous oxides, than using fossil fuels. Many conservationists advocate relying more on biomass energy, along with solar and wind power, as part of a strategy to combat global warming. Burning biomass and biofuels releases similar amounts of the greenhouse gas carbon dioxide as burning fossil fuels does—but overall the use of biomass energy results in significantly lower carbon dioxide emissions. This is because the crops used for biomass energy are replaced with more crops, which take carbon dioxide out of the air as part of their growth cycle. The net reduction varies, depending on how much energy was used in producing and transporting the plants. (The plants from which fossil fuels formed also took carbon dioxide from the air. That happened millions of years ago, however, so it does not balance emissions from the current use of fossil fuels.)   *Ed.*

Peter Menzel—Stock, Boston

Wind turbines generate electricity without polluting the environment.

releases the greenhouse gas carbon dioxide into the air; most scientists believe that this is the major cause of global warming. (*See also* Environmental Pollution; Global Warming; Greenhouse Effect.)

Energy Crisis and Alternative Fuels

Throughout most of its history the United States has had ample, inexpensive supplies of fuels to provide energy. During the 20th century the country gradually shifted from reliance on coal as its principal fuel to dependence on natural gas and petroleum. By the late 1970s the United States was consuming more than one third of the world's supply of these two fuels and was dependent on them for three fourths of its energy.

As it became more apparent during the 1970s that natural gas and petroleum resources might be depleted within the foreseeable future, energy conservation became an important government policy. Conservation measures were also adopted because of political and economic developments. About one half of the petroleum used by the United States was imported, much of it from Middle Eastern countries that opposed certain United States foreign policies. In addition, oil-exporting countries increased oil prices by more than 1,500 percent between 1970 and 1980.

In 1977 President Jimmy Carter established a Cabinet-level Department of Energy, formerly known as the Atomic Energy Commission, and proposed a comprehensive energy program. As passed by Congress in 1978, the program included measures to discourage energy consumption, particularly of natural gas and petroleum, and provided incentives for alternative energy sources. An Energy Security Act, to develop synthetic fuels, was passed in 1980.

Government, industry, and private citizens all took steps to conserve energy. To meet new government standards, smaller and more efficient automobiles were produced. There was renewed emphasis on improving the country's mass transportation systems. Grants,

loans, and tax credits were offered for the installation of insulation and other energy-saving devices in homes and commercial properties. Efficiency standards for appliances were adopted. The government mandated minimum and maximum temperatures for nonresidential buildings and suggested maintenance of similar temperatures in homes.

The energy crisis of the 1970s also led to increased emphasis on alternative sources of power. The government supported further development of solar, geothermal, and wind power. Industries and utilities were encouraged, and in certain circumstances required, to use coal as an alternative to natural gas and petroleum. The government encouraged long-range research programs, including the development of economical methods of producing gas and oil from coal and shale. Gasohol—a mixture of ethanol (alcohol produced from grain or other plant matter) and gasoline—was introduced as an alternative fuel for automobiles, and electric cars were developed.

With the election of Ronald Reagan as president in 1980, government support for most of those programs

---

CONSERVATION—ARE YOU INVOLVED?

Each member of a community bears some responsibility for safeguarding the natural resources of the area. If conservation efforts are lax or lacking in your community, you should help make local and national lawmakers aware that there is popular support for an effective program.

If You Live in the City or Suburbs

Does your community dump untreated sewage into streams or lakes?

Is groundcover or grass neglected in schoolyards, playgrounds, and parks?

Do the builders of housing developments, shopping centers, and highways let valuable topsoil wash away?

Do factories discharge waste into public waterways?

Is the air contaminated by incinerated garbage and industrial gases?

Does your family pollute the air by burning leaves and trash?

If You Live in a Farm Community

Are crops planted without using such practices as contouring, terracing, or rotation?

Are fields eroded because there are no windbreaks?

Are fertilizers and pesticides used indiscriminately, contaminating farm workers, harming wildlife, or destroying organisms in the waters into which field draining flows?

Do local farmers fail to consult soil scientists and other conservationists on the best use of their land?

If You Live in Forest or Rangeland Areas

Is timberland leveled without leaving immature trees for survival of the timber site or without provisions for reseeding the acreage?

Are cattle and sheep allowed to overgaze the grassland and thus jeopardize the range?

Bill Horsman—Stock, Boston
A program at an Earth Day celebration in the United States encourages people to recycle.

ended. Instead, the government promoted the expansion of nuclear energy and a return to imported petroleum. In the early 2000s the United States used fossil fuels to meet roughly 85 percent of its energy needs, with nuclear power accounting for about another 8 percent.

Worldwide, growing concern about global warming in the early 21st century led to greater efforts to reduce the use of fossil fuels and to rely increasingly on renewable, nonpolluting energy sources such as solar, wind, and geothermal power. New methods of using biomass energy, by burning plant matter or producing ethanol and other fuels from crops and agricultural wastes, were also investigated, and more electric and gasoline-electric hybrid automobiles were introduced.

THE U.S. CONSERVATION MOVEMENT

Conservation in the United States began as a movement to save the country's vanishing forests, but the concept was soon broadened to include other resources. Gifford Pinchot, the head of the United States Forest Service from 1898 to 1910, was an early conservationist. He strongly influenced President Theodore Roosevelt, who established the National Conservation Commission. Some 234 million acres (95 million hectares) of government-owned timber, coal, oil, and phosphate lands were set apart as public lands, never to be sold to private interests.

During President Franklin D. Roosevelt's first term, with a severe drought in the Plains states, reforestation and erosion control were undertaken by the Civilian Conservation Corps and the Soil Conservation Service. The government took over abandoned and nonproductive farms; many acres were reforested and set aside as game reserves. The Taylor Grazing Act of 1934 regulated livestock grazing on public lands to prevent overgrazing and soil deterioration.

Under President Harry S. Truman a national program was established to control water pollution. Later legislation required states to set and enforce standards to maintain clean natural waters.

Efforts to save native wildlife from extinction were aided by management programs provided in the Endangered Species Preservation Act of 1966. Beginning in 1969 the importation of endangered species and the interstate shipment of illegally captured wildlife were prohibited. Thus the pet, fur, and hide markets for native and foreign species facing potential extinction were outlawed.

The National Environmental Policy Act of 1969, a far-reaching conservation measure, was supported by President Richard M. Nixon. It reflected the need for a high-quality environment, emphasized recycling of nonrenewable resources, and advocated attempts to equalize population and resource use. In 1970 the Environmental Protection Agency (EPA) was formed to establish standards of environmental quality. Since then the EPA has been responsible for enforcing several major statutes, including such landmark environmental laws as the Clean Air Act of 1970 and what became known as the Clean Water Act of 1972, to protect the environment from air and water pollution. These acts have subsequently been amended and additional ones passed, but this basic framework of environmental protections remains in place. (*See also* Environmental Law.)

Various presidential administrations in the late 20th and early 21st century have taken different approaches toward the environment, with some favoring land development, resource exploitation, and deregulation of industries over conservation of wildlife and natural ecosystems and protections against environmental pollution. Contentious issues have included whether to prohibit new road construction in certain national forests in order to protect them from excessive timbering, whether to open large areas of key wildlife habitat in the Arctic National Wildlife Refuge to oil drilling, and whether to require automobiles to meet stricter fuel-efficiency standards. (For a history of the global conservation movement, *see* Environmentalism.)

FURTHER RESOURCES FOR CONSERVATION

Calhoun, Yael, ed. Conservation (Chelsea House, 2005).
Cruden, Gabriel. Energy Alternatives (Lucent, 2005).
Dalgleish, Sharon. Managing the Land; Protecting Forests; Protecting Wildlife; Renewing Energy; Saving Water (Chelsea House, 2003–04).
Desonie, Dana. Humans and the Natural Environment (Chelsea House, 2008).
Few, Roger. Animal Watch (DK, 2002).
Gallant, R.A. Wonders of Biodiversity (Benchmark, 2003).
Haddock, Patricia. Environmental Time Bomb: Our Threatened Planet (Enslow, 2000).
Mongillo, John, and Mongillo, Peter. Teen Guides to Environmental Science, 5 vols. (Greenwood, 2004).
Parker, Janice. The Disappearing Forests (Smart Apple Media, 2003).
Patent, D.H. Biodiversity (Clarion, 1996).
Penny, Malcolm. Endangered Species: Our Impact on the Planet (Raintree Steck–Vaughn, 2002).
Royston, Angela. Energy of the Future (Heinemann, 2007.)
Saunders, Nigel, and Chapman, Steven. Energy Essentials: Renewable Energy (Raintree, 2004).
West, Krista, ed. Critical Perspectives on Environmental Protection (Rosen, 2007).

Boy Scouts plant native tree seedlings in Puerto Princesa, Philippines, as part of the city's annual forest festival. Each June, several thousand volunteers participate in this massive reforestation campaign.

ENVIRONMENTALISM

The political and intellectual movement called environmentalism seeks to improve and protect the quality of the natural environment. It advocates curtailing or ending human activities that harm the environment. The movement also seeks to change political and economic systems so that human societies can prosper without causing pollution and other environmental damage.

The term environment is broad, as it refers to all the natural world. In various ways, environmentalists call for protecting or improving the quality of the air, the water, and the land, including the conservation of the soil and important natural areas such as rainforests and wetlands. Environmentalists are also concerned with protecting the biosphere, which consists of the animals, plants, and other living things and the ecosystems in which they live. (*See also* Ecology; Earth.)

However, the goals and methods of different environmentalists are quite varied. For example, some focus on raising public awareness of the need to "reduce, reuse, and recycle" materials in order to cut back on the resources consumed in making, packaging, and transporting consumer products. Others work to

enact local, national, or international laws that protect the environment, such as by requiring that motor vehicles meet certain fuel efficiency and emissions standards, by creating nature reserves, by banning the killing of endangered species, or by regulating the chemicals that businesses can emit into the air and water. Some environmentalists organize various kinds of protest actions to draw attention to or to disrupt activities by corporations and governments that harm the environment. Others seek to establish alternative communities that live in closer harmony with nature.

Despite the diversity of the movement, most environmentalists agree on four general principles: protection of the environment, democracy, social justice, and nonviolence. However, a small number of individuals and groups believe that violence in the name of environmentalism is justified if it is committed against businesses that damage the environment or that kill or abuse animals for profit, such as mining and logging companies and the makers of fur coats. Critics of this practice, many of whom are not themselves environmentalists, have referred to it as "ecoterrorism."

TWO BASIC APPROACHES

In many cases, environmentalists call for protecting the natural world in order to directly improve or maintain human health and well-being. However, many believe that the environment should also be protected in other cases. They claim that living things other than humans, and the natural environment as a whole, should also be taken into account when people reason about the morality of political, economic, and social policies.

Environmentalists are often divided into two intellectual camps: those whose thinking about the environment is anthropocentric, or "human-centered," and those whose thinking is biocentric, or "life-centered." This division has also been described as "shallow" ecology versus "deep" ecology.

Anthropocentric approaches focus on the negative effects that environmental damage has on human beings, including harm to human health and quality of life. They also tend to think of the value of the natural environment in terms of its usefulness to humans. According to this approach, for example, what is wrong with polluting the ocean or depleting the ozone layer is that doing so ultimately harms human beings, who use the ocean as a source of food and who rely on the ozone layer for protection against ultraviolet radiation from the Sun.

In contrast, proponents of biocentrism claim that it is wrong to treat the environment merely as a resource to be exploited for human purposes. They hold that nature is valuable for its own sake. Polluting the ocean or depleting the ozone layer would be wrong, therefore, even if the ocean or the ozone layer did not benefit human beings in any way. Advocates of biocentrism believe that anthropocentric approaches have been responsible for centuries of environmental destruction. The division between these two basic approaches played a central role in the development of environmental thought in the late 20th century.

ANTHROPOCENTRIC SCHOOLS OF THOUGHT

Apocalyptic environmentalism. The vision of the environmental movement of the 1960s and early '70s was generally pessimistic, reflecting a belief that Earth's long-term prospects were bleak. Apocalyptic, or "survivalist," environmentalism stressed the possible destruction of the planet. Works such as Rachel Carson's 'Silent Spring' (1962) and Paul Ehrlich's ' The Population Bomb' (1968) suggested that the natural environment was reaching the limits of what it could sustain. Influenced by such books, some environmentalists began to call for increasing the powers of central governments in order to limit human activities thought to be environmentally harmful. Robert Heilbroner's 'An Inquiry into the Human Prospect' (1974), for example, argued that human survival ultimately required the sacrifice of human freedom. Other viewpoints, such as those presented in Julian Simon and Herman Kahn's 'The Resourceful Earth' (1984), have emphasized humanity's ability to find or invent substitutes for resources that were scarce and in danger of being exhausted.

Emancipatory environmentalism. Beginning in the 1970s, many environmentalists began to develop strategies for limiting environmental damage through recycling, the use of alternative-energy technologies, and increasing government regulation of industries that harm the environment. They have also sought to increase popular participation in economic planning, such as by introducing citizen representation on the boards of major corporations and by allowing the public to vote on environmentally sensitive decisions by businesses and government. In contrast to apocalyptic environmentalism, so-called "emancipatory" environmentalism has taken a more positive and practical approach. One element of this approach has been to promote an ethic of stewardship, or responsible management, of the environment.

Activists from Greenpeace and ANSE try to stop the construction of a new harbor at La Manga, Spain, in a campaign to protect the region's coasts from overdevelopment, especially in ecologically important areas. Their signs say "Mar Menor free of cement" in Spanish.
AFP/Getty Images

© AFP/Corbis

Demonstrators protest deforestation at a World Trade Organization meeting in Seattle, Wash.

Some forms of emancipatory environmentalism have emphasized the development of small-scale farms and industries that would be more closely integrated with the natural processes of the surrounding environment. Prominent environmentalists advocating this approach included American ecologist Barry Commoner and German-born British economist Ernst Schumacher. Such environmentalists also encourage the use of renewable resources (those that can be replenished comparatively quickly, easily, and inexpensively), such as wind and solar power, rather than nonrenewable resources, such as fossil fuels. They also advocate organic farming, which uses biological methods of fertilization and pest control rather than chemical fertilizers and pesticides. The emancipatory approach was evoked through the 1990s in the popular slogan, "think globally, act locally."

Biocentric Schools of Thought

Social ecology. An emphasis on small-scale economic structures is also a feature of the school of thought known as social ecology. Social ecologists trace the causes of environmental damage to what they consider to be the unfair distribution of political and economic power in society. They see this problem as characteristic of modern capitalist societies, in which power is centralized in large government agencies or private businesses that are not accountable to the people who work in them or who are affected by them. They argue that the most environmentally beneficial political and economic system is one based on decentralized, small-scale communities and systems of production. A major proponent of social ecology was the American environmental anarchist Murray Bookchin.

Deep ecology. A more radical doctrine, known as deep ecology, also distrusts capitalism and favors decentralization. Deep ecologists claim that humans need to regain a "spiritual" relationship with nonhuman nature. They believe that people should reflect on the interconnectedness of all organisms—including humans—in the natural environment and cultivate in themselves a sympathy for nonhuman nature. By doing this, they argue, humans can develop an environmental consciousness and a feeling of environmental solidarity. Some more extreme forms of deep ecology have been strongly criticized, however, as "antihumanist" because they imply that one should oppose famine relief and immigration and accept the large-scale losses of life that have been caused by HIV/AIDS and other epidemics.

Animal rights. A belief in the intrinsic value of nature was fundamental to the development of the animal-rights movement. The movement was strongly influenced by works such as Peter Singer's 'Animal Liberation' (1977) and Tom Regan's 'The Case for Animal Rights' (1983). Animal-rights approaches go beyond a concern with cruelty to animals to demand an end to all forms of animal exploitation. For example, many animal-rights activists oppose the use of animals in scientific and medical experiments and as sources of food, clothing, and entertainment (such as in circuses, rodeos, and races).

Ecofeminism. The possibility of a spiritual relationship with nature has also been a concern of ecofeminism. Ecofeminists assert that there is a connection between the destruction of nature by humans and the oppression of women by men. Both, they argue, arise from political viewpoints and social practices in which both women and nature are treated as objects to be owned or controlled. Ecofeminists aim to establish a central role for women in the pursuit of an environmentally sound and socially just society. They hold that the relationship between nature and women is more intimate and more "spiritual" than the relationship between nature and men.

HISTORY OF THE ENVIRONMENTAL MOVEMENT

Concern for the impact on human life of problems such as air and water pollution dates to at least Roman times. Soil conservation was practiced in China, India, and Peru as early as 2,000 years ago. In general, however, such concerns did not give rise to public activism.

Early Environmentalism

The contemporary environmental movement developed in the late 19th century. It arose primarily from concerns about the protection of the countryside in Europe and of the wilderness in the United States and the health consequences of pollution during the Industrial Revolution. The dominant political philosophy of the time was liberalism. It held that all social problems, including environmental ones, could and should be solved through the free market—the exchange of goods and services in the economy without any government regulation. However, in opposition to this, most early environmentalists believed that government rather than the market should be responsible for protecting the environment and ensuring the conservation of resources.

In the United States a more strongly biocentric approach was advocated by the naturalist John Muir

Some Prominent Environmental Organizations

African Wildlife Foundation. International organization dedicated to conserving wildlife and habitats in Africa. Founded in 1961 as the African Wildlife Leadership Foundation, Inc. Its programs include establishing reserves, conducting scientific research, training local conservationists, and working with communities to develop ecotourism and other sustainable land-management projects. http://www.awf.org

Conservation International. Organization that works in more than 40 countries, especially developing ones, to protect biodiversity in land and marine ecosystems. Founded in 1987. Its scientists study global biodiversity and have identified hotspots, sites with exceptional biological richness that are most threatened. The organization works with governments, communities, farmers, and businesses in such places to adopt a wide variety of conservation measures. http://www.conservation.org

Environmental Defense. U.S. environmental organization working on such issues as climate change, pollution, and endangered wildlife. Founded in 1967 as the Environmental Defense Fund, it successfully fought for a U.S. ban on DDT in the courts. With a staff that includes scientists, economists, and lawyers, the group works with governments, corporations, and communities to find solutions to environmental problems, lobbies to enact environmental protection laws, and fights lawsuits to uphold them. http://www.environmentaldefense.org

Friends of the Earth International. Network of environmental and social-justice grassroots activist organizations in some 70 countries. Founded in 1971. The groups work on a wide range of environmental issues, such as fighting global warming, opposing genetically modified crops, and combating deforestation, as well as associated socioeconomic issues, such as protecting human rights, promoting fair trade, and fighting corporate globalization. http://www.foei.org

Greenpeace. International organization dedicated to preserving endangered species, preventing environmental abuses, and heightening environmental awareness. Founded in 1971. Its activists take direct, nonviolent actions, including confrontations with polluting corporations and governmental authorities—for example, steering small inflatable craft between the harpoon guns of whalers and their prey. It works to protect endangered whales and seals, to end the dumping of toxic chemicals into the oceans. to stop the construction of nuclear power plants, and to combat deforestation and global warming. http://www.greenpeace.org

National Resources Defense Council. U.S. organization focusing on environmental protection law, as well as environmental research and education. Founded in 1970. The group lobbies government officials to pass laws to protect the environment and files and fights lawsuits to ensure that such laws are enforced. Its lawyers, scientists, and other staff work on a wide range of issues, including

limiting environmental pollution in order to protect human health, preserving endangered species, and combating global warming. http://www.nrdc.org

Nature Conservancy. Conservation organization protecting wildlife and ecosystems in more than 30 countries. Founded in 1951. One of the group's strategies is to purchase important habitat areas in order to protect them. It also conducts scientific research and works with businesses, communities, and governments to develop effective and economically attractive conservation programs and policies. http://www.nature.org

Rainforest Alliance. International organization dedicated to conserving biodiversity and promoting environmentally sustainable and socially just practices in farming and forestry, in rainforests and elsewhere. Founded in 1986. The organization gives its "seal of approval" to certain consumer products, such as wood, paper, coffee, and bananas, that it certifies were produced in accordance with specific environmental and human-rights standards. http://www.rainforest-alliance.org

Sierra Club. U.S. grassroots organization for the conservation of natural resources. Founded in 1892, with naturalist John Muir as its first president. Its goals have included protecting wildlife and wilderness areas, keeping air and water clean, and curtailing global warming, such as by encouraging the reduction of fossil fuel use and the passage of laws that require better motor-vehicle fuel efficiency. It also mounts international campaigns related to overpopulation, international trade, and global climate change. http://www.sierraclub.org

World Conservation Union, or **IUCN.** International conservation and sustainable-development network formerly called the International Union for the Conservation of Nature and Natural Resources. Founded (under a different name) in 1948. The IUCN's membership includes about 1,000 organizations, including countries, government agencies, and nongovernmental organizations, and some 10,000 individual scientists. It supports and conducts scientific conservation research, manages ecosystems, and advises governments on conservation policy. It also prepares many databases, assessments, and guidelines, including a comprehensive list of global threatened species, called the 'Red List'. http://www.iucn.org

WWF. International conservation organization known as the World Wide Fund for Nature in some countries and the World Wildlife Fund in North America. Founded in 1961. Active in more than 100 countries, the WWF has focused on saving individual endangered species and protecting various ecosystems as well as providing a safe and sustainable habitat for the world's peoples. It addresses both local and global issues, the latter including climate change, safe agricultural practices, and responsible international trade. http://www.panda.org

(1838–1914), founder of the Sierra Club. and Aldo Leopold (1887–1948), a professor of wildlife management. Leopold introduced the concept of a "land ethic." According to him, humans needed to stop being conquerors of nature and to start being "citizens" of nature.

Environmental organizations established from the late 19th to the mid-20th century were primarily middle-class groups concerned with nature conservation, wildlife protection, and limiting the pollution that arose from industrial development and urbanization. Their emphasis was typically on lobbying, or trying to influence the decisions of legislators and government policy makers. In addition, various scientific organizations were concerned with natural history and the biological aspects of conservation efforts.

The Greens

Beginning in the 1960s, environmentalists began to establish activist organizations and political parties. The early activities of the "green" movement, as environmentalism came to be called, involved protest actions designed to obstruct and to draw attention to environmentally harmful policies and projects. Other activities included public-education campaigns and conventional lobbying of policy makers and political representatives. The movement also attempted to set public examples in order to increase awareness of environmental issues. Such projects included recycling and green consumerism, or "buying green," which means choosing products whose production, packaging, distribution, use, and disposal cause less harm to the environment than similar products.

Some Notable People Associated with Environmentalism

The people listed below were selected to show the wide range of goals, approaches, and backgrounds of people associated with environmentalism.

Bookchin, Murray (1921–2006). U.S. social ecologist. Born Jan. 14, 1921, in New York City. He believed that environmental problems could not be solved without also transforming society to be more egalitarian. A longtime leftist political theorist, activist, and teacher, he cofounded the Institute for Social Ecology in Vermont in 1974. His books include the prophetic 'Our Synthetic Environment' (1962), 'Post-Scarcity Anarchism' (1971), and 'The Ecology of Freedom' (1982).

Brower, David (1912—2000). U.S. environmental activist. Born July 1, 1912, in Berkeley, Calif. He worked nearly 70 years to protect wilderness areas in the United States, and his efforts led to the creation of several national parks and passage of the Wilderness Act in 1964. While he was executive director of the Sierra Club from 1952 to 1969, the organization's membership grew from 7,000 to 77,000. He later founded Friends of the Earth and the Earth Island Institute.

Brundtland, Gro Harlem (born 1939). Norwegian politician and physician. Born on April 20, 1939, in Oslo. After serving as Norway's minister of the environment in the 1970s, she served three terms as prime minister in the 1980s and '90s. She chaired the UN commission on the environment whose 1987 report introduced the idea of "sustainable development" and led to the first "Earth Summit." She was director general of the World Health Organization from 1998 to 2003.

Carson, Rachel (1907–64). U.S. biologist known for writings on pollution and the natural history of the ocean. Born on May 27, 1907, in Springdale, Penn. She earned an M.A. in zoology from Johns Hopkins University in 1932 and later had a long career as a marine biologist and editor for the U.S. government. Her 'The Sea Around Us' (1951) won a National Book Award. Her prophetic bestseller 'Silent Spring' (1962), a meticulously researched book about the dangers of DDT and other pesticides in the food chain, was a landmark work in the history of environmentalism.

Commoner, Barry (born 1917). U.S. biologist and educator. Born on May 28, 1917, in New York City. He studied at Harvard University and taught at Washington University and Queens College. His warnings, since the 1950s, of the environmental threats posed by modern technology (including nuclear weapons, pesticide use, and ineffective waste management) in such works as 'Science and Survival' (1966) made him one of the foremost spokespersons for environmentalism. He was a third-party candidate for U.S. president in 1980.

Fossey, Dian (1932–85). U.S. zoologist and top authority on mountain gorillas. Born on Jan. 16, 1932, in San Francisco, Calif. In 1967 she founded the Karisoke Research Center in Rwanda and began patiently observing mountain gorillas there. She earned a Ph.D. in 1974 and taught at Cornell University. In 1978 she began a public campaign against the poaching of gorillas, and her book 'Gorillas in the Mist' (1983) drew attention to their plight. She also herself actively protected them from poachers, who are suspected of her murder at Karisoke.

Gore, Al (born 1948). U.S. politician. Born on March 31, 1948, in Washington, D.C. A moderate Democrat, he served in the U.S. Congress (1977–93) before becoming U.S. vice-president (1993–2001). In the controversial 2000 election for the U.S. presidency, he won the popular vote but narrowly lost the electoral vote. A longtime environmentalist, he subsequently devoted much of his time to environmental advocacy. His writings include 'Earth in the Balance' (1992) and 'An Inconvenient Truth' (2006), a companion book to his Academy award–winning documentary about climate change. For their work on global warming, Gore and the International Panel on Climate Change jointly won the 2007 Nobel peace prize.

Rachel Carson

© Underwood & Underwood/Corbis

Dian Fossey

AP

David Brower

Roger Ressmeyer/Corbis

Barry Commoner

Time Life Pictures/Getty Images

Al Gore

Some Notable People Associated with Environmentalism—Continued

Jackson, Wes (born 1936). U.S. scientist working to revolutionize agriculture. Born on June 15, 1936, in Topeka, Kan., into a farming family. After receiving a Ph.D. in plant genetics in 1967, he founded the environmental studies program at California State University. He left academia in 1976 to found the Land Institute, an agricultural research organization. A critic of the soil erosion, biodiversity loss, and pesticide use associated with industrial farming, he worked to develop perennial crops and sustainable farming methods based on prairie ecosystems. He received a MacArthur fellowship in 1992 and a Right Livelihood Award in 2000.

Kelly, Petra (1947–92). German cofounder and leader of the West German Green party. Born on Nov. 29, 1947, in Günzburg. As a young woman she lived in the United States, where she was active in the civil rights and antiwar movements. She later worked for the European Communities and became an activist for nuclear disarmament, environmentalism, peace, and human rights. In 1979 she and a few others founded the Greens, which received enough votes in 1983 to send her and 26 others to the federal parliament. The Greens lost representation in 1990, but she continued to work ceaselessly as an activist until her death. She won the Right Livelihood Award in 1982.

Maathai, Wangari (born 1940). Kenyan environmentalist and politician who won the 2004 Nobel peace prize. Born on April 1, 1940, in Nyeri. She earned a Ph.D. in 1971 from the University of Nairobi, where she then taught veterinary anatomy. In 1977 she founded the Green Belt Movement, through which village women have planted millions of trees to combat deforestation and to raise their standard of living. She was elected to Kenya's parliament in 2002 and became an assistant minister of the environment.

Schumacher, Ernst Friedrich (1911–77). German-born British economist. Born on Aug. 16, 1911, in Bonn. During World War II, he worked on plans for Britain's welfare state under the government's chief economic adviser. As an adviser to Britain's nationalized coal industry from 1950 to 1970, he emphasized conservation. In 'Small Is Beautiful' (1973), he argued that capitalism brought higher living standards at the cost of deteriorating culture and that large industries and large cities would lead to the depletion of natural resources that should be conserved.

Scott, Peter Markham (1909–89). British conservationist and wildlife painter. Born on Sept. 14, 1909, in London. In 1946 he founded what became the Wildfowl and Wetlands Trust, which saved the nene from extinction in the 1950s. In 1961 he cofounded the World Wildlife Fund (WWF). As a member of a commission of the International Union for the Conservation of Nature and Natural Resources (1962–81), he created the 'Red Data' books, lists of endangered species. He also led expeditions, wrote travel and wildlife books, and promoted conservation issues on British television series. He was knighted in 1973.

Shiva, Vandana (born 1952). Indian physicist, ecofeminist, and social-justice theorist and activist. Born on Nov. 5, 1952, in Dehra Dun. After earning a Ph.D. in the philosophy of science, she founded an environmental research foundation. Through its Navdanya program, she led campaigns to conserve the biodiversity of crops by creating seed banks, to promote pesticide-free farming, and to protect the rights of farmers in developing countries against genetic engineering companies. She won the Right Livelihood Award in 1993.

Tamayo, José Andrés (born 1958?). Honduran environmental and social activist. Born in San Pedro, El Salvador. A Roman Catholic priest, he became the leader of the Environmental Movement of Olancho, a grassroots coalition of subsistence farmers, religious leaders, and others in Honduras opposing the rampant deforestation of their land and resulting water shortages. From 2003 he led mass marches and other nonviolent actions to protest illegal logging, land appropriation, and government corruption. He won the Goldman Environmental Prize in 2005.

Petra Kelly Bettmann/Corbis

Wes Jackson The Land Institute

Wangari Maathai AFP/Getty Images

Vandana Shiva AFP/Getty Images

Bob Krist/Corbis

A person dressed as the character "Recycle Pete" encourages citizens to recycle plastics at a recycling center in Ridgewood, New Jersey. (The acronym PETE stands for polyethylene terephthalate, a type of plastic commonly used to make plastic bottles.)

The political strategies of the green movement included forming its own political parties and nominating candidates to run for political office. Through these parties, the movement sought to make the environment a central concern of public policy and to render the institutions of government more democratic and accountable.

The world's first green parties were founded in the early 1970s in New Zealand and Tasmania, Australia. The most successful environmental party was the German Green party, founded in West Germany in 1980. In federal elections just three years later, the party won representation in the country's parliament. In 1998 it formed a coalition government of a united Germany with the Social Democratic party, and the party's leader, Joschka Fischer, was appointed the country's foreign minister.

In the late 20th and early 21st centuries, green party candidates won election to national parliaments in a number of countries—especially in Europe but also in such countries as Australia, New Zealand, Mexico, and Brazil—and some became government ministers. Green parties even claimed the office of mayor in European capital cities such as Dublin and Rome in the mid-1990s. In other places, including the United States, green party candidates were elected mayor of smaller cities or to other local offices.

International Environmental Movement

By the late 1980s environmentalism had become a global as well as a national political force. Some environmental nongovernmental organizations—for example, Greenpeace, Friends of the Earth, and the World Wildlife Fund—established a significant international presence. Such organizations had offices throughout the world and international headquarters to coordinate lobbying campaigns and to serve as information centers for their national affiliate organizations.

Through its international activism, the environmental movement has influenced the agenda of international politics. Only a small number of international environmental agreements were in force before the 1960s. However, since the 1972 United Nations Conference on the Human Environment in Stockholm, Sweden, there have been international agreements on most aspects of environmental protection. International agreements have also been made about practices that have environmental consequences, such as the trade in endangered species, the management of hazardous waste (especially nuclear waste), and armed conflict. In 1992 the United Nations Conference on Environment and Development (the "Earth Summit") in Rio de Janeiro, Brazil, was attended by some 180 countries and various business groups, nongovernmental organizations, and the media. An important international treaty called the Kyoto Protocol was adopted in 1997 and went into effect in 2005 (*see* Kyoto Protocol). Through this treaty, many countries agreed to reduce by specific amounts their emissions of certain gases that cause global warming.

At the beginning of the 21st century, the environmental movement combined the traditional concerns of conservation, preservation, and pollution with more contemporary concerns such as the environmental consequences of tourism and trade. The short- and long-term effects of global warming also became of increasing concern. (*See also* Conservation; Environmental Law; Environmental Pollution; Global Warming.)

FURTHER RESOURCES FOR ENVIRONMENTALISM

Archer, Jules. To Save the Earth: The American Environmental Movement (Viking, 1998).
Calhoun, Yael, ed. Environmental Policy (Chelsea House, 2005).
Connolly, Sean. Safeguarding the Environment (Smart Apple Media, 2006).
David, Laurie. The Solution Is You: An Activist's Guide (Fulcrum, 2006).
Eblen, R.A., and Eblen, W.R., eds. The Environment Encyclopedia (Marshall Cavendish, 2001).
Halpin, Mikki. It's Your World—If You Don't Like It, Change It: Activism for Teenagers (Simon Pulse, 2004).
Juniper, Tony. Saving Planet Earth (Collins, 2007).
McDaniel, C.N. Wisdom for a Livable Planet (Trinity Univ. Press, 2005).
Sonneborn, Liz. The Environmental Movement (Chelsea House, 2007).
Switzer, J.V. Environmental Activism: A Reference Handbook (ABC-CLIO, 2003).
Weyler, Rex. Greenpeace (Rodale, 2004).

AP

Emergency cleanup crews work to remove 2,000 liters of oil spilled from a ship on three Rio de Janeiro beaches in September 2005.

ENVIRONMENTAL LAW

The vast field of environmental law encompasses the principles and policies enacted by local, national, and international entities to regulate human treatment of the nonhuman world. The field covers a broad range of topics in diverse legal settings, such as state bottle-return laws in the United States, regulatory standards for emissions from coal-fired power plants in Germany, and international treaties for the protection of biological diversity and the ozonosphere. During the late 20th century environmental law developed from a modest adjunct of the law of public health regulations into an almost universally recognized independent field protecting both human health and nonhuman nature.

Historical Development

Throughout history national governments have passed occasional laws to protect human health from environmental contamination. About AD 80 the Senate of Rome passed legislation to protect the city's supply of clean water for drinking and bathing. In the 14th century England prohibited both the burning of coal in London and the disposal of waste into waterways. In 1681 the Quaker leader of the English colony of Pennsylvania, William Penn, ordered that one acre of forest be preserved for every five acres cleared for settlement, and in the following century Benjamin Franklin led various campaigns to curtail the dumping of waste. In the 19th century, in the midst of the Industrial Revolution, the British government passed

regulations to reduce the deleterious effects of coal burning and chemical manufacture on public health and the environment.

Prior to the 20th century there were few international environmental agreements. The accords that were reached focused primarily on boundary waters, navigation, and fishing rights along shared waterways and ignored pollution and other ecological issues. In the early 20th century, conventions to protect commercially valuable species were reached, including the Convention for the Protection of Birds Useful to Agriculture (1902), signed by 12 European governments; the Convention for the Preservation and Protection of Fur Seals (1911), concluded by the United States, Japan, Russia, and the United Kingdom; and the Convention for the Protection of Migratory Birds (1916), adopted by the United States and the United Kingdom (on behalf of Canada) and later extended to Mexico in 1936. In the 1930s Belgium, Egypt, Italy, Portugal, South Africa, Sudan, and the United Kingdom adopted the Convention Relative to the Preservation of Fauna and Flora in their Natural State, which committed those countries to preserve natural fauna and flora in Africa by means of national parks and reserves. Spain and France signed the convention but never ratified it, and Tanzania formally adopted it in 1962. India, which acceded to the agreement in 1939, was subject to the sections of the document prohibiting "trophies" made from any animal mentioned in the annex.

Some Notable Environmental Laws and Agreements

1959 Antarctic Treaty. Agreement in which the Antarctic continent was made a demilitarized zone to be preserved for scientific research. The treaty, originally signed by 12 nations, resulted from a conference held in Washington, D.C. Later other nations acceded to the treaty.

1969 National Environmental Policy Act. U.S. law that requires the preparation of an environmental impact statement for any "major federal action significantly affecting the quality of the human environment."

1972 Stockholm Declaration. A declaration of 26 principles that enjoined states to ensure that activities within their jurisdiction do not cause environmental damage to other states or areas. Issued at the UN Conference on the Human Environment in Stockholm, Sweden.

1973 Convention on International Trade in Endangered Species. Authorized signatory states to designate species "threatened with extinction which are or may be affected by trade." Once a plant or animal species has been designated as endangered, states are bound to prohibit import or export of that species except in specific limited circumstances.

1973 Endangered Species Act. Protects various species of fish, wildlife, and plants listed by the U.S. federal government as "endangered" or "threatened."

1977 Clean Water Act. Primary U.S. law for the protection of wetlands. Contains a prohibition against unpermitted charges of "dredged and fill material" into any "waters of the United States."

1980 Comprehensive Environmental Response, Compensation, and Liability Act. U.S. law that established a federal "Superfund" to clean up abandoned or uncontrolled hazardous waste sites.

1985 Vienna Convention for the Protection of the Ozone Layer. International treaty in which signatory states agreed to take "appropriate measures. . .to protect human health and the environment against adverse effects resulting or likely to result from human activities which modify or are likely to modify the Ozone Layer."

1989 Basel Convention on the Control of Transboundary Movements of Hazardous Wastes and Their Disposal. International treaty which sought to minimize the production of hazardous waste and to combat illegal dumping.

1990 Clean Air Act. U.S. law designed to reduce overall sulfur dioxide emissions by fossil-fuel-fired power plants.

1992 Rio Declaration. A set of 27 broad, nonbinding principles outlining global strategies for cleaning up the environment and encouraging environmentally sound development. Issued at the UN Conference on Environment and Development (popularly known as the "Earth Summit") in Rio de Janeiro, Brazil.

1997 Kyoto Protocol. International treaty, named for the Japanese city in which it was adopted in December 1997, that aimed to reduce the emission of gases that contribute to global warming.

1998 Århus Convention. Committed the 40 European signatory states to increase the environmental information available to the public and to enhance the public's ability to participate in government decisions that affect the environment.

2004 Stockholm Convention on Persistent Organic Pollutants (POPs). Global treaty to protect human health and the environment from POPs—widely distributed chemicals that can accumulate in the fatty tissue of living organisms and are toxic to humans and wildlife.

2007 Western Regional Climate Action Initiative. A regional initiative among a number of western U.S. states and Canadian provinces to collectively reduce greenhouse gas emissions in the region.

Beginning in the 1960s, environmentalism became an important political and intellectual movement in the West. In the United States the publication of biologist Rachel Carson's 'Silent Spring' (1962), a passionate and persuasive examination of chlorinated hydrocarbon pesticides and the environmental damage caused by their use, led to a reconsideration of a much broader range of actual and potential environmental hazards. In subsequent decades the U.S. government passed an extraordinary number of environmental laws—including acts addressing solid-waste disposal, air and water pollution, and the protection of endangered species— and created an Environmental Protection Agency to monitor compliance with them. These new environmental laws dramatically increased the national government's role in an area previously left primarily to state and local regulation.

In Japan rapid reindustrialization after World War II was accompanied by the indiscriminate release of industrial chemicals into the human food chain in certain areas. In the city of Minamata, for example, large numbers of people suffered mercury poisoning after eating fish that had been contaminated with industrial wastes. By the early 1960s the Japanese government had begun to consider a comprehensive pollution-control policy, and in 1967 Japan enacted the world's first such overarching law, the Basic Law for Environmental Pollution Control. Not until the end of the 20th century was Minamata declared mercury-free.

Thirty-four countries in 1971 adopted the Convention on Wetlands of International Importance Especially as Waterfowl Habitat, generally known as the Ramsar Convention for the city in Iran in which it was signed. The agreement, which entered into force in 1975, now has nearly 100 parties. It required all countries to designate at least one protected wetland area, and it recognized the important role of wetlands in maintaining the ecological equilibrium.

Following the United Nations Conference on the Human Environment, held in Stockholm in 1972, the UN established the United Nations Environment Programme (UNEP) as the world's principal international environmental organization. Although UNEP oversees many modern-day agreements, it has little power to impose or enforce sanctions on noncomplying parties. Nevertheless, a series of important conventions arose directly from the conference, including the London Convention on the Prevention of Pollution by Dumping of Wastes or Other Matter (1972) and the Convention on International Trade in Endangered Species (1973).

Until the Stockholm conference, European countries generally had been slow to enact legal standards for environmental protection—though there had been some exceptions, such as the passage of the conservationist

Twenty years after the 1986 accident at the nuclear power plant in Chernobyl, Ukraine, a preschool classroom remains abandoned in the nearby town of Pripyat in January 2006. Pripyat and the surrounding area will not be safe for human habitation for several centuries.

Daniel Berehulak/Getty Images

Countryside Act in the United Kingdom in 1968. In October 1972, only a few months after the UN conference, the leaders of the European Community (EC) declared that the goal of economic expansion had to be balanced with the need to protect the environment. In the following year the European Commission, the EC's executive branch, produced its first Environmental Action Programme, and since that time European countries have been at the forefront of environmental policy making. In Germany, for example, public attitudes toward environmental protection changed dramatically in the early 1980s, when it became known that many German forests were being destroyed by acid rain. The environmentalist German Green Party, founded in 1980, won representation in the Bundestag (national parliament) for the first time in 1983 and since then has campaigned for stricter environmental regulations. By the end of the 20th century, the party had joined a coalition government and was responsible for developing and implementing Germany's extensive environmental policies. As a group, Germany, The Netherlands, and Denmark—the so-called "green troika"—established themselves as leading innovators in environmental law.

During the 1980s the "transboundary effects" of environmental pollution in individual countries spurred negotiations on several international environmental conventions. The effects of the 1986 accident at the nuclear power plant at Chernobyl in Ukraine (then part of the Soviet Union) were especially significant. European countries in the pollution's downwind path were forced to adopt measures to restrict their populations' consumption of water, milk, meat, and vegetables. In Austria traces of radiation were found in cow's milk as well as in human breast milk. As a direct result of the Chernobyl disaster, two international agreements—the Convention on Early Notification of a Nuclear Accident and the Convention on Assistance in the Case of Nuclear Accident or Radiological Emergency, both adopted in 1986—were rapidly drafted to ensure

notification and assistance in the event of a nuclear accident. In the following decade a Convention on Nuclear Safety (1994) established incentives for countries to adopt basic standards for the safe operation of land-based nuclear power plants.

There are often conflicting data about the environmental impact of human activities, and scientific uncertainty often has complicated the drafting and implementation of environmental laws and regulations, particularly for international conferences attempting to develop universal standards. Consequently, such laws and regulations usually are designed to be flexible enough to accommodate changes in scientific understanding and technological capacity. The Vienna Convention for the Protection of the Ozone Layer (1985), for example, did not specify the measures that signatory states were required to adopt to protect human health and the environment from the effects of ozone depletion, nor did it mention any of the substances that were thought to damage the ozone layer. Similarly, the

Branches from a tree in Germany's Black Forest show needle loss and yellowed boughs caused by acid rain.

Ted Spiegel/Corbis

AP

A section of China's Yellow River is stained red from the polluted discharge flowing from a sewage pipe in Lanzhou, Gansu province, in October 2006.

Framework Convention on Climate Change, or Global Warming Convention, adopted by 178 countries meeting in Rio de Janeiro at the 1992 United Nations Conference on Environment and Development (popularly known as the "Earth Summit"), did not set binding targets for reducing the emission of the "greenhouse" gases thought to cause global warming.

In 1995 the Intergovernmental Panel on Climate Change, which was established by the World Meteorological Organization and UNEP to study changes in the Earth's temperature, concluded that "the balance of evidence suggests a discernible human influence on global climate." Although cited by environmentalists as final proof of the reality of global warming, the report was faulted by some critics for relying on insufficient data, for overstating the environmental impact of global warming, and for using unrealistic models of climate change. Two years later in Kyoto, Japan, a conference of signatories to the Framework Convention on Climate Change adopted the Kyoto Protocol, which featured binding emission targets for developed countries. The protocol authorized developed countries to engage in emissions trading in order to meet their emissions targets. Its market mechanisms included the sale of "emission reduction units," which are earned when a developed country

reduces its emissions below its commitment level, to developed countries that have failed to achieve their emission targets. Developed countries could earn additional emission reduction units by financing energy-efficient projects (*e.g.*, clean-development mechanisms) in developing countries. Since its adoption, the protocol has encountered stiff opposition from some countries, particularly the United States, which has failed to ratify it.

Levels of Environmental Law

Environmental law exists at many levels and is only partly constituted by international declarations, conventions, and treaties. The bulk of environmental law is statutory—*i.e.*, encompassed in the enactments of legislative bodies—and regulatory—*i.e.*, generated by agencies charged by governments with protection of the environment.

In addition, many countries have included some right to environmental quality in their national constitutions. Since 1994, for example, environmental protection has been enshrined in the German Grundgesetz ("Basic Law"), which now states that the government must protect for "future generations the natural foundations of life." Similarly, the Chinese constitution declares that the state "ensures the rational use of natural resources and protects rare animals and plants"; the South African constitution recognizes a right to "an environment that is not harmful to health or well-being; and to have the environment protected, for the benefit of present and future generations"; the Bulgarian constitution provides for a "right to a healthy and favorable environment, consistent with stipulated standards and regulations"; and the Chilean constitution contains a "right to live in an environment free from contamination."

Much environmental law also is embodied in the decisions of international, national, and local courts. Some of it is manifested in arbitrated decisions, such as the Trail Smelter arbitration (1941), which enjoined the operation of a smelter located in British Columbia, Canada, near the international border with the U.S. state of Washington and held that "no State has the right to use or permit the use of its territory in such a manner as to cause injury by fumes in or to the territory of another or the properties or persons therein." Some environmental law also appears in the decisions of national courts. For example, in Scenic Hudson Preservation Conference *vs.* Federal Power Commission (1965), a U.S. federal appeals court voided a license granted by the Federal Power Commission for the construction of an environmentally damaging pumped-storage hydroelectric plant (*i.e.*, a plant that would pump water from a lower to an upper reservoir) in an area of stunning natural beauty, demonstrating that the decisions of federal agencies could be successfully challenged in the courts. Significant local decisions included National Audubon Society *vs.* Superior Court (1976), in which the California Supreme Court dramatically limited the ability of the city of Los Angeles to divert water that might otherwise fill Mono Lake in California's eastern desert.

Current Trends and Prospects

Although numerous international environmental treaties have been concluded, effective agreements remain difficult to achieve for a variety of reasons. Because environmental problems ignore political boundaries, they can be adequately addressed only with the cooperation of numerous governments, among which there may be serious disagreements on important points of environmental policy. Furthermore, because the measures necessary to address environmental problems typically result in social and economic hardships in the countries that adopt them, many countries, particularly in the developing world, have been reluctant to enter into environmental treaties. Since the 1970s a growing number of environmental treaties have incorporated provisions designed to encourage their adoption by developing countries. Such measures include financial cooperation, technology transfer, and differential implementation schedules and obligations.

The greatest challenge to the effectiveness of environmental treaties is compliance. Although treaties can attempt to enforce compliance through mechanisms such as sanctions, such measures usually are of limited usefulness, in part because countries in compliance with a treaty may be unwilling or unable to impose the sanctions called for by the treaty. In general, the threat of sanctions is less important to most countries than the possibility that by violating their international obligations they risk losing their good standing in the international community. Enforcement mechanisms other than sanctions have been difficult to establish, usually because they would require countries to cede significant aspects of their national sovereignty to foreign or international organizations. In most agreements, therefore, enforcement is treated as a domestic issue, an approach that effectively allows each country to define compliance in whatever way best serves its national interest. Despite this difficulty,

Pollution and debris accumulate outside the Alco Pacífico plant, a maquiladora located near Tijuana, Mexico, in August 1993.

international environmental treaties and agreements are likely to grow in importance as international environmental problems become more acute.

Many areas of international environmental law remain underdeveloped. Although international agreements have helped to make the laws and regulations applicable to some types of environmentally harmful activity more or less consistent in different countries, those applicable to other such activities can differ in dramatic ways. Because in most cases the damage caused by environmentally harmful activities cannot be contained within national boundaries, the lack of consistency in the law has led to situations in which activities that are legal in some countries result in illegal or otherwise unacceptable levels of environmental damage in neighboring countries.

This problem became particularly acute with the adoption of free trade agreements beginning in the early 1990s. The North American Free Trade Agreement (NAFTA), for example, resulted in the creation of large numbers of maquiladoras—factories jointly owned by U.S. and Mexican corporations and operated in Mexico—inside a free trade zone 60 miles (100 kilometers) wide along the U.S.-Mexican border. Because Mexico's government lacked both the resources and the political will to enforce the country's environmental laws, the maquiladoras were able to pollute surrounding areas with relative impunity, often dumping hazardous wastes on the ground or directly into waterways, where they were carried into U.S. territory. Prior to NAFTA's adoption in 1992, the prospect of problems such as these led negotiators to append a so-called "side agreement" to the treaty, which pledged environmental cooperation between the signatory states. Meanwhile, in Europe concerns about the apparent connection between free trade agreements and environmental degradation fueled opposition to the Maastricht Treaty, which created the EU and expanded its jurisdiction.

Demonstrators stage an anti-global warming protest during the UN Climate Change Conference in Montreal on Dec. 3, 2005.

Ablestock/Jupiterimages

PART IV

EARTH

The third planet from the Sun is Earth, the home of all known life. While it shares many characteristics with other planets, its physical properties and history allow it to support life in its near-surface environment. In fact, life itself has greatly altered the planet in ways that generally help maintain the conditions for life. Scientists have come to view Earth as a dynamic world with many interacting systems. Understanding these relationships will surely be important as human activities increasingly affect the planet's surface, oceans, and atmosphere.

Shape and Size

Many ancient cultures, even sophisticated ones such as the Egyptians, pictured Earth as flat, with the sky above a separate abode of heavenly bodies: the Sun, Moon, planets, and stars. By 2500 BC, some people correctly thought Earth to be roughly spherical. The Greek mathematician Pythagoras is widely credited with reaching this conclusion in the 6th century BC. Two centuries later, Aristotle gave specific reasons for thinking Earth is round: (1) matter is drawn to Earth's center and would compress it into a sphere, (2) traveling south reveals new stars rising above the southern horizon, and (3) Earth's shadow on the Moon at lunar eclipses is circular.

After Aristotle, many people did not know about his teachings. Belief in a flat Earth could persist, and there was at least some debate on the issue. However, knowledge of the spherical shape of Earth has been widespread among astronomers for most of the last 2,000 years, at least. Greek and Indian astronomers accepted the concept, and by the 9th century AD Islamic astronomers were using it. Christian Europe had widely accepted the idea by the 13th century.

. . . .

This article was contributed by Thomas J. Ehrensperger, physics, astronomy, and meteorology upper school instructor.

The field of measurement of Earth is called geodesy. One of the earliest known attempts to calculate the circumference of Earth was that of Eratosthenes, a librarian at the library of Alexandria in Egypt, in about 250 BC. He knew that at about noon on the day of the summer solstice (the day the noon Sun was highest in the sky), a vertical stick in Alexandria would cast a shadow that made an angle of about 7 degrees with the stick. He also knew that in Syene (now Aswan), Egypt, the Sun would pass directly overhead on that day, shining to the bottom of a deep well. By using an estimate of the north-south distance between the two cities, and assuming that the Sun was very far away, Eratosthenes was able to calculate Earth's circumference within a relatively small percentage of the value now known.

It is now known that the circumference at the equator is 24,902 miles (40,075 kilometers). The diameter at the equator is 7,926 miles (12,756 kilometers). Actually, Earth is not quite spherical but is an oblate spheroid—squashed in the north-south direction so that the pole-to-pole diameter is only 7,900 miles (12,714 kilometers). The distance from the equator to the North Pole along Earth's surface is 6,214 miles (10,002 kilometers). In fact, the meter was originally defined (by the French

Academy of Sciences in 1791) to be one ten-millionth of the distance from the equator to the North Pole. This explains why this distance is almost exactly 10 million meters (10,000 kilometers).

Motions

For centuries, Earth was simply "the world"—the only one known. Even most believers in a spherical Earth thought it to be a one-of-a-kind object in the center of a spherical universe. The Sun, Moon, planets, and stars were generally thought to be of a very different nature from Earth. In fact, in the 4th century BC Aristotle proposed that they were made of a heavenly fifth element ("quintessence"), in addition to his supposed earthly elements of earth, water, air, and fire. The Sun and Moon, plus Mercury, Venus, Mars, Jupiter, and Saturn (all easily visible to the naked eye), were seen to gradually change position relative to the stars. This earned them the name planets, which meant "wanderers."

Most thinkers, including Aristotle, believed that Earth was motionless in the center of the universe. This is called the geocentric (Earth-centered) theory, and it was developed in greater detail by Ptolemy of Alexandria in around AD 150. Almost all astronomers accepted the theory for the next 1,400 years. In this view, Earth was certainly not a planet, because it was obviously not a wandering light in the sky.

In the 16th century AD Nicholas Copernicus of Poland proposed that Earth rotates on an axis through the North and South poles once a day—actually once a "sidereal" day, which is measured using the distant stars as a reference frame instead of the Sun. Earth's sidereal day is 23 hours, 56 minutes, and 4 seconds, which is a few minutes shorter than its "solar" day. Copernicus also said that Earth orbits, or revolves around, the Sun once a sidereal year (which is 365.256 days). He believed that the Moon orbits Earth but that the other wanderers (the planets, not including the Sun) revolve around the Sun like Earth does. In this, Earth is a planet, because it, too, is a wanderer—around the Sun.

Copernicus' heliocentric (Sun-centered) theory was slow to be accepted. However, Johannes Kepler of Germany assumed this basic view in developing his three laws of planetary motion in the early 17th century. One of these laws states that a planet's orbit, or path around the Sun, is an ellipse, with the Sun not at the exact center but at one of two points called foci. Earth's orbit turns out to be more nearly a circle than the orbits of most of the other planets. Earth's distance from the Sun varies by only a small percentage, from about 91.4 million miles (147.1 million kilometers) in early January to some 94.5 million miles (152.1 million kilometers) in early July.

In 1687 Isaac Newton of England published his law of universal gravitation in his major work, the 'Principia'. This explained the planets' motions as being caused by the Sun's gravitational pull on the planets.

Facts About Earth

Average Distance from Sun. 92,956,000 miles (149,600,000 kilometers).

Diameter at Equator. 7,926 miles (12,756 kilometers).

Diameter at Poles. 7,900 miles (12,714 kilometers).

Surface Area. 196,938,000 square miles (510,066,000 square kilometers). *Oceans and Seas*—about 139,400,000 square miles (361,100,000 square kilometers). *Land*—about 57,500,000 square miles (149,000,000 square kilometers).

Highest Point. Mount Everest, 29,035 feet (8,850 meters) above sea level.

Lowest Point. Mariana Trench, 36,201 feet (11,034 meters) below sea level.

Mass. 5.976×10^{24} kilograms.

Average Density. 5.5 grams per cubic centimeter.

Average Surface Gravity. 32.2 feet per second squared (9.8 meters per second squared).

Average Orbital Velocity. 18.5 miles/second (29.8 kilometers/second).

Year on Earth.* 365.3 Earth days.

Rotation Period.† 23.9 Earth hours.

Day on Earth (Solar Day). 24.1 Earth hours.

Tilt (Inclination of Equator Relative to Orbital Plane). 23.5°.

Atmospheric Composition. 78% molecular nitrogen; 21% molecular oxygen; 0.93% argon; small amounts of carbon dioxide, neon, helium, methane, krypton, and other gases; variable amounts of water vapor.

Average Pressure at Sea Level. 1 atmosphere, or 14.7 pounds per square inch (101,320 newtons per square meter).

General Composition. Iron core, silicate rocks.

Average Surface Temperature. 59° F (15° C).

Number of Known Moons. 1.

*Sidereal revolution period, or the time it takes the planet to revolve around the Sun once relative to the fixed (distant) stars.

†Sidereal rotation period, or the time it takes the planet to rotate about its axis once relative to the fixed (distant) stars.

By this point, almost all scientists accepted the heliocentric theory.

Newton showed that any two objects attract each other with this gravitational force. Its strength is proportional to the mass of each object, and it becomes weaker with increasing distance between the objects. A body's "weight" is simply the gravitational force exerted on it by Earth, or whatever planet it happens to be near. Objects naturally tend to fly off through space in a straight line at a constant speed, but a gravitational pull can curve the path into a closed orbit. The Moon orbits Earth, and likewise Earth orbits the Sun.

Earth's spin axis is tilted about 23.5 degrees with respect to the axis of its revolution around the Sun. This allows the Northern Hemisphere to get the most sunlight—and therefore its summer—on about June 21, when the North Pole is tipped toward the Sun. The North Pole points almost the same direction all year, toward the North Star. On about December 21 Earth is on the opposite side of the Sun, though, so the South Pole is tipped toward the Sun and the Southern Hemisphere gets the most sunshine and its summer at that time. These dates are called the solstices. The equinoxes, when day and night are of nearly equal length worldwide, occur in between, on around March 21 and September 23. Thus the seasons are controlled much more by the tilt of Earth's axis than by the rather small variation in distance from the Sun.

The spin axis itself wobbles, much like that of a top, slowly over time. This is the main cause of the "precession of the equinoxes," a roughly 26,000-year cycle in which the spin axis traces out a circle, 47 degrees wide, in the sky. On this circle lie several "candidates" for North Star. Polaris is the present North Star, since currently Earth's axis points almost directly at it. Some 13,000 years from now, though, the North Star will be the bright star Vega. The Greek astronomer Hipparchus recognized this subtle phenomenon in the 2nd century BC.

Even more subtle motions exist. The circle traced out in the sky by the North Pole has little wobbles on it, because of a sort of rocking motion called nutation. Over a cycle of about 41,000 years, the tilt of the spin axis actually varies from about 22 to 25 degrees. In the first part of the 20th century the Serbian mathematician Milutin Milankovitch proposed that such variations in tilt, along with slight changes in the shape of Earth's orbit, have triggered climate change in the past. Scientists now widely accept this theory as explaining one of the many triggers of the onset and ending of ice ages.

***

Earth's Place in Space

As originally proposed, the heliocentric theory held that the Sun was stationary. In the last hundred years or so, the perspective on this has changed dramatically. It turns out that the stars are actually other suns (so the Sun is a star), all of which move through space. Moreover, many of them may have planets of their own. The first extrasolar planet was discovered in 1995. Within 15 years, more than 200 more such planets were discovered, mainly using indirect methods such as analyzing the slight wobble of the parent star in response to the planet's gravitational tug on it.

The nearest star system is about 270,000 times as far from Earth as the Sun is. Most of the stars visible to the naked eye are over a million times as far as the Sun, thus explaining why they appear so faint. Many would appear much brighter than the Sun if placed where the Sun is. All the stars one can see with the naked eye are nearby neighbors in a gigantic disklike structure called the Milky Way galaxy, which contains over a hundred billion suns. The Sun ("our" Sun) is about 25,000 light-years from the center of the Milky Way. A light-year is the distance light travels in a year, almost 6 trillion miles (9.5 trillion kilometers). The Sun and its planets orbit the Milky Way's center with a period (the time it takes to complete one orbit) of about 250 million years. The Milky Way, in turn, is only one of billions of galaxies in the observable universe. The galaxies are generally

NASA

Astronauts aboard the Apollo 17 spacecraft captured a stunning image of Earth as the spacecraft headed to the Moon in 1972. Vast oceans and seas surround the continent of Africa, the island of Madagascar, and, at top, the Arabian Peninsula. Also visible are clouds in the atmosphere and the south polar ice cap.

flying apart from each other and are scattered across billions of light-years of space.

All this can make Earth seem like a tiny, insignificant dot in the vastness of space. However, as our home, it is highly significant to us, and furthermore it has many very special properties and processes that are unique among the planets discovered so far. Earth is a special place indeed.

***

Internal Structure

To know what Earth is like inside, one might imagine drilling all the way to the center. Nothing anywhere near close to this has ever been done, though. The deepest well, on the Kola Peninsula in Russia, is about 7.62 miles (12.26 kilometers) deep, reaching only about $1/500$ the distance to Earth's center. The question remains, then, how can humans discover the structure of the planet?

While scientists have almost literally "barely scratched the surface" of Earth, a great deal has been learned about Earth's interior. One approach is to consider Earth's average density and the density and chemical composition of the near-surface layers, including rocks conveniently brought to the surface by volcanoes. Another method is to study the vibrations called seismic waves, which travel through the planet after being produced by natural sources such as earthquakes and by manmade events such as nuclear weapons tests.

Earth's mass is known from its gravitational effects to be 5.976×10^{24} kilograms, which if it could be weighed on another "Earth," would amount to about 6.587 billion trillion tons. Combined with knowledge of Earth's

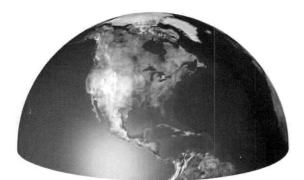

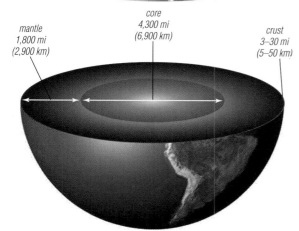

mantle
1,800 mi
(2,900 km)

core
4,300 mi
(6,900 km)

crust
3–30 mi
(5–50 km)

Earth's interior has three main layers: a metallic core; a thick, rocky mantle; and a thin, rocky crust. The measurements provided are broadly rounded averages.

are much like the rolling waves on the ocean surface. Love waves vibrate side-to-side, for example east-to-west for a northward traveling wave. Together, these waves produce most of the damage to buildings during earthquakes.

Other waves travel downward into Earth's interior. These waves are known as body waves, and they come in two basic types. *P*, or primary, waves have a "push-pull" motion parallel to the direction the wave is traveling. *S*, or secondary, waves make a side-to-side motion, perpendicular to the direction of wave motion. The *P* waves travel faster, hence the name primary, since they arrive first. Both types of waves generally travel faster in denser material. This not only affects arrival time but also allows the waves to bend (refract) and bounce (reflect) upon encountering changes in the density of the material. *S* waves have the additional property of not being able to travel through liquids.

By carefully analyzing data from thousands of earthquakes, using seismometers scattered across the globe, scientists have developed a rather detailed picture of Earth's interior. This technique is called seismic tomography. It is similar to the use of ultrasonic sound waves to produce images of unborn babies or computed tomography (CT) X-ray scans for diagnosing medical conditions.

A very notable result is that something inside the planet casts "shadows" for *S* waves on the side of Earth opposite a given earthquake. In other words, these

volume, this gives a density of 5.52 grams per cubic centimeter. This is denser than the typical 2 to 3 grams per cubic centimeter for rocks but less than the densities of iron and nickel, which are about 8 and 9 grams per cubic centimeter, respectively. These metals are commonly found in meteorites and may have been much of the raw material for Earth. Therefore, one might suppose Earth to be some mixture of rock and metal. Furthermore, iron and nickel, being denser than rock, would tend to sink toward the center.

When Earth is disturbed by an earthquake, several kinds of waves are produced, all of which can be recorded by instruments called seismometers. Some of these waves travel along Earth's surface. Rayleigh waves

Major Elements in Earth's Crust

Element	% by Weight
Oxygen	46.6
Silicon	27.7
Aluminum	8.1
Iron	5.0
Calcium	3.6
Sodium	2.8
Potassium	2.6
Magnesium	2.1

The planet's outer layers can be subdivided according to their physical properties. The crust and the uppermost part of the mantle form the rigid lithosphere. Below that is a partly molten zone, called the asthenosphere, which overlies another rigid zone.

Earth's Outer Layers

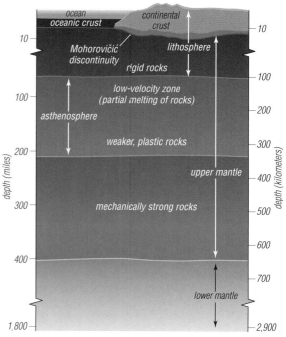

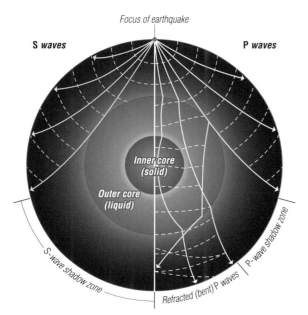

S waves

P waves

Focus of earthquake

Inner core (solid)

Outer core (liquid)

S-wave shadow zone

Refracted (bent) P waves

P-wave shadow zone

Scientists learned that Earth's core has separate liquid and solid layers by studying the waves produced by earthquakes. S waves do not travel through liquid, but P waves do. A simplified diagram shows the S waves on the left and the P waves on the right (but waves of both types would actually radiate in all directions).

waves are absent on the opposite side. Since *S* waves cannot travel through liquid, this indicates the existence of a large liquid layer deep inside Earth. *P* waves can travel through it, and the arrival times and refractions of these waves show that there is a solid core inside this liquid layer.

Seismic tomography also readily yields details of the outer layers of the planet. The outermost part, the crust, has rather low density rock in which waves travel somewhat slowly. The waves partially reflect upon reaching a boundary, called the Moho. This is short for the Mohorovičić discontinuity, named after Andrija Mohorovičić, the Croatian seismologist who discovered it in 1909. The depth at which this discontinuity occurs ranges from as little as 3 miles (5 kilometers) beneath some parts of the ocean bottom to up to about 45 miles (75 kilometers) beneath some continental surfaces.

The picture then is as follows. The outermost layer, the crust, consists of solid rock. The crust of the continents is thicker and less dense than that of the ocean bottom. The Moho marks the boundary between the crust and the denser rock of the layer beneath it, the mantle, which contains over half the planet's mass. The crust and outermost mantle together are called the lithosphere, from the Greek word *lithos*, meaning "rock."

Temperatures and pressures rise with increasing depth. At roughly 50 miles (80 kilometers) below the surface, the rock of the mantle is at about 2,500° F (1,370° C) and becomes partly molten. This is the beginning of the part of the mantle known as the asthenosphere. Below about 150 to 200 miles (250 to 350 kilometers), the mantle is under so much pressure that it becomes more rigid again, though it is still plastic enough to allow very

gradual motions. The mantle extends down to about 1,800 miles (2,900 kilometers) beneath the surface. The temperature at the bottom of the mantle is believed to be roughly 6,700° F (3,700° C).

Beneath the mantle, the material becomes much denser (as indicated by faster *P* waves) and liquefies (as evidenced by the lack of *S* waves). Scientists believe that this layer, called the outer core, consists of up to 90 percent molten iron and nickel (mostly iron), with some other elements such as sulfur mixed in. It makes up about 30 percent of Earth's mass. Finally, below about 3,200 miles (5,100 kilometers) is the inner core, which extends to the very center, about 3,960 miles (6,370 kilometers) down. It contains about 2 percent of Earth's mass. Despite extremely high temperatures, estimated to be between 8,000 and 12,000° F (about 4,400 and 6,600° C), the pressure is so high that the iron and nickel become solid.

Rocks and Minerals

Earth is largely a ball of rock. Rocks form on and beneath Earth's surface under a wide range of physical and chemical conditions. All rocks are made up of minerals. The minerals in some rocks are single chemical elements such as gold or copper, but the minerals in most rocks are compounds—combinations of elements with a definite chemical composition and a precisely patterned structure. Most minerals form crystals. Each crystal has a characteristic shape and structure that is determined by the type and arrangement of its atoms.

The most common atoms present in Earth's rocks are oxygen and silicon, which combine to make silicates such as quartz (SiO_2). Silicates make up about 95 percent of the planet's crust and upper mantle. Other common elements, present in lesser amounts, are aluminum, iron, calcium, sodium, potassium, and magnesium.

IGNEOUS ROCK

Igneous rock is the primary rock of Earth's crust in that most other kinds of rock found on Earth form from it. Igneous rock is rock that solidifies from a molten state. The molten rock material under Earth's surface is called magma. Magma that is forced out onto Earth's surface, onto either the ocean bottom or the land, as in volcanic action, is called lava.

Magma deep beneath the surface may cool slowly. When this happens, the minerals grow slowly and may reach a relatively large size. This slow-cooling process produces coarse-grained rocks such as granite or gabbro. The type of rock produced depends on the chemicals in the magma. Each type can be distinguished by its characteristic mineral composition.

Magma closer to the surface cools more quickly, giving the minerals little chance to grow. As a result, fine-grained rocks similar in composition to the coarse-grained ones are produced. The fine-grained rhyolite is the equivalent of the coarse-grained granite, and the fine-grained basalt is the equivalent of gabbro.

Columns of basalt, an igneous rock, make up the formation known as the Devils Postpile, part of a national monument in east-central California, U.S. It formed within the last 100,000 years, when a lava flow filled a valley floor and then very slowly cooled and cracked into many-sided columns. Glaciers later eroded most of the hardened lava, revealing the sides of the remaining columns.

Some materials ejected from volcanoes cool so quickly that they solidify before they strike the ground. Lava cools so rapidly that often gas bubbles are trapped within it. When such lava hardens, it is light and porous. Pumice is formed in this way. The natural glass obsidian is also formed from lava.

METAMORPHIC ROCK

Metamorphic rock results when heat and pressure change the original composition and structure of rock. The original rock may be of any type—igneous, sedimentary, or other metamorphic rock. Deep in Earth's crust the temperature is much higher than it is near the surface, and the hot rock is subjected to pressure from the weight of the crust above and from lateral movements of the crust. Sometimes liquids and gases also act on the rock to change it.

Limestone, a sedimentary rock, changes to marble as a result of such forces. Under stress, the mineral grains in the sedimentary rock shale grow in new directions to form slate, a metamorphic rock. Continued stress changes the slate to phyllite and then to schist, a rock that is very different in appearance, composition, and structure from the original shale. Quartzite, one of the hardest and most compact rocks, is the metamorphic form of the relatively soft, grainy sandstone, a sedimentary rock.

SEDIMENTARY ROCK

Sedimentary rocks form at or near Earth's surface, often through the weathering action of wind and running water. In fact, rocks of this type cover much of the surface, but they are often hidden by a thin layer of soil. For convenience, sedimentary rocks are divided into two major groups: clastic rocks and crystalline rocks. Clastic rocks are composed of sediment—particles or fragments of rock—of varying sizes that have been compacted or cemented together. Crystalline rocks are composed of minerals that have been precipitated out of solutions.

Particles of rock, eroded from exposed areas such as mountains, are transported by streams and rivers to the sea. There they slowly settle as fine silts or clays. Coarser particles, such as sands, are deposited nearer the shore, and the largest particles, such as pebbles and cobbles, settle at the shoreline. As these materials slowly accumulate over long periods, water is squeezed out from between the particles. Cementing agents carried in solution in the water—for example, calcium carbonate, silica, and iron oxide—may bind the particles together.

The pebbles close to shore are cemented together into a conglomerate. A little farther out shales form. In the

Blocks of marble, a metamorphic rock, are cut from a quarry in Carrara, Italy. Heat, pressure, and liquids cause limestone to metamorphose, or change, into marble.

Jeremy Woodhouse/Getty Images

The erosion of sandstone created spectacular formations in Arizona. A sedimentary rock, sandstone consists of grains of sand that have been cemented or compressed into rock.

open oceans limestones form from calcium carbonate and the shells of dead sea animals.

Crystalline rocks can form in shallow inland seas where access to open water has been restricted or cut off. In such places the seas may evaporate slowly, leaving behind compounds that form sedimentary rocks such as gypsum and rock salt.

Mineral resources such as coal, petroleum, and natural gas occur in sedimentary rocks. In addition, geologists can reconstruct the ancient geography and environment of a region by studying the distribution of its sedimentary rocks, which lie in layers, or strata. Correlating the sequences of rock layers in different areas enables them to trace a particular geologic event to a particular period. Fossils—the remains, imprints, or traces of organisms that once lived on Earth—are found almost exclusively in sedimentary rocks. They record the history of life on Earth, though only certain parts of a small percentage of ancient life, most often the solid skeleton or shell of animals with such parts or the woody structures of certain plants, are preserved as fossils. In unusual circumstances, the soft tissues of living things have been preserved.

Spheres and Cycles

EARTH'S SPHERES

One approach to understanding Earth, especially the outer parts, is to divide it into interacting spheres. One such scheme considers these to be the atmosphere, the hydrosphere, the lithosphere, and the biosphere.

Atmosphere

The atmosphere is the envelope of gases surrounding the planet. It clings to Earth because, having mass, it is gravitationally attracted to the mass of the rest of the planet. Gas molecules move quite rapidly at earthly temperatures, and a few of them actually escape into space. Fortunately, Earth's atmosphere is massive

enough so that this leakage has not caused a significant loss of its gases over the billions of years scientists believe it has existed. Smaller worlds, such as the Moon and Mars, have not been so successful at holding onto any air they might have ever had. The Moon has virtually no atmosphere, and that of Mars is much thinner (less dense) than Earth's.

The atmosphere's mass is just over 5×10^{18} kilograms (5 million gigatons, with a gigaton equaling a billion metric tons), which weighs more than 11×10^{18} pounds. This may sound impressive, but it is less than one millionth the mass of the whole planet. Traces of the atmosphere can be found 100 miles (160 kilometers) above the surface, but most of it lies within 3.5 miles (5.6 kilometers) of the ground. On the scale of a typical globe with a 12-inch (30-centimeter) diameter, this is little more than the thickness of a sheet of paper.

About 78 percent by volume of dry air consists of nitrogen (chemical formula N_2). Oxygen (O_2) makes up 21 percent. Most of the rest is argon (Ar), but small amounts of other gases, such as carbon dioxide (CO_2), methane (CH_4), and hydrogen (H_2), are present as well. Notice that these figures are for dry air; water vapor (H_2O) makes up varying amounts, usually between 0.1 and 4 percent.

The composition of the air is very nearly uniform across the globe and even at different heights. However, a small (a few parts per million) concentration of ozone (O_3) exists in the layer called the stratosphere, mostly more than about 6 miles (10 kilometers) above the ground. This "ozone layer" is vital to life on Earth because it absorbs most of the harmful ultraviolet rays reaching Earth from the Sun. This concentration of ozone has been reduced in recent decades, at least in part because of reactions with man-made chemical compounds called chlorofluorocarbons (CFCs), used in commerce and industry. Since 1992, production of these gases has been greatly restricted, so it is hoped that little further damage to the ozone layer will occur.

Though composition changes only slightly with height, the temperature and pressure of the air vary greatly. In the lower part of the atmosphere, called the troposphere, temperature generally drops with increasing height. At a height of about 7 miles (11 kilometers), but somewhat higher over the tropics and lower over the poles, the temperature has reached approximately –70° F (–57° C). This point, the "top" of the troposphere, is called the tropopause. Almost all of Earth's "weather" (meaning precipitation, especially) occurs in the troposphere.

Above that, however, temperatures stay about the same and then actually begin to rise with height. This zone is called the stratosphere. Most of its surprising warmth—up to the freezing point of water or slightly higher—results from the interception of ultraviolet solar energy by ozone. Because of this temperature structure, the air in the stratosphere is very stable, meaning very little vertical mixing can occur. For this reason, volcanic dust or man-made gases that reach the stratosphere can remain stuck there for years. This also makes the stratosphere very dry, since very little water vapor is able to mix up into it from below.

The stratopause, the top of the stratosphere, is about 30 miles (50 kilometers) up. Above this is the mesosphere, a zone in which temperatures fall once again. After bottoming out at the mesopause, at roughly 50 miles (80 kilometers) up, temperatures become very high in the thermosphere, reaching over 2,000° F (1,100° C). This is misleading, however, because by this point the air is so thin that there is almost nothing there to feel. It simply means that the relatively few particles (mostly ions, or electrically charged atoms) present are moving quite fast. Beyond the thermosphere, one can define another region, the exosphere. This is an extremely rarified gas of mainly hydrogen and helium, which merges with the near vacuum of interplanetary space.

The atmosphere's pressure drops considerably with height, for a very simple reason. The pressure exerted by the air at any height is due to the weight of all the air above it. At great altitudes, there is little air above, so the pressure, and in turn density, becomes quite low. Pressure at sea level averages about 14.7 pounds per square inch (101,320 newtons per square meter), or one "atmosphere" (a unit of pressure). Roughly speaking, pressure is cut in half with every additional 3.5 miles (5.6 kilometers) above the ground. At an altitude of 7 miles, air pressure is about one fourth that at sea level.

The atmosphere is constantly in motion, mainly because of pressure differences, which are in turn caused by differences in heating by the Sun. This solar energy is redistributed by winds, infrared radiation, and water vapor, resulting in the changing state of the atmosphere called the weather.

The circulation pattern of the atmosphere changes from day to day and from season to season. However, some definite overall patterns can be discerned. Air near the equator is generally heated the most, which makes it less dense and causes the atmosphere in that region to expand upward. This often produces clouds and rain, making the tropics relatively wet. Air at high altitudes then flows poleward. Earth's rotation comes into play, though, via the Coriolis effect, which deflects the air to

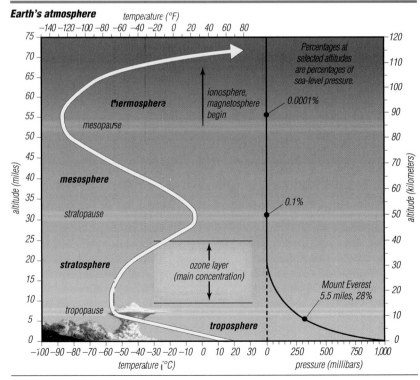

The temperature and pressure of the air vary with height. Temperatures, indicated by the yellow line, drop with altitude in some zones but rise in others. Pressures, indicated by the black line at right, decrease greatly with height.

the right of the winds' direction of motion in the Northern Hemisphere and to the left in the Southern Hemisphere. This results in high altitude winds mainly from west to east in the middle latitudes.

Some of the poleward-flowing air sinks back toward the surface at about 25 or 30 degrees of latitude from the equator in both hemispheres. This air then flows back toward the equator near the surface but is deflected by the Coriolis effect, becoming the trade winds. The trade winds blow from the northeast in the Northern Hemisphere and from the southeast in the Southern Hemisphere. Where the air is sinking, relatively high surface pressures are produced. The sinking air is compressed and warmed, so that clouds tend to evaporate and there is little rain. Most of the world's deserts are located in these subtropical regions.

Winds in the middle latitudes tend to be from the west on average. Closer to the poles winds tend to flow from the northeast in the Northern Hemisphere and the southeast in the Southern Hemisphere, much like the trade winds. A fairly distinct boundary between the relatively warm mid-latitude westerly (blowing from west to east) winds and the cold polar easterly winds can often be found. It is along this "polar front" that low-pressure systems called cyclones frequently form. An overall effect of these storms is to send colder air toward low latitudes and warmer air toward the poles.

In addition to mid-latitude cyclones, very strong tropical cyclones such as hurricanes and typhoons (two names for the same type of storm, applied to different regions) form in summer or fall. These storms eventually carry heat to high latitudes. In fact, the weather generally has the effect of making the equator cooler than it would otherwise be, and the poles warmer than they would be.

Hydrosphere

The hydrosphere includes all the liquid water on or just below the surface of the planet, the vast majority of which is in the oceans. Some of Earth's water is frozen, mainly in Antarctica and Greenland. This ice and snow is called the cryosphere and is often included with the hydrosphere (as is done in this article). About 71 percent of Earth's surface is covered by oceans, with only a few percent covered by smaller bodies of water or by ice. The water vapor in the atmosphere can also be considered part of the hydrosphere (as is done here).

The total mass of the hydrosphere is about 1.4×10^{21} kilograms (1.4 billion gigatons), which weighs about 3.1×10^{21} pounds. The mass of the hydrosphere is about 270 times the mass of the atmosphere. However, it is still less than $1/4,000$ of Earth's total mass. The oceans make up almost 98 percent of the hydrosphere's mass. By some estimates, ice caps and glaciers constitute almost 1.7 percent, with underground reservoirs accounting for about 0.37 percent. Freshwater in lakes and streams is only a tenth as abundant as groundwater, making up some 0.036 percent of the total. About 0.001 percent of Earth's water can be found in the atmosphere as water vapor or cloud droplets and ice crystals. If all the water vapor in the atmosphere at a given time were condensed

into liquid and spread over Earth's entire surface, it would form a layer about an inch (2.5 centimeters) thick.

The average depth of the oceans is about 12,400 feet, or 2.3 miles (3.8 kilometers). Even the deepest part, the Mariana Trench in the western North Pacific—6.86 miles (11.03 kilometers) deep—extends only about $1/600$ of the way to Earth's center. So, like the atmosphere, the hydrosphere forms a relatively thin skin on the planet's surface.

A notable feature of the oceans is that they contain a great deal of dissolved salts, mainly sodium chloride (ordinary table salt). On average, there are about 3.5 kilograms of salt for every 100 kilograms of seawater. If the oceans were to completely evaporate, the remaining compacted salt would form deposits averaging at least 200 feet (60 meters) thick.

Since water is much denser than air, pressure changes in the vertical are much more dramatic in water than in air. Pressure in water increases by the equivalent of one atmosphere, or 14.7 pounds per square inch, for every 33 feet (10 meters) of depth. The ocean bottom has several hundred atmospheres of pressure, or several hundred times the pressure at sea level on land.

Very little light penetrates more than about 100 feet (30 meters) into the water, so the depths of the ocean are pitch black. Temperatures become cold near the bottom, even in tropical seas, dropping as low as about 36° F (2° C). This is largely due to cold, dense salty water from the polar regions settling near the bottom of the world's oceans.

Like the atmosphere, the oceans have large scale motions, or currents, which play an important role in redistributing the heat Earth receives from the Sun. Huge ocean currents, driven mainly by winds, circulate basically clockwise in the Northern Hemisphere and counterclockwise in the Southern Hemisphere. These currents bring cold water toward the equator on the west coasts of continents and warm water toward the poles on east coasts. In North America the cold California Current makes places such as San Francisco surprisingly cool, most notably in summer. The warm Gulf Stream flowing north near the eastern coast of the continent keeps eastern beaches warmer and also strengthens hurricanes approaching the coast.

Evaporation of water from the oceans supplies almost all the moisture for precipitation. Rain falling on the continents dissolves minerals, such as salt, which flow into and become concentrated in the oceans. On land much of the water flows visibly at the surface as rivers, but a great deal also goes underground, saturating deep layers of rock in reservoirs called aquifers. Many desert regions have aquifers deep underground holding water from rain that fell thousands of years ago. Wells that tap into these aquifers have been used for thousands of years.

Lithosphere

"Lithos" means "rock," and the lithosphere consists of the outer, rocky parts of the planet. The name generally refers to Earth's crust and some of the upper mantle. The lithosphere has been found to make gradual movements,

Numerous kinds of green plants grow in profusion in a rainforest in Dominica. The existence of nearly the entire biosphere—including people and all other animals—depends on the photosynthesis carried out by the world's green plants and by certain algae and bacteria.
Randolph Femmer/NBII Image Gallery

which sometimes bring fresh material to the surface and also bury older parts of the surface. Over vast amounts of time, much of the material is therefore recycled. During this process, it affects, and is affected by, the atmosphere, hydrosphere, and biosphere.

The lithosphere is broken into several "plates" that essentially float on the denser material underneath and drift up against, alongside, over, or underneath other plates. This process, called plate tectonics, is discussed in greater detail later, in the section "Plate Tectonics."

Biosphere

The biosphere is the "zone of life," consisting of all of Earth's living things and their environments. It is not really a separate sphere from the others but includes parts of all three. Life obviously occupies the oceans and the surfaces of the continents, but it also exists in the atmosphere. Birds and insects are obvious examples, but smaller organisms such as bacteria that become airborne can be carried miles above the surface. Additionally, bacteria have been found in rock 1.7 miles (2.8 kilometers) underground.

The biosphere plays a vital role in the chemistry and geologic processes of the planet. Earth, especially the outer layers, is a very different world than it would be with no life. The biosphere is thought to have almost completely buried an ancient atmosphere of mainly carbon dioxide, replacing some of it with oxygen. It has also produced vast deposits of coal and oil and has even regulated the planet's temperature.

Most of the biosphere is based on the process of photosynthesis, by which plants and some microorganisms use sunlight to convert water, carbon dioxide (from the atmosphere), and minerals into oxygen (which then enters the atmosphere) and simple and complex sugars. Animals eat many of these plants and microorganisms, thus consuming much of their stored energy. Energy is concentrated further into a small number of carnivores, who eat other animals. Scavengers eat dead plants and animals. After all of the

above creatures die, they are gradually buried in the ground or sink to the seafloor. In this way, they are eventually incorporated into Earth's lithosphere, with some gases, such as methane, being released into the atmosphere or hydrosphere. (These phenomena are discussed in more detail below in several sections, including "Carbon Cycle" and "Carboniferous Period.")

In recent decades, scientists have found ecosystems (groups of interdependent organisms and their environment) independent of sunlight. An example is the communities of creatures thriving around hydrothermal vents in the deep ocean. These vents spew hot water, laden with sulfur dioxide gas, from the ocean floor. Bacteria called chemoautotrophs make their food (sugars, as in photosynthesis) by using these hot gases along with carbon dioxide. Other creatures, such as long, red tube worms, store the bacteria in their bodies and live off their energy. Bacteria that have been found in deep underground rocks may be using hydrogen to make their food. The hydrogen may come from water broken apart by the nuclear radiation from radioactive elements, such as uranium, trapped in the rock.

Recently, many biologists have decided that some microorganisms inhabiting extreme environments (such as those with very hot or salty conditions) are not true bacteria. A new kingdom of such creatures, called Archaea, has been proposed, with the creatures called the archaeans. Finding organisms in such surprising environments has led some scientists to speculate that life could exist beneath the surface of Mars or in the deep, ice-covered oceans of Jupiter's moon Europa. (*See also* Ecology; Biogeography.)

EARTH'S CYCLES

Many of Earth's materials are recycled in various ways through Earth's spheres. Life plays an essential role in many of these cycles, in effect regulating the environment, often in a way that is beneficial for life. Two of the most important cycles are the water cycle and the carbon cycle.

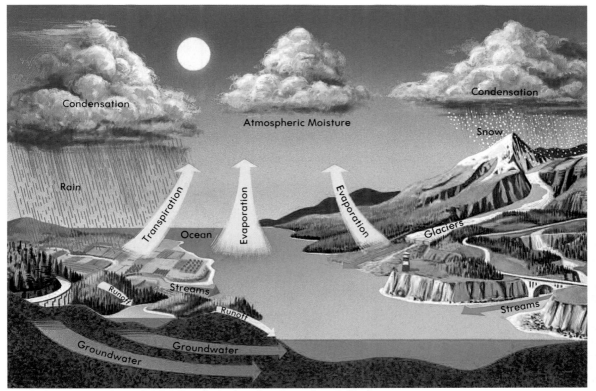

Earth's water is constantly recycled. It falls on the land as rain and snow, is carried by rivers or groundwater to the oceans, rises as water vapor, and travels inland again. This process is called the hydrologic cycle.

Water Cycle

The water, or hydrologic, cycle can be thought to begin—though cycles do not necessarily have a "beginning"—when the Sun's heat evaporates water from the oceans. This water enters the atmosphere as vapor. About 100,000 cubic miles (over 400,000 cubic kilometers) of seawater evaporate each year. If this water were not returned to the oceans and the water continued to evaporate at the same rate, the sea level would drop by almost 4 feet (about 1.2 meters) per year and the oceans would be gone within 3,500 years.

Of course, this water is eventually returned. Precipitation falling directly on the oceans amounts to just over 90 percent of the water evaporated from them. The remainder flows back into the ocean from land, carried mainly in rivers. Precipitation also falls on land—about the same amount per square mile as the ocean receives—totaling about 26,000 cubic miles (107,000 cubic kilometers). Plants draw water from the soil and, in a process called transpiration, release water vapor into the air through tiny pores in their leaves. About 17,000 cubic miles (70,000 cubic kilometers) of water enters the atmosphere over land in this way and from evaporation off the land. This leaves about 9,000 cubic miles (37,000 cubic kilometers) traveling from land to water via rivers each year.

Much of the water that falls on land does not immediately enter streams and rivers. Instead, it filters through porous soil and rock into the ground. At varying depths under the surface, it often saturates the porous rock, forming the "water table." Such water may remain underground for hundreds of years, but most of it eventually finds its way into streams and enters the oceans after all.

As a material—in this case water—moves among various reservoirs, any given molecule will spend a characteristic time, called the residence time, in each reservoir. Typically, a water molecule will remain in the atmosphere a bit over a week before falling to the ground as precipitation (or possibly forming dew or frost). Shallow soil moisture or seasonal snow cover may last months. Glaciers and lakes hold water for decades. Residence time in the ocean is a few thousand years.

Carbon Cycle

Carbon makes up only about 0.03 percent of Earth's crust by weight. Its principal form in the atmosphere—carbon dioxide—makes up only about 0.04 percent of the atmosphere. However, this element is the basis of all known life and also plays a vital role in maintaining habitable conditions on Earth. How it is cycled through the environment is therefore of great interest.

The vast majority—over 99.9 percent—of Earth's near-surface carbon (carbon in the lithosphere and above) is stored in sedimentary rock. Estimates vary, but this reservoir probably holds roughly 80 million gigatons of carbon. This carbon was deposited over billions of years, partly by the weathering of silicate rocks to form carbonate rocks, which contain carbon compounds. It also accumulated from the remains of marine organisms that had used carbon to build calcium carbonate shells or body parts.

The next most abundant storage site is the deep ocean, which holds about 38,000 gigatons of carbon. Fossil fuels—coal, oil, and natural gas—make up an estimated 5,000 gigatons. The rest of the carbon is divided roughly equally among living plants (about 600 gigatons), organic debris in soil (about 1,600 gigatons), the near-surface ocean (about 1,000 gigatons), and the atmosphere (nearly 800 gigatons and increasing).

The carbon cycle is quite complex, partly because life plays many roles in it, but also because of the huge range of residence times involved. The largest reservoir, sedimentary rock, also has the longest residence time. Carbon has been steadily buried in rock throughout Earth's history and is released a little at a time, primarily through volcanic activity. A carbon atom might spend hundreds of millions of years locked away in rock before being released in the gases of a volcano. Probably most carbon atoms ever trapped in rock have never been released and may never be. Nevertheless, this geologic carbon cycle is of great importance. Over long periods the burial and release of carbon dioxide (and also methane) largely control Earth's surface temperature (*see* Greenhouse Effect). Higher amounts of these gases in the distant past likely helped warm the planet when the Sun was less bright in its youth.

The deep ocean and the near-surface ocean were listed separately above because the two do not mix very quickly. Thousands of years may be needed for changes near the surface to work their way down to the bottom. The oceans in general have a great capacity to store carbon. However, the short-term (such as decades) storage is mainly in the upper layers, which have limited capacity.

Fossil fuels are a complicated case because they took millions of years to be formed and buried but are being released by humans rather quickly. From the beginning of the Industrial Revolution in the mid-18th century to the start of the 21st century, roughly 300 gigatons of carbon were released by humans burning these fuels—over half of that after 1970. In the early 21st century such use was releasing over 6 gigatons of carbon per year, a rate thousands of times that at which it was originally buried.

Carbon travels rather quickly—generally a matter of months, years, or decades—among the remaining reservoirs. Plants take about 120 gigatons of carbon per year from the atmosphere during photosynthesis, which releases oxygen. However, they return about half of that carbon by respiration, which uses oxygen, largely at night. Also, some of the carbon in plants is eaten by herbivores and released during the herbivores' respiration, or during the respiration of carnivores that eat the herbivores. Much of the dead plant and animal matter in the soil is consumed by bacteria and fungi, which release carbon dioxide (or methane, if deprived of oxygen).

Just over 90 gigatons of carbon enter the ocean each year, largely by being dissolved from the air. Plankton in the ocean perform photosynthesis on a scale similar to that of land plants. Some of the carbon that enters the ocean is buried in ocean sediments, but much is released, some through the respiration of creatures that eat the plankton. All but perhaps two gigatons is released back into the atmosphere per year.

While human-induced release of carbon accounts for only a few percentage of the total entering the atmosphere, it is important to understand that this disrupts an otherwise fairly delicate balance. Much, perhaps half, of it ends up as excess carbon dioxide in the atmosphere. Besides burning fossil fuels, humans alter the balance in other ways. Deforestation, some farming practices, and the manufacture of cement also contribute to increasing the carbon content of the atmosphere. (*See also* Global Warming; Deforestation.)

Magnetic Field

Over 1,000 years ago, the Chinese discovered a curious property of certain metallic rocks. If floated on a piece of wood in water, such rocks (or similarly magnetized iron needles) would rotate into a specific orientation relative to north and south. These rocks also had the ability to attract bits of iron. This was the discovery of magnetism (and the invention of the compass) and also that Earth itself is a giant magnet.

This invisible effect is now described as due to a magnetic field, a region of influence around any magnet. Earth has north and south magnetic poles that are near, but not quite on, the actual geographic North and South poles. The planet's magnetic field can be illustrated by lines, called magnetic field lines, that connect the magnetic poles and curve out and around the edges of the field, forming closed loops.

Earth's magnetic field has far more important effects than just deflecting compass needles. It shields Earth by steering and trapping electrically charged particles, such as protons and electrons, ejected by the Sun. This stream of particles is called the solar wind. The particles in it travel about 1 million miles (1.6 million kilometers) per hour, reaching Earth in a few days. Once trapped, the particles travel in a corkscrew pattern and effectively bounce back and forth between the poles. Some of the particles are guided into Earth's upper atmosphere, where they strike atoms and cause them to glow. This colorful display is called an aurora, also known as the northern or southern lights.

The region of space in which Earth's magnetic field dominates the environment and traps particles from the solar wind is called the magnetosphere. Many of the charged particles remain trapped there. The greatest concentrations of these particles are in two regions called the Van Allen belts, located mainly between 5,000 and

Surtsey Island, off the coast of the Vestmann Islands in the North Atlantic Ocean, was born rather suddenly from volcanic action. The island rose from the sea on Nov. 14, 1963, with explosive eruptions of ash and steam. Thin streams of basaltic lava created towering steam clouds. By the end of 1964, the island was 568 feet high and covered an area of a mile square.

20,000 miles (8,000 and 32,000 kilometers) above the ground. The radiation (consisting of these high-energy charged particles) in the belts would be harmful to humans over time. In the direction away from the Sun, Earth's magnetic field lines are effectively blown far downwind, reaching over a million miles into space.

A beneficial effect of the magnetic field is that it prevents many of the solar wind particles from striking the atmosphere. Without the field, the solar wind might gradually erode away much of the planet's atmosphere. Mars, which is almost devoid of a magnetic field, has an atmosphere only about one hundredth as dense as Earth's. Mars's weaker gravity would probably have left it with less of an atmosphere anyway, but its exposure to the solar wind very likely helped remove some of its air.

Scientists believe that Earth's magnetic field is generated by huge currents of molten metal flowing in the liquid outer core. Interestingly, the field's orientation occasionally—very roughly once every million years—reverses, so that the north and south magnetic poles more or less switch. This process is not fully understood, but it is of critical importance to geologists, who use correlations between the magnetism of rocks to document and date the drifting of the continents.

The Changing Face of Earth

PLATE TECTONICS

A number of distinctive features on Earth beg for an explanation. Earthquakes and volcanoes are concentrated in certain regions of the world, especially the Ring of Fire—basically the edges of the continents facing the Pacific Ocean. The Hawaiian Islands form a long chain of mostly extinct volcanoes, with the southeastern tip of the chain (the big island of Hawaii) still volcanically active. An undersea ridge of mountains running north-south splits the Atlantic Ocean roughly in half, and some parts of the ridge, such as Iceland, rise above the surface. Fresh magma (molten rock) has been seen oozing from the ocean floor in the middle of this range. The east coast of South America and the west coast of Africa seem like they would fit together like pieces of a jigsaw puzzle and have similar rocks and fossils of about the same age. It would also be desirable to account for the existence of huge mountain ranges such as the Himalayas and the Andes.

For many years, most of these facts were known, but no one had a good explanation for them. In 1912 the German meteorologist Alfred Wegener proposed that in fact the continents had once been joined as a gigantic landmass, which he called Pangea, meaning "all land." According to this theory, called continental drift, this supercontinent long ago broke into pieces—the present continents—which have since drifted to their current positions. Wegener was not the first to suggest that the continents might move, but he developed the theory in greater detail than before.

The idea seemed ridiculous to many geologists. How could a continent, made of rock, just get up and move? Wegener had no convincing explanation for the motion, but later researchers realized that the partly molten asthenosphere (part of the upper mantle, as described earlier) could allow motion of rock basically floating on top of it. Giant convection cells (churning motions) in Earth's hot interior might be able to drive continents or the seafloor apart where the material surfaces, such as at the Mid-Atlantic Ridge. These churning motions should really be expected. Many bodies, such as a pan of boiling water, naturally exhibit them as an "effort" to rid themselves of heat. Some of the heat in Earth's interior is left over from the planet's formation, and some is released from the outer core as the iron and nickel slowly solidifies. Most of it, though, is believed to result from the decay of long-lived radioactive elements such as uranium.

As Wegener's ideas were developed more fully by others, the moving pieces of lithosphere became known as plates. Carried by convection currents from below, the plates could rub alongside each other, causing earthquakes as they grabbed and slipped. Plates striking each other head on would cause huge wrinkles in Earth's crust—mountain ranges. In some cases, a plate carrying seafloor crust, which consists of denser rock than that of continents, could be forced underneath a plate carrying continental crust—a process called subduction. Some of the subducted plate would then melt and perhaps force its way up through the other plate's edge as volcanoes. Most volcanoes and earthquakes, then, occur near the borders of plates, where they interact. The Ring of Fire, it turns out, lies along part of the edges of the Pacific Plate.

By the 1960s most geologists had accepted this idea, now known as plate tectonics. It is now thought that the crust of the ocean bottom is gradually formed as magma rising up in convection currents reaches the surface (the ocean bottom) and cools to form relatively new, dense rock. This creates undersea mountain chains called oceanic ridges, such as the Mid-Atlantic Ridge, which extend in an interconnected network through every ocean basin. The rock of the ocean bottom is mainly of a type called basalt, while the lighter rock of the continents is mostly granite. Continental crust is also thicker than oceanic crust, and it floats higher on the asthenosphere, so that most continental land has a higher elevation than the ocean surface. Radioactive dating of continental rocks has shown some to be about 4 billion years old. Rocks of the ocean crust are usually dated to less than 200 million years, and some are brand new, such as the freshly cooled magma in the Mid-Atlantic Ridge.

CONTINENTAL DRIFT

The configuration of Earth's continents has changed dramatically over hundreds of millions of years and is still changing today. The plates typically move about 2 to 4 inches (5 to 10 centimeters) per year, which is about 30 to 60 miles (50 to 100 kilometers) every million years.

Scientists believe that until about 240 million to 200 million years ago all the major landmasses were joined together in a supercontinent called Pangea. At that time, Pangea began to break apart because of gigantic convection currents rising up under it from the mantle. At first it fractured into a northern continent called Laurasia and a southern one called Gondwana, which were separated by an equatorial sea called Tethys.

Later, Gondwana broke apart to form Africa, South America, Antarctica, Australia, and India. Laurasia was

At the San Andreas Fault in California, the North American and Pacific plates slide past each other along a giant fracture in Earth's crust. Their movement sometimes causes earthquakes.

torn apart to form North America and Eurasia (Europe and Asia considered as a single landmass). Open water—the young Atlantic Ocean—separated South America from Africa and North America from Eurasia. Magma rising from the interior surfaced along the Mid-Atlantic Ridge and formed new seafloor, steadily widening the Atlantic and separating the continents.

Meanwhile, Australia and Antarctica drifted farther apart. India traveled north and began to collide with Asia about 40 million years ago, wrinkling the crust to form the world's highest mountain system, the Himalayas. The Tethys Sea narrowed as Africa and Eurasia approached and made contact. The Mediterranean Sea was left as a remnant. Only about 3 million years ago, North America and South America met for the first time since being part of Pangea, as the Isthmus of Panama formed a bridge between them.

As North and South America drifted westward, the Pacific Plate was subducted underneath their western coasts. As a result, the continents crumpled, helping raise the Rocky and Andes mountains. Earthquakes and volcanoes are common near these coasts.

The Pacific Plate itself drifted slowly northwestward. A plume of hot material rising from deep within the mantle burned through the oceanic crust in the North Pacific, forming a volcanic island. As the plate moved, it carried the new island to the northwest and brought a

Dan Morrill—EB, Inc.

Materials eroded from the Calico Mountains formed an alluvial fan in California's Mojave Desert.

different section of the crust above the hot plume. The plume broke through the crust again to form another island, and the process repeated, forming the Hawaiian Island chain.

There is much evidence that Pangea itself formed from previous versions of the current continents colliding. As this occurred, smaller pieces of Earth's crust, called terranes, collided with and attached to the major continents. Pangea was probably fully formed by about 250 million years ago. As it formed, what would eventually become North America collided with what would later become Africa. This raised the Appalachians. These mountains are now so old (about 300 million years) that the forces of rain and wind have smoothed them and worn them down to about half their former height.

Tracing back even further, it appears that most of Earth's land was combined into an earlier supercontinent called Rodinia, which began to break up over 700 million years ago. This eventually produced an earlier version of the Atlantic Ocean, called Iapetus. By 470 million years ago, the seafloor of Iapetus had become more compacted and dense, and its edges began to be subducted under the adjacent continents. These continents began to slide toward each other, gradually narrowing Iapetus and eventually forming Pangea. Many scientists believe that other supercontinents formed and broke up even before Rodinia. Even earlier, the major continental masses themselves were likely formed by collisions of smaller pieces of crust.

OTHER FORCES THAT SHAPE EARTH'S SURFACE

The positions of the continents are determined almost entirely by processes within Earth's interior, but the forces of water, ice, wind, and gravity also help shape Earth's surface. Rocks are weathered, or broken into fine particles, by both physical and chemical processes. Water seeping into cracks and alternate cycles of freezing and thawing help break rocks into smaller pieces over time.

Chemical reactions may occur when acidic water makes contact with rock, leading to more rapid fragmentation.

Once rocks have broken into fine pieces, water, wind, and ice can transport the material great distances—a process called erosion. Over time, rivers can carve deep canyons and carry vast amounts of debris, depositing it in valleys, on the seafloor, or in large river deltas. Ice has significant effects as well, as glaciers carve valleys and transport large boulders. In some areas, wind has a strong influence, creating large dune fields and scouring the surface with airborne dust or sand. Gravity produces landslides, packs sediment together, and causes denser rocks to slide under less dense ones, as in the case of subduction.

Wind-driven waves as well as the rising and lowering of the tides greatly erode the shoreline. Such erosion sometimes produces chains of sandy barrier islands separated from the coast by saltwater marshes. Lava from volcanoes resurfaces the land in some areas as it covers existing land and cools to form rock. Winds carry volcanic ash great distances, with the ash eventually settling to the surface.

Life also plays an enormous role in shaping Earth's surface. Plants help break rocks into soil, which can be washed away, but they also reduce erosion by holding the soil. Ancient forests and swamps were buried and eventually became coal. Shellfish and other marine organisms build shells of calcium carbonate, which continually settle to the ocean floor, forming vast deposits of chalk. Over time, these sediments— combined with various minerals—have formed layers many miles thick. In short, much of Earth's crust has been formed or at least altered by life.

Earth Through Time

FORMATION AND AGE OF EARTH

By the late 1800s, geologists and biologists had collected evidence suggesting that Earth is at least hundreds of millions of years old, much older than had earlier been thought. Geologists reasoned that vast stretches of time were needed for the slow work of erosion and sedimentation to have had the effects they apparently had. Biologists felt that a similarly long time was needed for evolution to have resulted in the great diversity of life seen today.

There were dissenting opinions, though. Physicists such as Lord Kelvin calculated that Earth, apparently still molten inside, should have cooled to a solid throughout if it were more than about 40 million years old. Similarly, astronomers figured that the Sun could not be more than a few tens of millions of years old. They believed that the

Maps on the following three pages show the changing face of Earth's surface at various points in geologic time, from about 450 million years ago to the present, and what it might look like 250 million years in the future. The smaller, inset maps show the locations over time of the present-day continents.

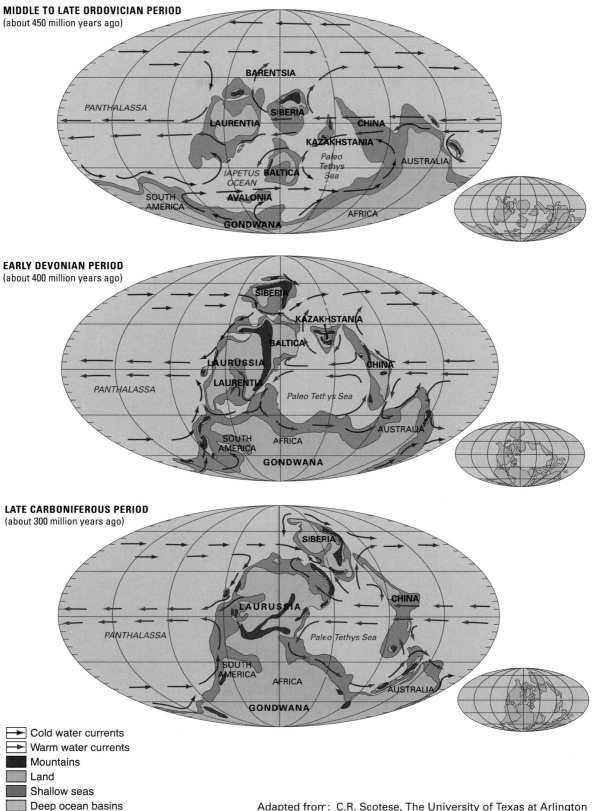

MIDDLE TO LATE ORDOVICIAN PERIOD
(about 450 million years ago)

BARENTSIA
SIBERIA
PANTHALASSA
LAURENTIA
CHINA
KAZAKHSTANIA
Paleo Tethys Sea
AUSTRALIA
IAPETUS OCEAN
BALTICA
SOUTH AMERICA
AVALONIA
AFRICA
GONDWANA

EARLY DEVONIAN PERIOD
(about 400 million years ago)

SIBERIA
KAZAKHSTANIA
BALTICA
PANTHALASSA
LAURUSSIA
LAURENTIA
CHINA
Paleo Tethys Sea
SOUTH AMERICA
AFRICA
AUSTRALIA
GONDWANA

LATE CARBONIFEROUS PERIOD
(about 300 million years ago)

SIBERIA
CHINA
LAURUSSIA
PANTHALASSA
Paleo Tethys Sea
SOUTH AMERICA
AFRICA
AUSTRALIA
GONDWANA

Cold water currents
Warm water currents
Mountains
Land
Shallow seas
Deep ocean basins

Adapted from: C.R. Scotese, The University of Texas at Arlington

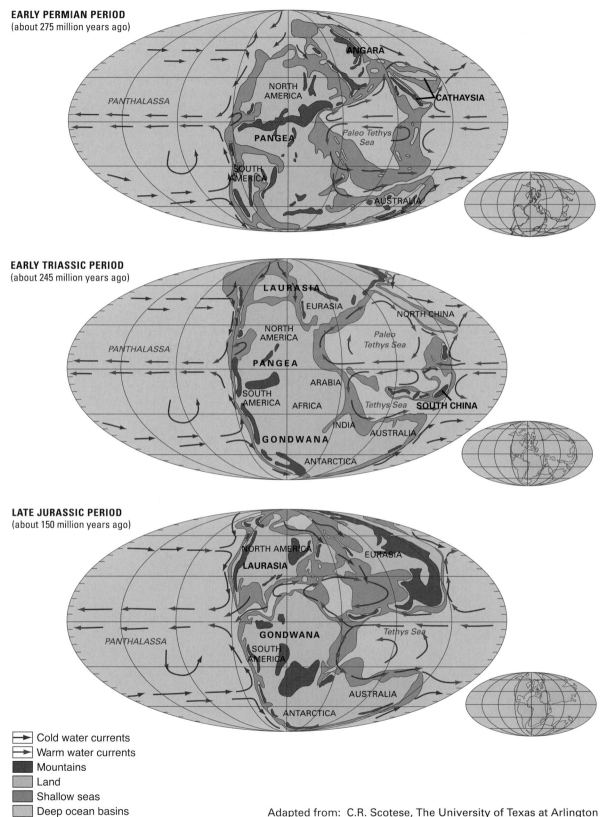

EARLY PERMIAN PERIOD
(about 275 million years ago)

PANTHALASSA

ANGARA

NORTH
AMERICA

CATHAYSIA

PANGEA

Paleo Tethys
Sea

SOUTH
AMERICA

AUSTRALIA

EARLY TRIASSIC PERIOD
(about 245 million years ago)

LAURASIA

EURASIA

NORTH CHINA

NORTH
AMERICA

PANTHALASSA

Paleo
Tethys Sea

PANGEA

ARABIA

SOUTH
AMERICA

AFRICA

Tethys Sea

SOUTH CHINA

INDIA

AUSTRALIA

GONDWANA

ANTARCTICA

LATE JURASSIC PERIOD
(about 150 million years ago)

NORTH AMERICA

EURASIA

LAURASIA

GONDWANA

Tethys Sea

PANTHALASSA

SOUTH
AMERICA

AUSTRALIA

ANTARCTICA

Cold water currents
Warm water currents
Mountains
Land
Shallow seas
Deep ocean basins

Adapted from: C.R. Scotese, The University of Texas at Arlington

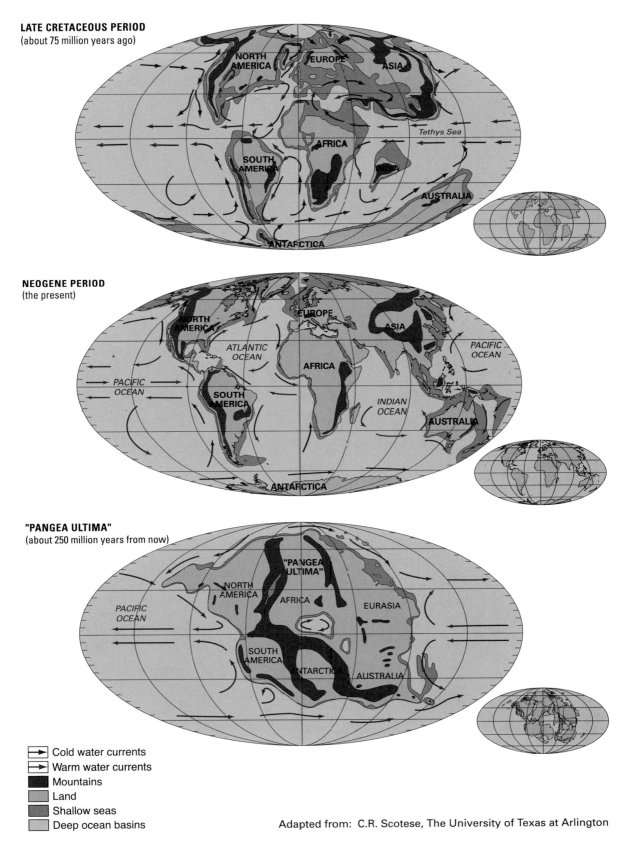

LATE CRETACEOUS PERIOD
(about 75 million years ago)

NORTH AMERICA · EUROPE · ASIA · AFRICA · SOUTH AMERICA · INDIA · AUSTRALIA · ANTARCTICA · Tethys Sea

NEOGENE PERIOD
(the present)

NORTH AMERICA · EUROPE · ASIA · ATLANTIC OCEAN · PACIFIC OCEAN · AFRICA · PACIFIC OCEAN · SOUTH AMERICA · INDIAN OCEAN · AUSTRALIA · ANTARCTICA

"PANGEA ULTIMA"
(about 250 million years from now)

"PANGEA ULTIMA" · PACIFIC OCEAN · NORTH AMERICA · AFRICA · EURASIA · SOUTH AMERICA · ANTARCTICA · AUSTRALIA

Cold water currents
Warm water currents
Mountains
Land
Shallow seas
Deep ocean basins

Adapted from: C.R. Scotese, The University of Texas at Arlington

Types of Erosion

River carving a valley

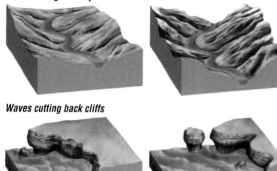

Waves cutting back cliffs

Wind blowing topsoil

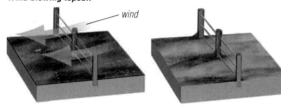

— wind

Glacier moving rocks

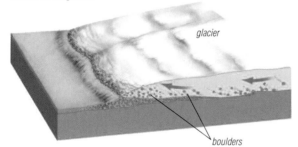

glacier

boulders

Landslide

The action of water, wind, glaciers, and gravity can wear away rock and shape land surfaces in a variety of ways, gouging out valleys, sculpting the shoreline, and redistributing topsoil, boulders, and masses of rock, earth, and debris.

Sun shone because of energy from gravitational contraction and so could not have sustained its energy output for so long without a drastic reduction in size.

The discovery of radioactivity by Henri Becquerel in 1896 led to a solution to both problems. Earth could be heated internally by radioactive decay of elements such as uranium deep inside, and this could last billions of years. The Sun, it turned out, shines by nuclear fusion, giving it a potential lifetime of at least 10 billion years.

Radioactive dating of rocks played a crucial role in calculating Earth's age. Some isotopes (forms of an element with different atomic masses) of some elements, such as uranium, decay by emitting radiation in the form of smaller particles, such as electrons and alpha particles. This leaves behind a succession of "daughter" products, such as lead. The rates of decay have been measured with great precision in laboratories. By measuring the ratios of the daughter products to the original radioactive elements, and assuming that the materials were trapped in a rock from the time it solidified, the age of the rock can be calculated.

Rocks from the seafloor are rarely found to be older than 200 million years, but those from the continents are occasionally found to date back over 3 billion years. In 2001 Australian researchers announced the discovery of a small grain of zircon (a mineral containing zirconium) that they dated to 4.4 billion years ago. Moreover, meteorites, which likely formed at about the same time as Earth, have been dated to about 4.5 billion years ago. These findings help pin down a likely age of about 4.55 billion years for Earth itself.

It is believed that Earth formed, along with the rest of the solar system, from a cloud of gas and dust called a nebula. Nebulae are seen today in other parts of the Milky Way and also in other galaxies. Astronomers have found evidence of stars and planetary systems forming in many of these nebulae, as the mutual gravitational attraction of the nebula's particles pulls them together.

According to this theory, called the nebular hypothesis, the cloud consisted mainly of hydrogen and helium, the vast majority of which ended up in the Sun. The outer planets—Jupiter, Saturn, Uranus, and Neptune—are quite different from Earth. They were far enough from the Sun and therefore cold enough that these gases, along with other compounds such as methane, ammonia, and water, were able to gravitationally collect around small, rocky or metallic cores.

The inner planets—Mercury, Venus, Earth, and Mars—were warmer and also exposed to a stronger solar wind. These effects drove most of the light gases out into space, leaving these planets as solid bodies. Venus and Earth, and to a lesser extent Mars, were able to retain atmospheres, but only as fairly thin envelopes surrounding the rock and metal.

The planets formed by accretion—a collecting together of smaller objects—mainly due to gravity. The late stages of accretion took the form of impacts of meteoroids and comets. Some of these impacts must have been tremendously energetic, likely melting much or all of Earth's early crust. The most widely accepted theory of the Moon's formation suggests that a "protoplanet" at least half of Earth's diameter struck, blasting material from both it and Earth into space. Some of this material then collected together to form the Moon. This event likely happened sometime during Earth's first 100 million years.

FIRST BILLION YEARS

The earliest period of Earth's history has been called the Hadean, after Hades, the underworld abode of the dead in ancient Greek religion. It has been believed that the leftover heat of formation, combined with frequent impacts, would have rendered Earth a hellish place, with red-hot seas of glowing magma. However, the existence of the 4.4-billion-year-old zircon crystal suggests the surface may have cooled more quickly than previously thought. The ratio of certain oxygen isotopes in the zircon also suggests it formed in the presence of water. This means temperatures must have been below the boiling point—and some water present—in at least some areas by the time the crystal formed.

Much of Earth's first billion years is shrouded in mystery, partly because so few rocks remain from that time. Most of them have been through repeated cycles of being subducted and melted, with the material eventually surfacing in the middle of oceans. The Moon bears witness to a very violent period in its own history, and surely Earth's as well. Results from the Apollo Moon exploration program show that most lunar craters (which are the results of impacts) formed prior to 3.8 billion years ago, with many of them from just before that time. Scientists believe that around 3.9 billion years ago impacts by comets and meteoroids were quite frequent. This event, called the late heavy bombardment, may have resulted from migrations of Uranus and Neptune disturbing the orbits of smaller bodies in the outer solar system and sending them sunward, so that they would then strike the inner planets.

What look like rock formations in Western Australia are actually living stromatolites—mats of microbes called cyanobacteria and layers of deposits formed by their growth. Similar organisms were once among the most abundant life-forms on Earth. Many scientists also believe that certain layered deposits from an astonishing 3.5 billion years ago are fossils of stromatolites, making them some of the earliest known life-forms.

After this period, certain pieces of crust were able to survive. A good example is the Canadian Shield, which constitutes much of that country. Several places there have rocks about 3.8 billion years old (with some dating back about 4 billion years). Oceans very probably existed, but instead of large continents, it appears there were smaller bodies of land, such as arcs of volcanic islands. Eventually, many of these drifted together and combined to form the first continents.

Fossils help geologists establish the relative geologic ages of layers of rock. In this diagram, sections A and B represent rock layers 200 miles apart. Their respective ages can be established by means of the fossils in each layer.

Geologic Time Scale

Eonothem/Eon	Erathem/Era	Sub-Era	System/Period	mya[1]
Phanerozoic	Cenozoic	Quaternary	Neogene	
				23.0
		Tertiary	Paleogene	
				65.5
	Mesozoic		Cretaceous	
				145.5

Eonothem/Eon	Erathem/Era	System/Period	mya[1]
			145.5
Phanerozoic	Mesozoic	Jurassic	
			199.6
		Triassic	
			251.0
	Paleozoic	Permian	
			299.0
		Carboniferous	
			359.2

Eonothem/Eon	Erathem/Era	System/Period	mya[1]
			359.2
Phanerozoic	Paleozoic	Devonian	
			416.0
		Silurian	
			443.7
		Ordovician	
			488.3
		Cambrian	
			542.0

Eonothem/Eon	Erathem/Era	System/Period	mya[1]
Precambrian	Proterozoic	Neoproterozoic — Ediacaran	542
			~630
		Neoproterozoic — Cryogenian	
			850
		Neoproterozoic — Tonian	
			1,000
		Mesoproterozoic — Stenian	
			1,200
		Mesoproterozoic — Ectasian	
			1,400
		Mesoproterozoic — Calymmian	
			1,600
		Paleoproterozoic — Statherian	
			1,800
		Paleoproterozoic — Orosirian	
			2,050
		Paleoproterozoic — Rhyacian	
			2,300
		Paleoproterozoic — Siderian	
			2,500
	Archean	Neoarchean	
			2,800
		Mesoarchean	
			3,200
		Paleoarchean	
			3,600
		Eoarchean — Lower limit is not defined	

[1] Millions of years ago.

Adapted from information provided by the International Commission on Stratigraphy (ICS). International chronostratigraphic units, ranks, names, and formal status are approved by the ICS and ratified by the International Union of Geological Sciences (IUGS).
Source: 2006 International Stratigraphic Chart produced by the ICS.

A time scale indicates the names and time ranges of different eons, eras, periods, and other divisions of geologic time, from the Archean eon more than 3.6 billion years ago, at bottom right, to the present Neogene period, at upper left.

Astronomers studying and modeling the life cycles of stars believe that at that time the Sun was only about 75 percent as bright as it is now. This should have made Earth quite cold, at least when large impacts were not occurring. Without something to trap the Sun's heat, the oceans might have completely frozen over, with the early continents covered in snow. Calculations show that the white surface would have reflected away so much of the Sun's light that even now the planet would be in a deep freeze.

In fact, it appears there was something to keep the planet warm—Earth's early atmosphere. Carbon dioxide and methane—both greenhouse gases, which let visible light in but absorb much of the outgoing infrared ("heat") rays—are believed to have been much more abundant than now. These gases were probably released mainly through volcanic activity. This was sufficient for the planet to avoid a frozen fate. Oxygen made up only a tiny fraction of the atmosphere's present day concentration.

LIFE APPEARS

Some of Earth's oldest rocks (up to about 3.8 billion years old) show signs of organic compounds—carbon-containing molecules likely produced by living organisms. More definite evidence appears in rocks about 3.5 billion years old. Microscopic casts of what some scientists believe to be ancient bacteria that resembled cyanobacteria (also called blue-green algae) have been found from then. Also, certain layered rock formations dating to about that same time are thought to be stromatolites, which are formed by the growth of matlike colonies of microorganisms, especially cyanobacteria. These layered columns are still being formed by living organisms today, such as in a few spots on the western coast of Australia.

The first organisms may have been prokaryotes—single-celled organisms with no cell nucleus. Some of them started carrying out photosynthesis, which uses sunlight as an energy source to take carbon (needed to build the organisms' bodies) from carbon dioxide in the air, releasing oxygen in the process. These bacteria are thought to have been quite similar to the cyanobacteria that are still abundant today. It is likely that cyanobacteria were not the only type, and perhaps not the first type, of organism during this period. Chemoautotrophs (discussed earlier) likely existed in the depths of the sea and even in rock. Some of these early organisms may have been archaeans, rather than true bacteria.

For hundreds of millions of years, the oxygen released by photosynthesizing organisms quickly reacted with materials in the environment. Oxygen therefore could not accumulate in the air to any great extent. Much of this oxygen likely combined with iron, essentially producing rust. The long time period, or eon, just described—from about 4 billion to 2.5 billion years ago—is called the Archean (not to be confused with the organisms called archaeans).

THE OXYGEN REVOLUTION

Most scientists agree that the Archean atmosphere contained very little oxygen, probably less than 1 percent of present-day levels. That changed during the first part of the next eon, the Proterozoic, from about 2.5 billion to 542 million years ago. Much of the material that could combine with oxygen (that is, to be oxidized) had already done so. From about 2.5 to 1.9 billion years ago, vast deposits called banded iron formations were laid down on the ocean bottom. The deposits consist of alternating, very thin layers of iron-rich minerals and silica minerals such as chert. The process by which they formed is not completely understood. However, it appears to have occurred in response to increasing, and perhaps fluctuating, amounts of free oxygen in the atmosphere and oceans. These formations are the source of most of the iron ore used today, so people are reaping the harvest of an event that occurred when Earth was only half its present age.

By 1.5 billion years ago, oxygen levels had reached perhaps 10 percent of current levels. One effect of this is that "red beds" began to form. These are areas where iron in the soil has been oxidized, producing a rusty appearance. This process happens mainly in dry, hot climates, such as the present-day Australian outback, often called the "red center."

A more important consequence of increased oxygen levels was a dramatic change in Earth's life. Oxygen is poisonous to many microorganisms (such as the tetanus bacterium, which thrives in closed wounds with little oxygen). Much of this life perished, but some of it found refuge deep in the sea or underground. A more complex type of single-celled living thing arose at about this time—eukaryotes. These organisms have a cell nucleus and many other structures not present in prokaryotes. More complex, multicellular eukaryotes also evolved later. In fact, all animals, plants, fungi, and protists are eukaryotes.

Eukaryotes require something that prokaryotes do not—oxygen at levels at least 1 percent of the present level. Once sufficient oxygen was present, eukaryotic cells became very numerous. For most of the remainder of the Proterozoic, all life on Earth consisted of single-celled organisms, including both prokaryotes and eukaryotes.

Near the end of the Proterozoic eon, the climate changed dramatically. Since the Hadean eon, temperatures had apparently been much like today's. About 750 million years ago, however, conditions became drastically colder. Rocks from that time show evidence of the action of glaciers, and some of these rocks appear to have formed near the ancient equator. Many scientists believe that Earth froze over, even at the equator, for millions of years—a state called "snowball Earth." This seems to have occurred at least twice, probably about 710 million years ago and 640 million years ago. (Some evidence also points to widespread glaciation much earlier, about 2.2 billion years ago). Other scientists do not believe the glaciation was quite this extensive, so that open water and some bare land were present in the tropics. In either case, the climate was probably colder than at any time since.

The following is how this may have occurred. By this time, the supercontinent Rodinia had begun to break apart, with many of the fragments likely being in tropical regions. Carbon dioxide, dissolved in rain falling on the continent and also in water in waves smashing against the shores, weathered the rocks. This washed calcium ions into the sea, where they combined with carbon dioxide to make limestone. Photosynthesizing organisms in the ocean continued to take carbon dioxide from the air and to bury the carbon as they died and sank to the bottom. With less of this greenhouse gas present, and the Sun at only about 94 percent of its present brightness, temperatures began to drop. Once snow and ice began to form, they reflected more of the Sun's light away. This vicious circle is an example of "positive feedback," in which an effect itself causes more of the same effect to occur, and it allowed the world's average temperature to plunge to perhaps −60° F (−50° C).

After perhaps millions of years in this state, continuing volcanic activity continued to release carbon dioxide. However, now there was little or no rain to weather rocks, and almost all rocks were covered by ice or snow anyway. This allowed carbon dioxide levels to increase in the air again, perhaps reaching hundreds of times the present-day concentration. Temperatures became warm enough for some of the ice to start to melt, exposing darker surfaces that could absorb more sunlight. A positive-feedback warming process then sent the planet into a very hot state, with Earth reaching

Major Evolutionary Events, 650 million years ago to the present

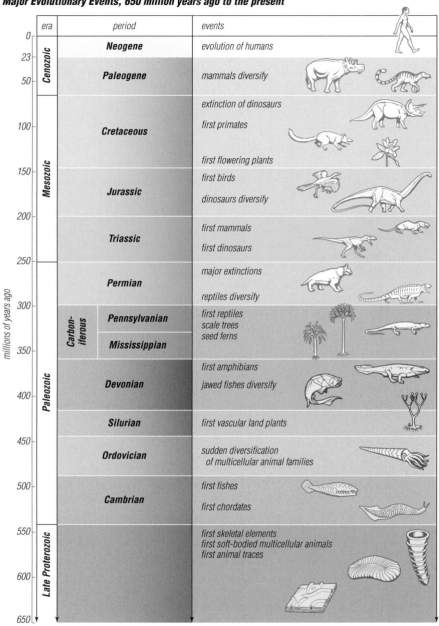

era	period	events
Cenozoic	**Neogene**	evolution of humans
Cenozoic	**Paleogene**	mammals diversify
Mesozoic	**Cretaceous**	extinction of dinosaurs first primates first flowering plants
Mesozoic	**Jurassic**	first birds dinosaurs diversify
Mesozoic	**Triassic**	first mammals first dinosaurs
Paleozoic	**Permian**	major extinctions reptiles diversify
Paleozoic (Carboniferous)	**Pennsylvanian**	first reptiles scale trees seed ferns
Paleozoic (Carboniferous)	**Mississippian**	
Paleozoic	**Devonian**	first amphibians jawed fishes diversify
Paleozoic	**Silurian**	first vascular land plants
Paleozoic	**Ordovician**	sudden diversification of multicellular animal families
Paleozoic	**Cambrian**	first fishes first chordates
Late Proterozoic		first skeletal elements first soft-bodied multicellular animals first animal traces

millions of years ago — 0, 23, 50, 100, 150, 200, 250, 300, 350, 400, 450, 500, 550, 600, 650

average temperatures of perhaps 100° F (38° C). The freeze-over had reduced the amount of life available to take the carbon dioxide back out of the air. Earth may have gone through at least two such freeze-thaw cycles in the late Proterozoic.

These stresses may have played a role in the next revolution of the biosphere—the appearance of multicellular life. Evolution can occur rapidly when the environment changes dramatically. Fossils from as much as 600 million years ago appear to be the imprints of soft-bodied creatures. Some of these, referred to as the Ediacarans, appear as round, fanlike, or "quilted"

impressions. Their relationship, if any, to later animals is unclear. Relatively little is known about these creatures, but as the Proterozoic ended, an explosion of new life-forms was about to take place.

PALEOZOIC ERA

Dramatic changes occurred on Earth around 542 million years ago, heralding the beginning of the Paleozoic (meaning "old life") era. The glaciers of the late Proterozoic melted. This, combined with changes on the seafloor, led to a rise in sea level, which flooded the coastlines of the ancient continents. Earth became

At left are photographs of brachiopod (top) and trilobite (bottom) fossils as they appear in rocks. Drawings of these animals (at right) show details of their form and structure.

(Top and bottom left) Bill Ratcliffe; (top and bottom right) Historical Geology, 3rd edition, by Dunbar and Waage

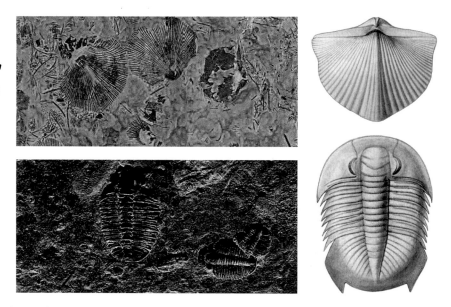

warmer—somewhat warmer than today. Oxygen had recently increased to perhaps half its present-day level (though there is considerable uncertainty regarding the amount). These changes set the stage for a rapid phase of evolution called the Cambrian explosion.

Cambrian Period

The Cambrian period lasted from about 542 million to 488 million years ago. Fossils are very scarce in older rock layers but suddenly quite abundant in the Cambrian. It was once thought that no life, or at least nothing other than single-celled organisms, preceded it. Some fossils from earlier times have now been found, but the dramatic increase requires an explanation.

One factor is that at about this time animals developed the ability to form hard parts, such as exoskeletons or shells. These structures are much more easily preserved than the soft parts of creatures. However, it is likely that the actual numbers of animals, and certainly the number of types of animals, increased greatly. Many scientists believe that almost all of the large groups called phyla in the animal kingdom appeared at this time. For example, the ancestors of arthropods (such as today's crabs, spiders, and insects), mollusks (snails, clams, squid), poriferans (sponges), and echinoderms (starfish, sea urchins) are present in Cambrian sediments. These creatures lived in the sea. The first fishes, which were jawless, also appeared. There is only limited evidence of any life on land during this time, and any land dwellers that did exist were probably single-celled organisms such as bacteria.

Though the creatures of the Cambrian were mostly related to those of today, some would look very unfamiliar, even bizarre, to people today. A very common animal in the sea was the trilobite, an early arthropod. There were thousands of species of these segmented creatures, which looked something like a rib cage. They varied from the size of a coin to about 18 inches (46 centimeters) long. Many of them may have fed on algae or other small organisms, though some may have eaten larger prey. The trilobites appeared very early in the Cambrian period and lasted nearly 300 million years, almost through the entire Paleozoic era.

Trilobites apparently had at least one creature to fear—*Anomalocaris*—meaning "strange shrimp." These creatures were evidently predators, with two curved, spiny appendages protruding from the front, a mouthlike feature on the underside, and two large eyes. They generally grew up to 2 feet (about 60 centimeters) in length. Some fossilized trilobites have been found with apparent bites taken out of them, possibly by *Anomalocaris*.

The rest of the Paleozoic era consisted of periods called the Ordovician (488 million to 444 million years ago), the Silurian (444 million to 416 million years ago), the Devonian (416 million to 359 million years ago), the Carboniferous (359 million to 299 million years ago), and the Permian (299 million to 251 million years ago). Earth, and life itself, went through many changes during this time. These periods are distinguishable by significant changes in the sediments and in the fossil records, corresponding to environmental changes and extinctions of many species.

Rodinia broke apart, with the continents becoming most widely scattered about 470 million to 450 million years ago, during the Ordovician period. Then, the increasingly compacted seafloor started to be subducted

Anomalocaris canadensis

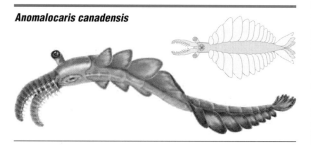

under the edges of plates carrying the continents as they turned around and began to approach each other.

ORDOVICIAN PERIOD

During the Ordovician period the continents were generally spread apart. Most of Earth's land was in the Southern Hemisphere, and most of this was concentrated in the large continent of Gondwana. For most of the period the sea level was high and temperatures were warm. Many of the groups of marine organisms that had appeared in the Cambrian became more diverse. Arthropods, as well as primitive plant life and fungi, are thought to have begun to colonize the land. Toward the end of the Ordovician, though, a large part of Gondwana lay near the South Pole. Glaciation developed there, the sea level dropped, and the world became colder. This led to the extinction of many species.

Silurian Period

During the Silurian period the continents were beginning to approach each other once again. Most of the late Ordovician ice melted, and the world became relatively warm. Large coral reefs were very common. Jawless fish became plentiful, and some fish with jaws appeared late in the period. Vascular plants—that is, plants with a system for transporting water and nutrients—were living on land, though they did not have definite stems and leaves. Worms, centipedes, and spiders added to the growing biological communities on land.

Devonian Period

The Devonian saw the continued approach of the continents. Plant life spread on land, and carbon dioxide levels in the air probably dropped because of the increasing photosynthesis. There is evidence of glaciers in southern Gondwana late in the period. The Devonian is sometimes called the Age of Fishes, because many new kinds, including sharks, appeared. Near the end of this time, tetrapods—four-legged animals likely descended from fish—first appeared on land. The first ones were similar to amphibians and are believed to be the ancestors of modern amphibians, reptiles, birds, and mammals.

Carboniferous Period

The Carboniferous period is so named because it was during this time that vast amounts of carbon were buried by plant life in forests and swamps. This same plant life liberated huge amounts of oxygen, which may have made up as much as 35 percent of the atmosphere. Forest fires must have burned with particular intensity.

Another interesting effect was that high oxygen levels are thought to have allowed some insects to become larger. Insects do not have lungs but absorb oxygen through their exoskeletons. This severely limits their maximum size. If the height, length, and width of an insect are all doubled, it will have eight times the volume and mass and will need eight times the energy. However, it will have only four times the surface area through which to absorb oxygen. Such an underpowered insect might not be able to function or even survive.

With twice as much oxygen in the air, though, it would have enough energy after all. Perhaps because of this, certain huge insects, such as dragonflies with wingspans of up to 30 inches (76 centimeters), were able to thrive.

The carboniferous swamp forests featured tall, fast-growing treelike plants, such as the *Lepidodendron*, or "scale trees." Some grew to heights of more than 100 feet (30 meters). Giant horsetails and ferns were also present. When these treelike plants died and fell, they formed dense mats of logs that were slow to rot, perhaps because appropriate microbes had not yet evolved to rapidly consume the dead matter. The logs and other plant matter were gradually buried and became the coal beds from which people extract so much fuel today.

Some of the largest forest belts were in what are now eastern North America and northwestern Europe. These regions were apparently in the tropics at the time. Southern Gondwana had reached the South Pole, and millions of years of snow had built an ice cap there. The planet as a whole was colder than it had been. The large temperature difference between the poles and the equator produced strong trade winds, which brought moisture from the ocean well inland. The resulting heavy rains enabled the rapid growth of these forests.

Permian Period

As the Permian began, the continents reassembled to form Pangea. Much of the land was then very far from any water. Much of Pangea became desert, and plant life on land was reduced. The southern ice cap diminished or disappeared, and the world became warmer. The great carboniferous forests diminished and were largely replaced by ferns and early conifer trees. Broad-leaved deciduous trees called *Glossopteris* became common in the south. A drop in sea level exposed sediments containing materials such as iron, which could then take oxygen from the atmosphere.

Land animals included early reptiles as well as creatures with characteristics of both reptiles and mammals. The latter included the curious *Dimetrodon*, which had a sail-like membrane protruding from its back, and predators called gorgonopsids. The gorgonopsids were part of the group called the therapsids, from which mammals likely evolved.

THE GREAT DYING

Geologic periods in general are defined by fairly sharp differences in the strata, or layers, of sediment. One of the differences seen is the fossils that predominate. In other words, the periods tend to be separated by extinction events, and the major eras by especially large extinction events. The Paleozoic ("old life") and Mesozoic ("middle life") eras are separated by the most dramatic extinction event known—that which separates the Permian period from the Triassic period. Roughly 95 percent of all marine species and 70 percent of all land-based species became extinct. Even those species that survived probably experienced significant loss of population.

This "great dying," known as the Permian-Triassic extinction, occurred about 251 million years ago. There were actually a series of extinctions in the middle and

A rock contains the fossilized skeleton of a dicynodont, or "two-tusker," that was found in the Karoo region of South Africa. The dicynodonts were plant eaters that thrived during the Permian and Triassic periods. They belonged to the group called the therapsids, which had characteristics of both reptiles and mammals.

Heinrich van den Berg—Gallo Images/Getty Images

late Permian. The final extinction event took place over a period of less than a million years, and possibly as little as several thousand years. The cause is not known with any certainty, but many ideas have been put forth. Quite possibly it was a combination of factors. A tremendous amount of volcanic activity occurred in what is now Siberia, Russia, at about that time, lasting about a million years. This released between 250,000 and 1 million cubic miles (1 million and 4 million cubic kilometers) of lava, which hardened into basalt. That would have been enough to cover the world in a layer about 6 to 25 feet (about 2 to 8 meters) deep, if the basalt had been spread out evenly. Such an event would likely cause large climate changes and acid rain, disrupting ecosystems.

Scientists also believe that oxygen was reduced at the time, to perhaps as little as half its present abundance. It has been suggested that there was a large release of methane that had been trapped underground and under the sea. Such a release of methane could have caused an intense greenhouse effect and warming and could also lower oxygen levels (*see* Greenhouse Effect). Also, the assembly of Pangea may have reduced the amount of shallow seas, which were needed to sustain many marine communities.

Another possibility is that a large comet or asteroid struck Earth at that time, triggering an environmental catastrophe. Some scientists believe that a feature found under the Antarctic ice or one found on the sea bottom off the coast of Australia could be the resulting crater. It may be that all of these suggested causes played a role, or were interrelated—such as the impact triggering the volcanic activity. Even though no consensus has been reached on this, scientists agree that studying such extinctions is important, since life on Earth could be similarly threatened in the future.

MESOZOIC ERA

The Mesozoic ("middle life") era lasted from 251 million to about 66 million years ago. It is divided into three periods: the Triassic (251 million to 200 million years

ago), the Jurassic (200 million to 146 million years ago), and the Cretaceous (146 to 66 million years ago). This era is more familiar to most people than the Paleozoic is, because the Mesozoic was the age of the dinosaurs. Each of the periods ended with some degree of extinctions, but the most dramatic event occurred at the end of the Cretaceous. While not as extensive as the Permian-Triassic event, it nonetheless put an end to the dinosaurs and paved the way for the rise of mammals.

Triassic Period

The early Triassic saw the continued existence of Pangea and a slow recovery from the preceding extinctions. The world rapidly became populated by large numbers of individuals of relatively few species, so that there was little biological diversity. With Pangea straddling the equator, much of the continent was hot and dry. Areas farther from the equator probably had fairly harsh seasons, with hot summers and fairly cold winters, along with large seasonal differences in rainfall. In the late Triassic, Pangea began to break apart.

The northern and southern parts of Pangea had rather different sorts of plants and animals. In the south, forests of seed-ferns replaced the *Glossopteris* that had dominated the Permian. In the north, cycads (looking something like a cross between a fern and a palm), ginkgos, and primitive evergreen conifers were common. In the south, the animal life featured therapsids, while in the north, primitive reptiles known as archosaurs were predominant. In the sea, fish were plentiful, but aquatic reptiles such as ichthyosaurs appeared as well. Late in the Triassic, early dinosaurs became common, apparently having evolved from the archosaurs. The small shrewlike creatures that were the first mammals also appeared late in the period. They are thought to have descended from the therapsids.

Jurassic Period

The Jurassic saw a continuation of the breakup of Pangea. The rifts between the splitting continents became shallow seas, and rising sea levels flooded parts of the continents. Reefs grew in the seas. The climate was generally warmer than today. Conifers and ginkgos were common plants, and cycads were very abundant. Forests grew where Australia and Antarctica began to separate, eventually becoming coal deposits.

Some of the dinosaurs reached enormous sizes, with plant-eating sauropods such as *Brachiosaurus* growing up to 40 feet (12 meters) tall and weighing up to 80 tons. The herbivores were pursued by carnivorous theropods such as *Allosaurus*. Some herbivores, such as *Stegosaurus*, developed self-defense features such as armored plates and bony spikes. The featherless flying and gliding dinosaurs called pterosaurs were common. Some of the smaller carnivores developed feathers and may also have begun to fly, evolving into the first birds. Mammals existed but were small.

Cretaceous Period

During the Cretaceous (meaning "chalk-bearing") period, the Atlantic Ocean widened. The southern continent of Gondwana broke apart completely, and the equatorial Tethys Sea began to narrow as Africa drifted north toward Europe. India moved north toward Asia. The climate was warm, perhaps in part because of the way the continents were distributed, but also likely from high levels of carbon dioxide released in the air from frequent volcanic activity. Forests, rather than ice, were to be found in the Arctic and Antarctic regions.

Thick deposits of chalk—the bodies of countless shell-producing marine organisms—were laid down in the shallow seas. Much of the deep ocean was largely devoid of life, though, as poor ocean circulation deprived the depths of oxygen. Large reef systems developed, but many of these were apparently built by large mollusks called rudists, rather than by corals. Large reptiles, such as plesiosaurs, swam in the sea.

Flying reptiles were common but declining in number, with the huge *Pteranodon* and *Quetzalcoatlus* remaining

Reptiles such as dinosaurs dominated Earth during the Mesozoic. Scientists at Dinosaur National Monument in Colorado carefully dig the fossil bones of one of these ancient creatures from the rocky face of a quarry wall.

until the end. Primitive birds continued to evolve from the theropod dinosaurs. Other theropods included the fearsome *Tyrannosaurus rex*. Plant eaters such as *Ankylosaurus* and *Triceratops* evolved defensive plates and spikes.

A major revolution in plants occurred during the Cretaceous—angiosperms, or flowering plants, first appeared. The landscape, formerly probably all shades of green, may have begun to take on other hues as these plants developed attractive flowers to lure insects, which could carry pollen. In response, insects themselves rapidly diversified into new forms.

Fairly modern reptiles, such as crocodiles and turtles, are seen in Cretaceous strata. Mammals developed into all three of their current groups: placentals, marsupials, and monotremes. The dinosaurs still dominated, though, and mammals remained quite small, with many burrowing into the ground.

THE END OF AN ERA

The Cretaceous ended rather suddenly 65–66 million years ago with a major extinction event that put an end to the dinosaurs (except for their apparent descendents—the birds). The rudist reefs also disappeared from the shallow seas. While not quite as severe as the Permian-Triassic event, this extinction is one of the worst known, as nearly 80 percent of all species were destroyed.

As with the end of the Permian, the causes of this environmental catastrophe are debated. A huge volcanic outpouring in what is now India formed the Deccan Traps. This may have produced climate change and acid rain. For this extinction, though, many scientists believe there is a "smoking gun" to support the theory that the impact of an extraterrestrial body, probably an asteroid, played a role. Geologist Walter Alvarez discovered an excess concentration of the element iridium in the sediment layer deposited at the boundary between the Cretaceous and Tertiary periods, known as the K-T boundary. In about 1980 he and his father, physicist Luis Alvarez, proposed an explanation. They said that, since iridium is common in meteorites, the layer could be

A dragonfly from Bavaria dates back to the Jurassic. Body imprints of these creatures are quite rare.

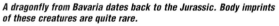

Crinoid fossils (top), found in Kansas, date back to the Cretaceous, when a shallow sea covered the inland plains. Dinosaur eggs (bottom), found in Mongolia, are also from the Cretaceous. They were probably buried in warm sand and left to hatch.

explained as debris from the impact of a large body, perhaps 6 miles (10 kilometers) across. The devastation produced by such an impact could have easily caused mass extinctions.

By the mid-1990s other researchers had accumulated strong evidence that a major impact occurred about 65 million years ago in shallow seas at what is now the northern coast of Mexico's Yucatán Peninsula. Surveys of gravitational and magnetic fields in the region show a huge circular feature, now known as the Chicxulub crater, roughly 100 miles (160 kilometers) in diameter. Cores drilled there by an oil company years before had revealed unusual, glassy rock at a depth of about 4,200 feet (1,300 meters). In addition, the types of rocks called breccias and tektites had been found at numerous sites around the Caribbean and North America. The breccias consisted of a mixture of fragments of different rock types fused together by heating. Tektites are believed to be material ejected from impact sites that melted and then resolidified. These samples were determined by radioactive dating to have formed at the time of the supposed impact.

The environmental consequences must have been severe. The energy of the impact is estimated to have been about 100 million megatons—the equivalent of 2 million of the most powerful nuclear bombs ever detonated. Huge tsunamis, earthquakes, and intense heat would have been almost immediate effects. Within half an hour, material ejected from the site would have

reentered the atmosphere over a large fraction of the globe. The shock heating of the air would have set off huge forest fires. Longer-term effects would have included an almost complete cutoff of sunlight reaching the ground over much of the world, lasting for months. Chemicals produced by the event could have poisoned the air and oceans. Carbon dioxide released by the vaporization of seafloor sediment could have caused a large greenhouse effect for hundreds of years afterward.

In spite of this, there is still debate regarding the main causes of the extinction. The question also remains as to why some species survived. It is likely, though, that the impact played a role. In any case, asteroid or comet impacts can and do occur over geologic time and are a threat to life on Earth.

CENOZOIC ERA

The Cenozoic ("recent life") era began about 66 million years ago and continues today. It has traditionally been divided into two rather unequal periods: the Tertiary and the Quaternary. Now, however, the periods are usually defined as the Paleogene (66 million to 23 million years ago) and the Neogene (23 million years ago until the present). The periods are divided into several epochs, with the current epoch being the Holocene (11,800 years ago to the present). The Cenozoic is often called the Age of Mammals, because mammals quickly replaced reptiles as the most prominent land animals.

During the Cenozoic, plate tectonics brought the continents to their modern positions. India rammed into Asia, producing the Himalaya Mountains. South America—once part of Gondwana—made contact with North America for the first time since Pangea broke apart, just in the last few million years.

The climate started out very warm, with global temperatures peaking at an average of about 77 to 86° F (25 to 30° C), compared to the present 59° F (15° C). At that time, tropical conditions extended at least 45 degrees from the equator, and even the Arctic Ocean may have had temperatures as high as 68° F (20° C). Gradual cooling occurred after that, with ice eventually forming on Antarctica and Greenland.

In just the last million years or so, Earth's climate entered a new and dramatic phase. Severe ice ages have occurred roughly every 100,000 years. These ice ages have been interrupted by relatively mild intervals called interglacials lasting roughly 20,000 years. The last major cold spell peaked about 18,000 years ago, with ice sheets over a mile thick covering much of northwestern Europe and North America (as far south as Ohio). Global temperatures averaged some 9 to 14° F (5 to 8° C) colder than at present, with high northern latitudes much more strongly affected. The ice began to melt rapidly about 14,000 years ago, and the present time is in the Holocene interglacial. For perspective, Earth is now considerably warmer than it has been for most of the last 100,000 years but still significantly cooler than the average of the last 250 million years.

Early in the Cenozoic, mammals and birds quickly filled many of the ecological niches previously occupied

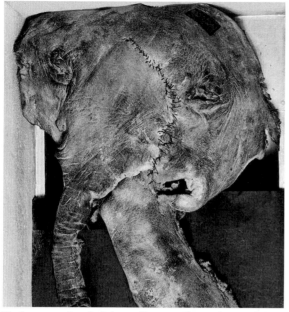

American Museum of Natural History, New York

The frozen remains of a baby woolly mammoth were dug out of the ground in Alaska. It may have been born more than 20,000 years ago when mammoths roamed the Arctic tundra.

by dinosaurs and other reptiles. Some mammals became quite large. *Indricotherium*, which ate leaves and looked something like a combination of a rhinoceros and a giraffe, stood up to about 15 feet (4.5 meters) high at the shoulder and weighed up to 15 tons. Some land mammals gradually adapted to aquatic life, eventually evolving into whales and dolphins. Mammals even entered the air, as bats evolved.

Huge carnivorous and flightless birds, some up to 10 feet (3 meters) tall, took over some of the predatory roles formerly played by the dinosaurs. Actually, since most biologists now believe birds to be descended from certain types of dinosaurs, in a sense, the dinosaurs never totally died out. In fact, they diversified into the huge number of bird species alive today.

Plant life changed, too. Flowering plants became dominant over much of the planet. These include grasses, which had appeared late in the Cretaceous but now spread and started a whole new ecosystem.

Primates became more common, eventually developing into monkeys, apes, and the ancestors of humans. Modern humans appeared probably in the last 150,000 years or so, after the cycle of ice ages and interglacials began. Human civilization, including farming and cities, did not develop until the Holocene, after the great northern ice sheets had largely receded.

EARTH AS A SYSTEM

Throughout Earth's history, its spheres and cycles have interacted in various ways. The water and carbon cycles discussed above, along with others (such as the nitrogen cycle and the phosphorous cycle) can be understood as parts of a system, of which the biosphere is a crucial part. In some ways, this system seems to be self-

regulating. In fact, some researchers, such as British scientist James Lovelock, think of Earth (mainly the biosphere) almost as a sort of organism, dubbed Gaia. The basic idea is that life has tended to help maintain the conditions necessary for its own continued existence. Many scientists have criticized the Gaia hypothesis for being teleological—meaning "purpose driven"—as if life somehow "meant" to act in this way. In response, Lovelock himself has pointed out that he did not intend the idea to be taken in this way.

Despite the controversy, it is clear that life has greatly shaped the planet's outer parts, at least. An important concept to use here is that of feedback, both positive and negative. Positive feedback occurs when an effect is in some way its own cause. The classic example is having a microphone too close to a speaker. The sound from the speaker is picked up by the microphone, which then produces even more sound from the speaker, in a vicious cycle. Such a system is regarded as unstable.

Negative feedback involves processes that are self-correcting. A simple example is a pendulum; the more it is displaced to one side, the greater the force trying to send it back where it was. The natural result is oscillatory behavior about an "equilibrium" state, or at least a tendency for things to "not get out of hand." This behavior is termed stable.

Negative feedback is vital to maintaining fairly constant conditions. For example, perhaps excess carbon dioxide in the air stimulates the growth of plants, which thereby absorb more carbon dioxide from the air. This would tend to keep the amount from changing too much. An example of positive feedback is the idea that rising global temperatures will release methane—a greenhouse gas—from storage in permafrost or in sediment in the deep ocean. This would cause a "bootstrap effect," with temperatures rising in an uncontrolled way.

The Earth system (regardless of whether one chooses to call it Gaia) certainly has many feedback loops, both positive and negative. Understanding these is crucial not only to understanding the planet's past, but also in predicting—or altering—its potential future.

THE FUTURE OF EARTH

Taking into account all that has been learned about Earth's past and present, one can speculate in an informed way about what the future may hold for the planet. This involves exploring two basic scenarios: one in which humans have no effect or role and another in which people influence the course of events in various possible ways.

Plate tectonics should continue at least through the reassembly and breakup of one more supercontinent. However, the radioactive isotopes that help power convection currents in the mantle are decaying all the time. Eventually, the continents will assume their final positions, and volcanoes and earthquakes will largely cease.

Assuming no human (or other intelligent creature's) intervention, some forms of life might continue for a billion years or more. The recent series of ice ages and interglacials might continue for millions of years. Eventually, however, changing continental positions, plus a slowly brightening Sun, would bring warm, ice-free climates like those of the Mesozoic. Plants and animals would develop into new forms, but probably with some familiar types surviving.

There will likely be asteroid and comet impacts from time to time. A few of these could trigger significant extinctions and alter the course of life's development. However, if the past is any clue, some species would almost certainly survive to populate a new and somewhat different world.

Within a few hundred million years, Earth should become very warm, perhaps with rainforests even near the poles. However, some models predict that weathering rates of silicate rocks will increase, thus reducing atmospheric carbon dioxide levels enough to threaten plant life.

By a billion years out, conditions would become so hot that multicellular life-forms would succumb, and the oceans would begin to evaporate at an ever higher rate. Only single-celled eukaryotes and prokaryotes might find conditions tolerable. Later, even the eukaryotes would perish, leaving only prokaryotes or other hardy single-celled organisms. In other words, basic types of life-forms would become extinct in approximately the reverse order in which they appeared.

By perhaps 1.2 billion years from now, the oceans may have completely evaporated. Even the resulting water vapor will eventually be lost, as ultraviolet radiation from the Sun breaks off water's hydrogen atoms, which will then escape into space. By 7 billion years from now, the Sun will be swelling toward its red giant stage, with its outer layers eventually reaching Earth's orbit. Earth will likely recede somewhat from the Sun as the Sun loses mass into space. In any case, however, the planet will become a ball of magma, glowing at thousands of degrees. Interestingly, the moons of Jupiter and Saturn (including Titan) should melt and offer at least the chance of having biospheres of their own, though not for as long as Earth had.

If Earth survives the Sun's red giant phase, it will then become a cold, barren rock when the Sun's nuclear reactions cease and the Sun shrinks to a faint white dwarf star. Earth would continue to orbit, as it had for over 12 billion years, but with a cold, dark future.

If the above comes to pass, the biosphere will have lasted about 5 billion years—about three quarters of which is already past. This scenario is not certain, though, largely because humans or other intelligent descendants could play a vital role. In the short term, the release of buried carbon from human activities threatens to warm the planet to levels that modern civilization has not had to deal with (*see* Global Warming). Among the changes such global warming could cause are the extinctions of other species—possibly on a scale rivaling the extinctions separating adjacent geologic periods discussed earlier.

In the very long term, though, the biosphere would probably adjust to the new conditions. Eventually, in the very distant future, our descendants would face the problem of the very gradual brightening of the Sun. It may be feasible to redirect an asteroid so that it swings by Earth and Jupiter every few thousand years, giving Earth a gentle tug to increase its orbital radius. Another option would be to place a large disk between Earth and the Sun to shade Earth and keep it cooler. If our descendants were actually to execute such plans, the lifetime of the biosphere might be extended by billions of years. In that case, life would have indeed helped determine its own fate.

FURTHER RESOURCES FOR EARTH

Books for Children

Arato, Rona. Fossils: Clues to Ancient Life (Crabtree, 2005).
Donnelly, K.J. Biomes of the Past and Future; Ice Ages of the Past and Future; Rising Temperatures of the Past and Future (PowerKids, 2003).
Ganeri, Anita, and others. Earth and Space (Parragon, 2004).
Hall, Cally, and O'Hara, Scarlett. 1001 Facts About Planet Earth (DK, 2003).
Harman, Rebecca. Earth's Changing Crust (Heinemann, 2005).
Hopkins, Ellen. Countdown to Yesterday: Earth's Prehistoric Past (Perfection Learning, 2002).
Mattern, Joanne. Igneous Rocks and the Rock Cycle; Metamorphic Rocks and the Rock Cycle; Sedimentary Rocks and the Rock Cycle (PowerKids, 2006).
Phelan, Glen. Uncovering Earth's History (National Geographic, 2003).
Simon, Seymour. Earth (Simon & Schuster, 2003).
Spilsbury, Louise, and Spilsbury, Richard. The Future—Bleak or Bright? (Raintree, 2006).
Trumbauer, Lisa. To the Core: Earth's Structure (Raintree, 2007).

Books for Young Adults and Adults

Bjornerud, Marcia. Reading the Rocks: The Autobiography of the Earth (Westview, 2005).
Blashfield, J.F., and Jacobs, R.P. When Life Took Root on Land: The Late Paleozoic Era (Heinemann, 2006).
Coenraads, R.R. Rocks and Fossils (Firefly, 2005).
Colson, Mary. Shaky Ground: Earthquakes (Raintree, 2006).
Edwards, John. Plate Tectonics and Continental Drift (Smart Apple Media, 2006).
Fothergill, Alastair. Planet Earth as You've Never Seen It Before (Univ. Calif. Press, 2006).
Johnson, R.L. Plate Tectonics (Lerner, 2006).
Kerr Casper, Julie. Water and Atmosphere: The Lifeblood of Natural Systems (Chelsea, 2007).
Knoll, A.H. Life on a Young Planet: The First Three Billion Years of Evolution on Earth (Princeton Univ. Press, 2005).
Levin, H.L. The Earth Through Time, 8th ed. (Wiley, 2006).
Margulis, Lynn, and Dolan, M.F. Early Life: Evolution on the Precambrian Earth (Jones and Bartlett, 2002).
Marshak, Stephen. Earth, 2nd ed. (Norton, 2005).
Miller, Ron. Earth and the Moon: Worlds Beyond (Twenty-First Century Books, 2003).
Nield, Ted. Supercontinent: Ten Billion Years in the Life of Our Planet (Harvard Univ. Press, 2007).
Pollock, Steve. Ecology, rev. ed. (DK, 2005).
Rogers, J.J.W., and Santosh, M. Continents and Supercontinents (Oxford Univ. Press, 2004).
Schneider, S.H., ed. Scientists Debate Gaia (MIT Press, 2004).
Stille, D.R. Erosion: How Land Forms, How It Changes (Compass Point, 2005).
Stille, D.R. Plate Tectonics (Compass Point, 2007).
Stow, D.A.V. Oceans (Univ. of Chicago Press, 2006).
Sussman, Art. Dr. Art's Guide to Planet Earth: For Earthlings Ages 12 to 120 (Chelsea Green, 2000).
Thompson, D.M. Processes That Shape the Earth (Chelsea, 2007).
Vernon, R.H. Beneath Our Feet: The Rocks of Planet Earth (Cambridge Univ. Press, 2000).
Vogt, G.L. The Atmosphere; The Biosphere; Earth's Core and Mantle; The Hydrosphere; The Lithosphere (Twenty-First Century, 2007).

INDEX

Page numbers in **bold** indicate main subject references; page numbers in *italics* indicate illustrations.

Page numbers in **bold** indicate main subject references; page numbers in *italics* indicate illustrations.

Page numbers in **bold** indicate main subject references; page numbers in *italics* indicate illustrations.